easy
Windows® 8.1

Mark Edward Soper

que®

800 East 96th Street
Indianapolis, Indiana 46240

Introduction..Pg. xix

PART I   Introducing Windows

CHAPTER 1
What's New and Improved in Windo..........................Pg. 2

CHAPTER 2
Upgrading to Windows 8.1.......................................Pg. 12

PART II   Using the Windows 8.1 Modern UI

CHAPTER 3
Essential Windows 8.1 Tasks....................................Pg. 22

CHAPTER 4
Using the Windows 8.1 Start Screen.........................Pg. 48

CHAPTER 5
Browsing the Web from the Modern UI.....................Pg. 62

CHAPTER 6
Using Alarms, Calculator, and Sound Recorder..........Pg. 80

CHAPTER 7
Enjoying Music and Video.......................................Pg. 98

CHAPTER 8
Using Movie Moments...Pg. 112

CHAPTER 9
Viewing and Taking Photos with Photos and Camera....Pg. 124

CHAPTER 10
Working with Files..Pg. 134

CHAPTER 11
Mail, Skype, and Information Services......................Pg. 146

CHAPTER 12
Customizing the Start Screen..................................Pg. 182

CHAPTER 13
Managing Windows with PC Settings.......................Pg. 194

CHAPTER 14
Using the Windows Store.......................................Pg. 228

CHAPTER 15
Playing Games...Pg. 244

D0517845

PART III   Using the Windows 8.1 Desktop

CHAPTER 16
Running Desktop Apps.. Pg. 252

CHAPTER 17
Managing Storage with File Explorer............................... Pg. 272

CHAPTER 18
Networking Your Home with HomeGroup..................... Pg. 296

CHAPTER 19
Working with Photos and Music from Your Desktop..... Pg. 318

CHAPTER 20
Web Browsing from Your Desktop................................. Pg. 350

PART IV   Managing Windows 8.1

CHAPTER 21
Advanced Configuration Options................................... Pg. 382

CHAPTER 22
User Accounts and System Security .... Pg. 396

CHAPTER 23
Protecting Your System .... Pg. 420

CHAPTER 24
System Maintenance and Performance........................... Pg. 434

Glossary .... Pg. 446
Index .... Pg. 454

ONLINE CONTENT

APPENDIX A
Installing Windows to an Empty Drive

CONTENTS

CHAPTER 1 **WHAT'S NEW AND IMPROVED IN WINDOWS 8.1** 2

Start Screen 4

Live Tiles 5

Supercharged Search 6

Powerful, Flexible Calculator 7

Enhanced Split Screen 8

Internet Explorer 11 9

Easy Photo Editing 10

Windows 8.1 Shortcut Keys 11

CHAPTER 2 **UPGRADING TO WINDOWS 8.1** 12

Starting the Installation 14

Reviewing Settings 16

Completing the Installation 18

CHAPTER 3 **ESSENTIAL WINDOWS 8.1 TASKS** 22

Logging In to Windows 24

Using the On-Screen Keyboard to Log In 25

Moving Around the Start Screen 26

Opening the Charms Bar 27

Using the Touch Keyboard 28

Entering Emoticons and Special Symbols 30

Using a Stylus for Handwriting 32

Using Your Touchscreen 34

Using Your Mouse or Integrated Touchpad 40

Using Keyboard Shortcuts 44

Locking and Unlocking Your PC 46

Choosing Sleep, Shut Down, or Restart 47

CHAPTER 4   USING THE WINDOWS 8.1
START SCREEN **48**

Working with the Start Screen 50

Opening an App 51

Switching Between Apps 52

Closing an App 53

Comparing Modern UI Apps and
Desktop Programs 54

Connecting a Drive 55

Viewing and Using Apps 56

Using Search to Find "Everything" 58

Using Search to Find Specific Types of Content ... 59

Zooming the Start Screen 60

CHAPTER 5   BROWSING THE WEB FROM THE
MODERN UI **62**

Starting Internet Explorer 11 64

Entering a Website Address (URL) 65

Working with Tabs in IE11 66

Creating a New Tab in IE11 67

Using InPrivate Browsing 68

Reopening a Frequently Used Web Page 70

Removing an Entry from the Frequent List 71

Pinning a Page to the Start Screen 72

Unpinning a Page from the Start Screen 74

Closing a Tab in IE11 75

Printing a Web Page 76

Viewing a Page on the Windows Desktop 78

Closing IE11 79

CHAPTER 6 **USING ALARMS, CALCULATOR, AND SOUND RECORDER** 80

Using Alarms as an Alarm Clock 82

Using Timer 86

Using Stopwatch 88

Starting Calculator and Switching Modes 90

Converting Values with Calculate 92

Recording Audio with Sound Recorder 94

Editing Recorded Audio 96

CHAPTER 7 **ENJOYING MUSIC AND VIDEO** 98

Playing Your Music Collection with Music 100

Exploring Your Music Library 102

Creating a Radio Station 103

Explore Featured and Top Music 104

Playing Music from Explore 105

Starting the Video App 106

Learning More About a Highlighted Video 107

Buying Music and Videos 108

Searching for TV Shows and Movies 110

Playing and Downloading Your Purchase 111

CHAPTER 8 USING MOVIE MOMENTS 112

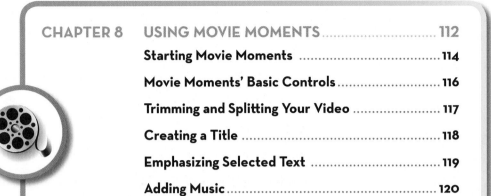

Starting Movie Moments 114

Movie Moments' Basic Controls 116

Trimming and Splitting Your Video 117

Creating a Title 118

Emphasizing Selected Text 119

Adding Music 120

Previewing and Saving Your Video 121

Sharing Your Video 122

CHAPTER 9 VIEWING AND TAKING PHOTOS
WITH PHOTOS AND CAMERA 124

Shooting Photos with Camera 126

Using the Self Timer 128

Using Video Mode 129

View Your Photos with Camera Roll 130

Crop Your Photos 131

Making and Saving Other Changes 132

CHAPTER 10 WORKING WITH FILES 134

Viewing Files on SkyDrive 136

Creating Folders and Adding Files in SkyDrive 138

Delete and Rename Files or Folders on
SkyDrive and This PC 140

Cutting and Pasting Files and Folders in
This PC or SkyDrive 142

Copying and Pasting Files in the Same Folder 143

Using Open With 144

**CHAPTER 11   MAIL, SKYPE, AND INFORMATION
SERVICES** **146**

   Starting Mail **148**

   Reading a Message in Mail **150**

   Marking a Message as Junk **152**

   Viewing a Newsletter **153**

   Writing and Sending a Message **154**

   Starting and Using Calendar **156**

   Scheduling Appointments with Calendar **158**

   Getting Directions with Maps **160**

   Trip Planning with Maps **162**

   Using the People App **164**

   Checking Weather with the Weather App **166**

   Using Finance **168**

   **Creating a Shopping List from a Recipe
with Food & Drink** **170**

   **Using Health & Fitness for Nutritional
Information** **172**

   Starting and Joining Skype **174**

   Selecting Favorites **176**

   Receiving a Call with Skype **177**

   Placing a Call with Skype **178**

   Text Messaging with Skype **180**

CHAPTER 12   CUSTOMIZING THE START SCREEN............ 182

Relocating Tiles on the Start Screen 184

Setting Up Name Groups 185

Pinning an App to the Start Screen 186

Unpinning an Object from the Start Screen 187

Pinning a Folder to the Start Screen 188

Personalizing the Start Screen 189

Adjusting the Size of Start Screen Tiles 190

Turning Live Tiles Off and On 192

**CHAPTER 13   MANAGING WINDOWS WITH
PC SETTINGS** 194

Adjusting System Volume 196

Changing Screen Brightness and Notifications.... 197

PC Settings Overview... 198

Customize the Lock Screen................................ 199

Setting Display Resolution................................. 200

Adjusting Mouse and Touchpad Settings............. 201

Changing AutoPlay Settings............................... 202

Viewing PC Info 203

Managing SkyDrive Storage Settings 204

Setting Camera Roll Options 206

Sync Settings 207

Metered Connections 208

Setting Search Options...................................... 209

Setting App Share Options 210

General Notification Settings 211

App-Specific Notification Settings......................... 212

App Sizes and Uninstall Options........................... 213

General Privacy Settings 214

Configuring Location Settings 215

Configuring Webcam Usage................................ 216

Configuring Microphone Usage 217

Configuring Time Zone.................................... 218

Configuring Ease of Access 220

The Recent Settings Pane................................. 226

CHAPTER 14   USING THE WINDOWS STORE................... 228

Going to the Store.. 230

Searching for Apps by Name 231

Browsing for Apps by Category........................... 232

Learning More about an App 234

Searching for Apps by Keyword Phrase 236

Installing an App... 237

Rating an App 238

Uninstalling an App from the Start Screen.........239

Adding a Payment Method to Your Account........ 240

Viewing Your Apps 242

CHAPTER 15   PLAYING GAMES.............................. 244

Shopping for Games..246

Managing Your Online Gaming Experience 248

Revisiting the Xbox Games Page for
Your Game... 250

CHAPTER 16 RUNNING DESKTOP APPS 252

Opening the Apps Screen 254

Searching for "Hidden" Apps 255

Using Sort Options to Find an App 256

Starting a Desktop App from the Apps Screen 258

Pinning a Desktop App to the Start Screen 260

Adding an App to the Desktop Taskbar 261

Switching Between Apps 262

Using the Snipping Tool 264

Using Sticky Notes 266

Using Character Map with WordPad 268

Printing 270

CHAPTER 17 MANAGING STORAGE WITH
FILE EXPLORER 272

Starting File Explorer 274

Introduction to File Explorer 275

Using the Home Tab 276

Using the View Tab 278

Copying and Moving Files or Folders 280

Dealing with Filename Conflicts 282

Burning Data Discs 284

Selecting, Viewing, and Grouping Options 288

Creating Compressed Files with the Share Tab ... 292

Using Frequent Places 293

Managing Drives 294

CHAPTER 18 NETWORKING YOUR HOME WITH
HOMEGROUP 296

Connecting to an Unsecured Wireless
Network..**298**

Connecting to a Secured Private Network **300**

Connecting to a Hidden Network **302**

Disconnecting and Disabling Wireless Access **303**

Creating a HomeGroup from the Start Screen ..**304**

Viewing the Password for Your HomeGroup **306**

Joining a HomeGroup from the Start Screen.....**307**

Opening the Network and Internet Window
in Control Panel..**308**

Setting Up a HomeGroup from Network
and Internet...**310**

Joining a HomeGroup from Network
and Internet...**312**

Opening HomeGroup Files................................**314**

Customized Sharing for Folders You Choose **315**

Viewing a Folder's Sharing Settings **316**

Leaving a HomeGroup from the Network
Screen **317**

CHAPTER 19 WORKING WITH PHOTOS AND MUSIC FROM YOUR DESKTOP **318**

Adding Pictures to Your Pictures Library 320

Importing Pictures 322

Selecting Import Options 324

Using Windows Photo Viewer 326

Printing Photos with Windows Photo Viewer 328

Starting Windows Media Player 330

Playing an Audio CD 332

Using Playback Controls in Windows Media
Player 334

Ripping (Copying) an Audio CD 336

Selecting and Playing Albums and Individual
Tracks 340

Setting Up Playlists 344

Syncing Files to a Media Player 346

Burning (Creating) a Music CD 348

CHAPTER 20 WEB BROWSING FROM YOUR DESKTOP **350**

Starting IE11 from the Desktop 352

Entering a Website Address (URL) 353

Working with Tabs 354

Setting Your Home Page 355

Opening a Link 356

Using Page Zoom 358

Previewing and Printing a Web Page 359

Opening the Favorites Center 360

Adding Favorites to the Favorites Bar 361

Adding Favorites to the Favorites Center 362

Organizing Favorites 364

Saving a Tab Group as a Favorite 366

Opening a Favorite Website or Tab Group 368

Using Accelerators 369

Using InPrivate Browsing from the Desktop 370

Managing Popups 372

Setting Internet Privacy Features 374

Deleting Selected Items from Your History List .. 376

Deleting All Items from Your History List 377

Saving a Web Page 378

Emailing a Web Page or Link 380

CHAPTER 21 ADVANCED CONFIGURATION OPTIONS 382

Configuring Windows Update 384

Adding and Using an Additional Display 386

Personalizing Your Desktop Background 388

Selecting a Standard Window Color 390

Creating a Customized Window Color 391

Selecting a Screen Saver 392

Saving a Desktop Theme 393

Managing Devices and Printers from the
Windows Desktop 394

Seeing What Programs Are Running with
Task Manager 395

CHAPTER 22 USER ACCOUNTS AND SYSTEM
SECURITY 396

Setting Up Windows 8 for Multiple Users........... 398

Changing an Account Type 400

Selecting an Account to Log In To 402

Setting Up PIN Number Access 404

Configuring Parental Controls with
Family Safety... 406

Reviewing Family Safety Logs............................. 412

Setting Up and Using a Picture Password............ 416

CHAPTER 23 PROTECTING YOUR SYSTEM 420

Looking at User Account Control 422

Configuring Windows Update............................. 424

Protecting Your Files with File History............... 426

Recovering Files with File History 428

Checking Security Settings with Windows
Action Center.. 430

Checking for Viruses and Spyware with
Windows Defender... 432

Setting Windows Defender Options..................... 433

CHAPTER 24 SYSTEM MAINTENANCE
            AND PERFORMANCE 434

Selecting a Power Scheme 436

Viewing Disk Information 437

Checking Drives for Errors 438

Using Windows Troubleshooters 440

Using System Restore 442

Displaying System Information .... online

Testing Memory .... online

Scheduling Tasks .... online

Opening the Troubleshoot Startup Menu .... online

Using Refresh .... online

Glossary 446

Index 454

ONLINE ELEMENTS
Appendix A: Installing Windows to an Empty Drive

EASY WINDOWS® 8.1

ISBN-13: 978-0-7897-5225-3
ISBN-10: 0-7897-5225-5

Library of Congress Control Number: 2013950630

Printed in the United States of America

First Printing: November 2013

TRADEMARKS

WARNING AND DISCLAIMER

BULK SALES

Que Publishing offers excellent discounts on this book when ordered in quan-tity for bulk purchases or special sales. For more information, please contact

U.S. Corporate and Government Sales
1-800-382-3419
corpsales@pearsontechgroup.com

For sales outside the United States, please contact

International Sales
international@pearsoned.com

Editor-in-Chief
Greg Wiegand

Acquisitions Editor
Michelle Newcomb

Development Editor
Todd Brakke

Managing Editor
Sandra Schroeder

Senior Project Editor
Tonya Simpson

Indexer
Erika Millen

Proofreader
Kathy Ruiz

Technical Editor
Vince Averello

Editorial Assistant
Cindy Teeters

Interior Designer
Anne Jones

Cover Designer
Alan Clements

Compositor
Bumpy Design

ABOUT THE AUTHOR

Mark Edward Soper has been using Microsoft Windows ever since version 1.0, and since 1992 he has taught thousands of computer troubleshooting and network students across the country how to use Windows as part of their work and everyday lives. Mark is the author of *Easy Windows 8*, *Easy Microsoft Windows 7*, *Teach Yourself Windows 7 in 10 Minutes*, and *Using Microsoft Windows Live*. Mark also has contributed to Que's *Special Edition Using* series on Windows Me, Windows XP, and Windows Vista; *Easy Windows Vista*; *Windows 7 In Depth*, and has written two books about Windows Vista, including *Maximum PC Microsoft Windows Vista Exposed* and *Unleashing Microsoft Windows Vista Media Center*.

When he's not teaching, learning, or writing about Microsoft Windows, Mark stays busy with many other technology-related activities. He is a longtime contributor to *Upgrading and Repairing PCs*, working on the 11th through 18th, 20th and 21st editions. Mark has co-authored *Upgrading and Repairing Networks*, Fifth Edition, written several books on CompTIA A+ Certification (including two titles covering the current 2012 exams), and written two books about digital photography, *Easy Digital Cameras* and *The Shot Doctor: The Amateur's Guide to Taking Great Digital Photos*. Mark also has become a video content provider for Que Publishing and InformIT and has posted many blog entries and articles at InformIT.com, MaximumPC.com, and other websites. He also teaches digital photography, digital imaging, and Microsoft Office for Ivy Tech Corporate College's southwest Indiana campus in Evansville, Indiana and Windows 8 for the University of Southern Indiana's continuing education department.

DEDICATION

For Zoe, who brings new joy into our lives.

ACKNOWLEDGMENTS

My name's on the cover, but a lot of people, including you, my valued readers, have helped put it there. I thank you for reading this book, and I want you to know who helped me.

"Every good and perfect gift comes from above," and I have seen the goodness and encouragement of God expressed in many ways and many people, most particularly my wife, Cheryl. She saw my gift for writing and teaching when no one else did, and has been blessed along with me to see it grow.

I started using Windows back when it was a graphic overlay over MS-DOS, and there are plenty of people who helped me learn more about Windows through the years. Thanks go to Jim Peck and Mayer Rubin, for whom I taught thousands of students how to troubleshoot systems running Windows 3.1, 95, and 98; magazine editors Edie Rockwood and Ron Kobler, for assigning me to dig deeper into Windows; Ed Bott, who provided my first opportunity to contribute to a major Windows book; Scott Mueller, who asked me to help with *Upgrading and Repairing Windows*; Ivy Tech Corporate College and University of Southern Indiana, for teaching opportunities; Bob Cowart, and Brian Knittel for helping continue my real-world Windows education. And, of course, the Microsoft family.

Thanks also to my family, both for their encouragement over the years and for the opportunity to explain various Windows features and fix things that go wrong. Even though some of them have joined the "dark side" (they have Macs), we still get along, and thanks to Microsoft's determination to "play nicely with others," we can share photos, chat, and enjoy each other's presence from across the room or across the country.

I also want to thank the editorial and design team that Que put together for this book: Many thanks to Michelle Newcomb for bringing me back for another *Easy* series book, and thanks to Todd Brakke, Vince Averello, and Tonya Simpson for overseeing their respective parts of the publishing process. Thanks also to Cindy Teeters for keeping track of invoices and making sure payments were timely.

I have worked with Que Publishing and Pearson since 1999, and I'm looking forward to many more.

WE WANT TO HEAR FROM YOU!

As the reader of this book, *you* are our most important critic and commentator. We value your opinion and want to know what we're doing right, what we could do better, what areas you'd like to see us publish in, and any other words of wisdom you're willing to pass our way.

We welcome your comments. You can email or write to let us know what you did or didn't like about this book—as well as what we can do to make our books better.

Please note that we cannot help you with technical problems related to the topic of this book.

When you write, please be sure to include this book's title and author as well as your name and email address. We will carefully review your comments and share them with the author and editors who worked on the book.

Email: feedback@quepublishing.com

Mail: Que Publishing
         ATTN: Reader Feedback
         800 East 96th Street
         Indianapolis, IN 46240 USA

READER SERVICES

Visit our website and register this book at quepublishing.com/register for convenient access to any updates, downloads, or errata that might be available for this book.

INTRODUCTION

WHY THIS BOOK WAS WRITTEN

Que Publishing's *Easy* series is famous for providing accurate, simple, step-by-step instructions for popular software and operating systems. Windows 8.1 is a major update to its predecessor (already the biggest change in Windows in years), and *Easy Windows 8.1* is here to help you understand and use it. Whether you're a veteran Windows user or new to Windows and computers, there's a lot to learn, and we're here to help.

Easy Windows 8.1 gives you a painless and enjoyable way to discover Windows' essential features. We spent months with Windows 8.1 to discover what's changed from Windows 8, and you get the benefit: an easy-to-read visual guide that gets you familiar with the latest Microsoft product in a hurry.

Your time is valuable, so we've concentrated our efforts on features you're likely to use every day. Our objective: help you use Windows to make your computing life better, more productive, and even more fun.

HOW TO READ *EASY WINDOWS 8.1*

So, what's the best way to read this book?

You have a few options, based on what you know about computers and Windows. Try one of these:

- Start at Chapter 1, "What's New and Improved in Windows 8.1," and work your way through.

- Go straight to the chapters that look the most interesting.

- Hit the table of contents or the index and go directly to the sections that tell you stuff you don't know already.

Any of these methods will work—and to help you get a better feel for what's inside, here's a closer look at what's in each chapter.

BEYOND THE TABLE OF CONTENTS— WHAT'S INSIDE

Chapter 1, "What's New and Improved in Windows 8.1," provides a quick overview of the most important new and improved features in Windows 8.1. If you're reading this book mainly to brush up on what's new and different, start here and follow the references to the chapters with more information.

Chapter 2, "Upgrading to Windows 8.1," is designed for users of Windows 7 or previous versions who are upgrading to Windows 8.1. This chapter covers the process and helps you make the best choices along the way.

Chapter 3, "Essential Windows 8.1 Tasks," shows you how to log in to Windows 8.1, how to use the touch keyboard or handwriting interface, how to use shortcut keys, how to work with a touchscreen, how to lock and unlock your computer, and how to shut it down or put it into sleep mode.

Chapter 4, "Using the Windows 8.1 Start Screen," helps you understand how to use the tile-based user interface on the Start screen. Learn how to start programs, switch between programs, close programs, and search for files and programs.

Chapter 5, "Browsing the Web from the Modern UI," provides step-by-step instructions on how to use Internet Explorer 11 when you run it from the Start screen.

Chapter 6, "Using Alarms, Calculator, and Sound Recorder," introduces you to three new Windows 8.1 apps and how they work.

Chapter 7, "Enjoying Music and Video," helps you discover your favorite music and video sources, download and buy music and video, and enjoy your personal collection.

Chapter 8, "Using Movie Moments," shows you how to use this new Windows 8.1 feature to create and upload short videos.

Chapter 9, "Viewing and Taking Photos with Photos and Camera," is your guide to the Photos and Camera apps. Whether you use your tablet's built-in webcam and backward-facing camera or a digital camera, learn how to view and edit your pictures.

Chapter 10, "Working with Files," shows you how Windows 8.1 brings local and cloud-based file storage to the Start screen.

Chapter 11, "Mail, Skype, and Information Services," introduces you to key features in the new and improved Mail, Skype, People, Calendar, Maps, Weather, Reader, Finance, and Food & Drink apps to stay in touch with the world around you.

Chapter 12, "Customizing the Start Screen," shows you how to pin folders and websites to the Start screen, how to change its background and color scheme, and how to rearrange tiles.

Chapter 13, "Managing Windows with PC Settings," helps you manage everything from screen resolutions and app settings to lock screen, PC information, and date/time settings from the Start screen.

Chapter 14, "Using the Windows Store," takes you on a tour of the preferred way to get free and commercial apps for your device. Learn how to search for apps, download free apps, and buy new apps.

Chapter 15, "Playing Games," shows you how to build a gaming library from the Windows Store and enjoy yourself.

Chapter 16, "Running Desktop Apps," helps you run and manage programs that run from the Windows desktop, use built-in apps such as Snipping Tool, Sticky Notes, Character Map, and WordPad, and print files.

Chapter 17, "Managing Storage with File Explorer," helps you manage files, folders, and drives, burn data discs, and copy/move files safely.

Chapter 18, "Networking Your Home with Home-Group," shows you how to use the HomeGroup feature to set up and manage a network with Windows 7, Windows 8, and Windows 8.1 computers. This chapter also helps you understand which network functions can be performed from the Start screen and which ones run from the Windows desktop.

Chapter 19, "Working with Photos and Music from Your Desktop," helps you use Windows apps for photo viewing and Windows Media Player for playing music and ripping CDs.

Chapter 20, "Web Browsing from Your Desktop," shows you how to use Internet Explorer 11's desktop-only features for tab, home page, and favorites management.

Chapter 21, "Advanced Configuration Options," shows you how to add a second display, personalize your desktop, manage devices and printers, and use Task Manager to find out what's happening inside your PC.

Chapter 22, "User Accounts and System Security," introduces you to different ways to set up a Windows 8 login for users, how to add additional users, and how to use parental controls to keep an eye on what young users are up to.

Chapter 23, "Protecting Your System," shows you how to keep Windows 8 updated, protect your files, create a restore point, and check for spyware.

Chapter 24, "System Maintenance and Performance," helps you improve system speed and solve problems that can prevent your system from running properly.

Baffled by PC and Windows terminology? Check out the Glossary!

Also be sure to check out additional tasks available online at quepublishing.com/register.

Enjoy!

WHAT'S NEW AND IMPROVED IN WINDOWS 8.1

Microsoft Windows 8.1 is a significant update of the eighth generation of the world's most popular desktop and laptop computer operating system. Windows 8.1 extends the reach of Windows not just to standard desktop and laptop PCs and full-size tablets (11-inch and larger), but also to a newer generation of tablet devices as small as eight inches. It also brings along big improvements in functionality, ease of use, and customization to existing Windows 8 users.

Windows 8.1 makes switching between its default Modern UI tile-based interface and the classic Windows desktop easier than ever before, while adding more customization and management features to the Modern UI. If you prefer to boot directly to the Windows desktop, you can. However, you can toggle between the Windows Start screen and the Windows desktop at any time with just a click or two of the new Start button.

Familiar Windows 8 features, such as Search, the Windows Store, and Start menu apps, are also more powerful and easier to use in Windows 8.1. This chapter takes a deeper look at the most notable of these improvements.

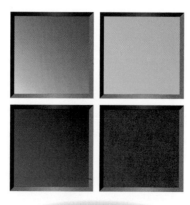

The Windows 8.1 Start screen provides live updates and lets you customize colors, patterns, and program groups.

Use Calculate for immediate numeric and financial calculations.

Search brings you a world of information with a single search.

Alarms provide you with visual and audible reminders.

START SCREEN

When you start or log in to Windows 8.1, the Windows Start screen appears by default. Use your touchscreen, touchpad, or mouse to scroll horizontally through the tiles to access the programs or features you want.

Start

1 Click or tap a program tile or icon to start it.

2 Scroll to the right to see more program tiles.

3 Click the down arrow, or flick downward to see Apps.

4 The Apps menu displays Start screen (Modern UI) apps to the left; scroll to the right for apps provided by your device vendor and for Windows desktop apps.

End

NOTE

Windows 8 Start Screen To learn more about working with the Start screen, see Chapter 4, "Using the Windows 8.1 Start Screen." ■

LIVE TILES

Many of the programs shown on the Start screen are live tiles—that is, they contain some form of continually updated information. This section highlights some of these live tiles; other live tiles include Photos, Travel, News, and Finance.

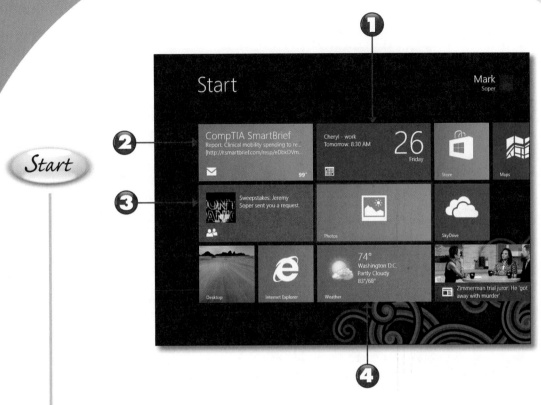

Start

1 Use your Microsoft account to sign in to your computer, and Calendar provides a live feed of events.

2 Mail also brings you your latest emails.

3 The People tile brings you social network messages from your friends and contacts.

4 Configure Weather with your preferred location for the current conditions and forecast.

End

SUPERCHARGED SEARCH

Windows 8.1 makes searching for everything from the web to a specific file easier than ever before. Just start typing from the Start screen, and Windows 8.1 automatically opens the Search window. You've never seen a single search bring you so much information before.

1 Type what to search for, and the Search box opens and displays the text you type.

2 Matching files on your computer.

3 Related searches from which you can choose.

4 Selected search and search details.

5 Photos, songs, and other media.

End

NOTE

More About Searching To learn more about the Search feature, see "Using Search to Find 'Everything'," and "Using Search to Find Specific Types of Content," both in Chapter 4. ■

POWERFUL, FLEXIBLE CALCULATOR

Windows 8.1 includes lots of new and extremely useful apps, including a triple-threat calculator that includes an amazing number of conversions. No more racking your brain to convert liters to ounces or anything else from volume to speed.

Start

1 Choose the conversion type.

2 Select what to convert from.

3 Select what to convert to.

4 Enter the amount to convert

5 Get the answer—instantly!

End

NOTE

More About Calculator To learn more about using Calculator, see Chapter 6, "Using Alarms, Calculator, and Sound Recorder." ■

ENHANCED SPLIT SCREEN

Windows 8.1 enables you to adjust how you split the screen, so you can display two programs on screen the way you like.

Start

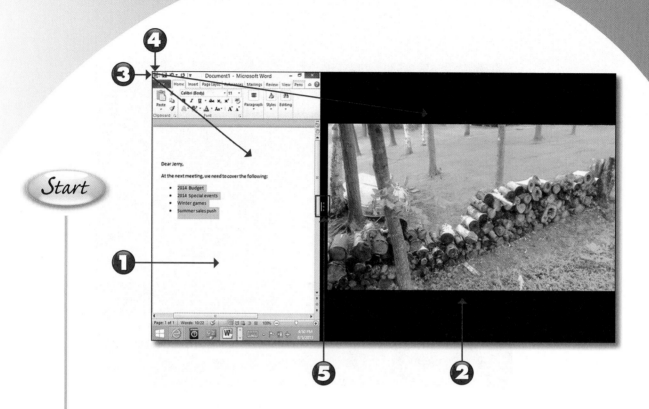

1 Start an app.

2 Start another app.

3 Drag and release an app to one side of the screen.

4 Drag and release an app to the other side of the screen.

5 Adjust the border between the apps.

End

INTERNET EXPLORER 11

Windows 8 includes Internet Explorer 11 (IE11), the latest version of Microsoft's popular web browser. When launched from the Start screen, IE11 provides a streamlined view of the Web. When you start IE11 from the Windows desktop, the program offers full support for plug-ins and tabbed browsing.

Start

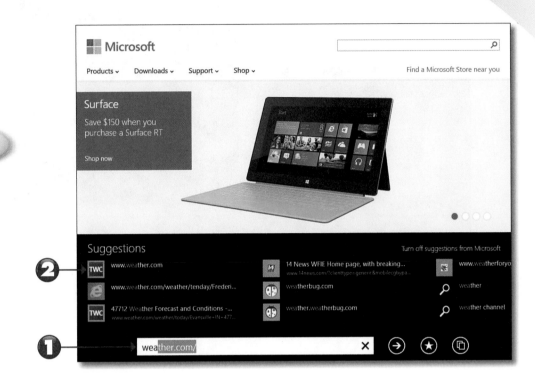

1 Enter the website address (URL) or part of the website name.

2 If one of the suggested sites is the one you want, click it.

End

NOTE

Web Browsing in the New UI To learn more about using Internet Explorer 11 from the Start screen, see Chapter 5, "Browsing the Web from the Modern UI." ■

EASY PHOTO EDITING

Windows 8.1 includes an updated Photos app and a new Camera app. Both of them enable you to fix color, contrast, and brightness and add special effects to pictures you shoot with a digital camera or your device's built-in camera.

Start

1 Rotate, crop, and edit options.

2 Click to take more photos with Camera.

3 Click to use the photo on the lock screen.

4 Here is the same photo after adding color, light, and selective-focus effects via the Edit button.

5 Click to convert the photo to black and white.

End

NOTE

Shopping at the Windows 8 Store For more details about shopping for apps at the Windows 8 Store, see Chapter 14, "Using the Windows Store." ∎

WINDOWS 8.1 SHORTCUT KEYS

Windows 8.1 includes shortcut keys you can use to start Windows desktop apps and utilities. One of these helpful shortcuts enables you to quickly access a list of common Windows desktop applications.

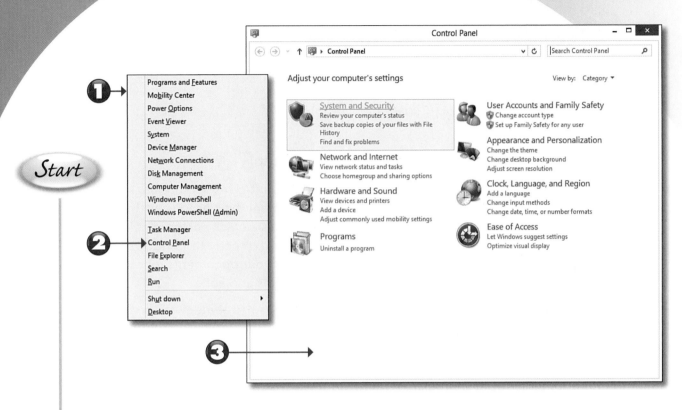

1 Press the **Windows key** and the **X key**, and a list of Windows desktop programs appears.

2 Click a program.

3 The program opens on the Windows desktop.

End

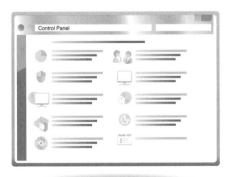

UPGRADING TO WINDOWS 8.1

If you're a Windows 8 user, congratulations! Microsoft gives you the upgrade to Windows 8.1 for free. You don't even have to do anything as long as the Windows Automatic Updates feature is enabled. It's a quick and painless process. If you're using Windows 7, you can upgrade directly to Windows 8.1—but at a cost. Upgrading to Windows 8.1 preserves your documents, photos, videos, downloads, and music but *not* your programs and apps.

If you can, we recommend upgrading from Windows 7 to Windows 8 first, and then upgrading from Windows 8 to Windows 8.1.

An upgrade from Windows 7 to Windows 8 gives you the option to keep your existing programs and apps. The process of upgrading from Windows 7 to Windows 8 is covered in detail in Chapter 2 of our book *Easy Windows 8* (first edition), which is available for free online on this book's web page at www.informit.com/title/9780789752253.

However, if you want to go directly from Windows 7 to Windows 8.1 (or don't have any other choice in the matter), read on.

Starting the upgrade
from Windows 7

Selecting the
files to save

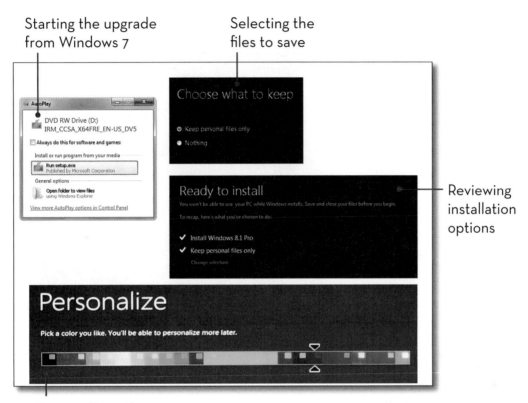

Reviewing
installation
options

Personalizing the
Start screen

STARTING THE INSTALLATION

To install Windows 8.1 on a computer running Windows 7 and have the option to keep your files (but not your programs), you must start Windows 7 and then launch the installation process from the Windows desktop. Follow these steps if you install from a DVD. If you install from a downloadable executable file or a USB flash memory drive, step 1 will vary. See the instructions provided with the download or flash media for details.

Start

Continued

1 Insert the Windows 8.1 DVD into the optical drive on your computer and click **Run setup.exe** from the AutoPlay dialog box when it appears.

2 Click **Download and install updates**.

3 Click the **I want to help make the installation of Windows better** checkbox if it's empty.

4 Click **Next**.

TIP

What Will You Need to Reinstall? Ask Belarc First! If you don't know what programs are installed on your system, the free (for personal use) Belarc Advisor is a terrific way to find out. Learn more at http://www.belarc.com/free_download.html. Run it *before* you start the upgrade (which will remove all of your installed apps) so you know what programs will be removed. Then, you can decide which ones to reinstall. ■

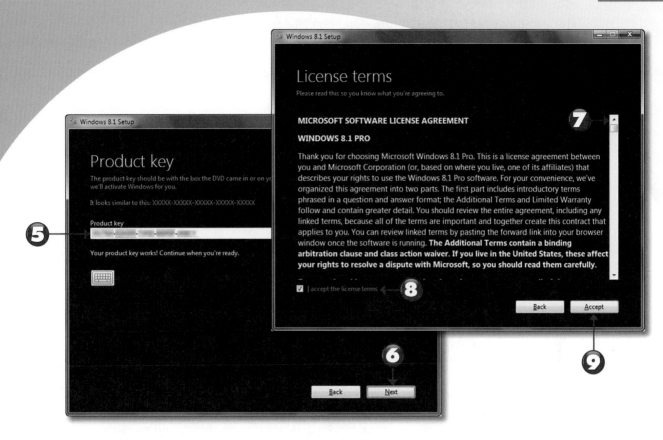

5 Enter the product key (it's provided in your upgrade disc package).

6 Click **Next**.

7 Scroll through and read the license terms.

8 Click the **I accept the license terms** checkbox.

9 Click **Accept**.

End

TIP

Starting the Upgrade Manually If the AutoPlay dialog box shown in step 1 doesn't appear, open Computer, navigate to the optical drive where the Windows 8.1 disc is located, view the contents of the drive, and double-click Setup.exe. ■

REVIEWING SETTINGS

The last decision to make before you start the upgrade is whether to keep your personal files. Unless you are setting up a computer to be used by another person, I recommend you use the "keep personal files" option to keep your files.

1 Select **Keep personal files only**.

2 Click **Next**.

Continued

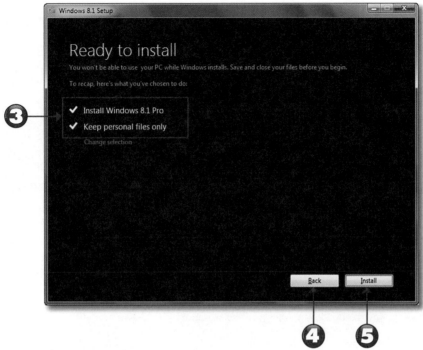

3 Review your settings.

4 Click **Back** if you need to make any changes.

5 Click **Install**.

End

COMPLETING THE INSTALLATION

Windows does most of the work during the installation process and restarts your computer a few times. However, near the end of the installation process, you will be prompted to provide a few responses.

1 Select the Start screen color scheme you prefer.

2 Click **Next**.

3 Click **Use express settings**.

Continued

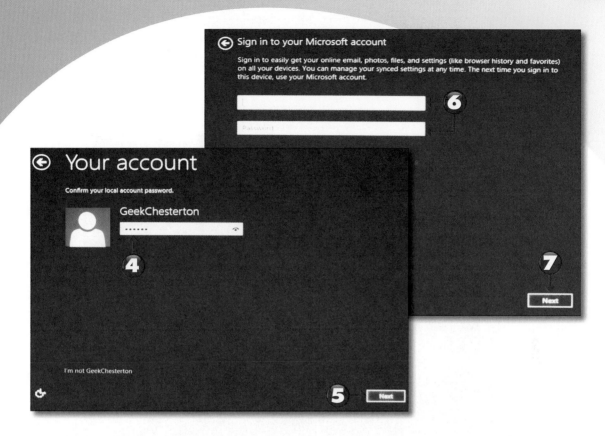

4 Enter the password for your local account.

5 Click **Next**.

6 Enter your preferred email address and password for your Microsoft account.

7 Click **Next**.

Continued

NOTE

What Is a Microsoft Account? Windows Live, Messenger, Xbox 360, and Hotmail accounts are all Microsoft accounts. ■

NOTE

Getting a Microsoft Account If you don't have a Microsoft account, you can get one by clicking the **Create a new account** link. ■

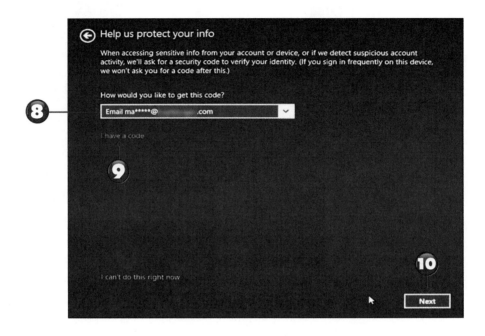

8 If prompted, select how you'd like to receive your security code.

9 If you already have a security code, click **I have a code**.

10 Click **Next**.

Continued

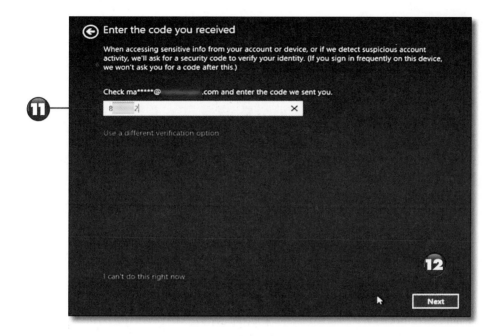

 If prompted, enter the security code.

 Click **Next**. Your account is created, and Windows starts.

End

NOTE

Logging In to Windows 8 If there is only one user on your system, Windows 8 logs you in automatically. If there is more than one user, you must select the user and log in manually. To learn how to log in to Windows 8, see Chapter 3, "Essential Windows 8.1 Tasks." ■

NOTE

Software and Hardware Compatibility In general, software and hardware that work with Windows 7 also work with Windows 8. Check the Microsoft Windows 8 page at http://windows.microsoft.com for more information. ■

Chapter 3

ESSENTIAL WINDOWS 8.1 TASKS

If you've upgraded from Windows 7 or earlier versions, the new and improved Windows 8.1 user interface is like nothing you've seen before on a PC. Even if you've upgraded from Windows 8, Windows 8.1 provides improved ways to use your PC. You'll notice the changes as soon as you log in to the system. In this chapter, you learn how to log in, how to interact with the new user interface through a mouse, keyboard, or touch interface, how to lock your computer, and how to shut it down.

Login Screen

Preparing to put the computer into low-power sleep mode.

Charms Bar

Entering symbols with the touch keyboard.

Using the handwriting panel.

Displaying the Run dialog box with Windows key+R.

LOGGING IN TO WINDOWS

To log in to Windows 8.1, you must know the username and password (if any) set up for your account. If you installed Windows 8.1 yourself, be sure to make note of this information when you are prompted to provide it during the installation process. You also log in to Windows 8.1 when you are waking up the computer from sleep, unlocking it, or restarting it.

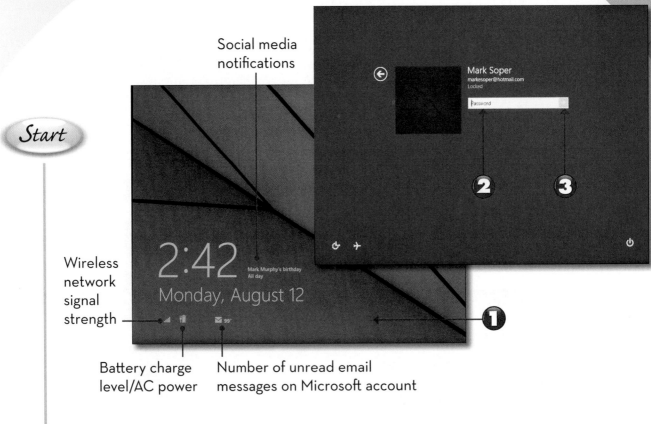

Social media notifications

Wireless network signal strength

Battery charge level/AC power

Number of unread email messages on Microsoft account

 Start

1 Press the **spacebar**, click your mouse, or tap your touchscreen or touchpad.

2 Type your password.

3 Press **Enter** or click the arrow. The Start screen appears.

End

NOTE

Seeing Your Password To see the characters you are entering, click the eye icon next to the arrow in step 3. You must enter at least one character before the eye icon is visible. See the next exercise for an example of the eye icon. ■

USING THE ON-SCREEN KEYBOARD TO LOG IN

You can also use the Accessibility menu's on-screen keyboard to log in. Here's how to open and use this menu.

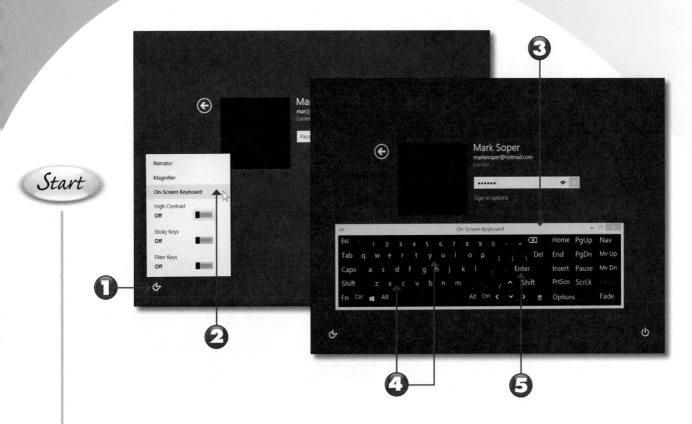

Start

1. Click the accessibility icon.

2. Click **On-Screen Keyboard**.

3. Click and drag the keyboard down so you can see the password window.

4. Click each character in your password.

5. Click the **Enter** key, and the Start screen appears.

End

NOTE

Forget Your Password? Check the Hint If you are using a local account (as you specified during the Windows 8.1 installation) and mistype your password, a password hint is displayed if you provided one during installation. ■

MOVING AROUND THE START SCREEN

The Start screen appears after you log in. In this lesson, you learn how to navigate the Start screen.

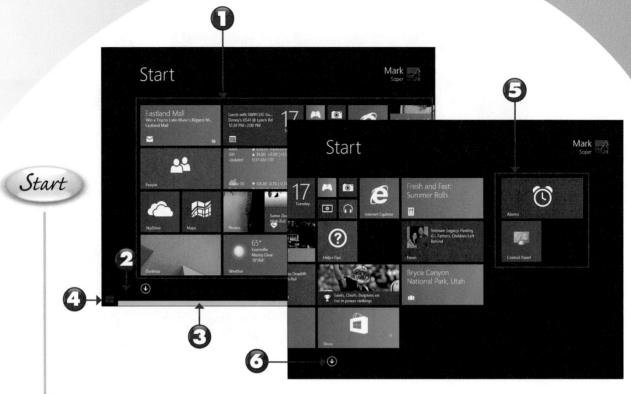

1 Internet-enabled and social-media program tiles are on the left side of the Start screen, as is the Windows Desktop tile.

2 Move the mouse to display the scrollbar.

3 Click and drag the scrollbar to the right.

4 Move the mouse to the lower-left corner to display the Start button.

5 Tiles for programs you pinned to the Start screen appear on the right end of the Start screen.

6 Click the down arrow to see the Apps menu, which lists all installed apps.

End

TIP

Personalize Your App Listing and More To learn more about placing your favorite apps on the Start screen and changing the Start screen's color, see Chapter 12, "Customizing the Windows 8 Start Screen." ■

OPENING THE CHARMS BAR

Windows includes a Charms bar with five charms: Search, Share, Start, Devices, and Settings. You'll use these charms for many tasks throughout this book. If you want to access the on-screen keyboard or stylus, you must open the Charms bar first. Here's how.

Start

① Hover the mouse over or point to the upper-right or lower-right corner of the screen. With a touch screen, swipe in from the right.

② The Charms bar appears on the right side of the screen. Move your mouse or pointer into the Charms bar to select an option.

③ Current date and time.

④ Network connection status.

⑤ Power/charge connection status.

End

NOTE

Date, Time, and Network Connection Status The date, time, network connection status, and power/charge connection status appear when you move your mouse or pointer into the Charms bar in step 3. ■

USING THE TOUCH KEYBOARD

If you have a tablet computer without a physical keyboard, you can access the touch keyboard from the Settings charm and use it for text entry and searches.

 Start

1 Click the **Settings** charm.

2 Click **Keyboard**.

3 Click **Touch keyboard and handwriting panel**.

Continued

NOTE

Accessing the Touch Keyboard from the Desktop The on-screen keyboard is also available from the Desktop taskbar. ■

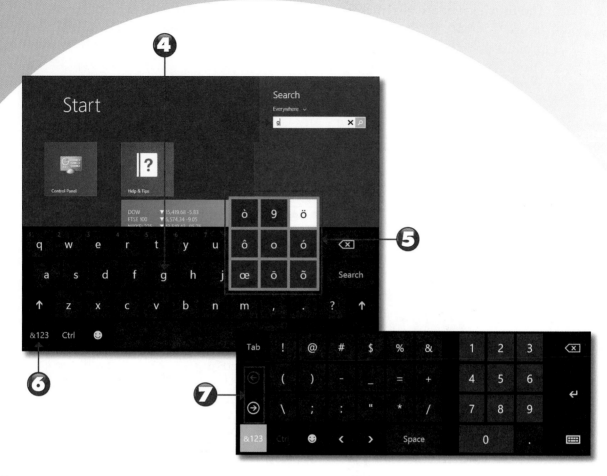

4 Select characters and they appear in the Search box.

5 Click and hold or tap and hold an on-screen key and select from accented or other characters listed.

6 Select to switch between text and numbers or symbols.

7 Select to switch to another symbol set.

End

TIP

Configuring the Touch Keyboard Click Change PC Settings (available from the Settings charm), PC and Devices, and select Typing to make changes to how the Touch Keyboard works. ■

ENTERING EMOTICONS AND SPECIAL SYMBOLS

The touch keyboard also makes entering emoticons and special symbols easy. Here's how to use this feature to enhance your messages and documents. We'll use the WordPad word processor included with Windows for this example.

Start

1 Click to select from various symbols keyboards.

2 Click the **emoticon** keyboard key.

3 Emoticons entered from the emoticon keyboard.

4 Click the **holiday and celebration** key.

5 Holiday and celebration symbols entered from the holiday and celebration keyboard.

Continued

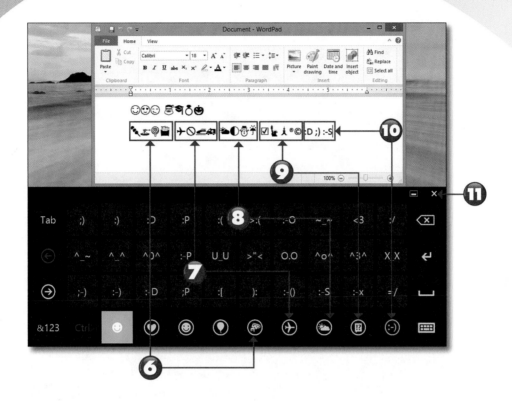

6 **Food** key and characters.

7 **Travel** key and characters.

8 **Sky and weather** key and characters.

9 **Icons** key and characters.

10 **Character emoticon** key and character.

11 Click to close the keyboard.

End

USING A STYLUS FOR HANDWRITING

If you have a stylus with your tablet or touchscreen PC, or you have a touch pad with a stylus, you can use it for text input. Here's how to switch to and use the stylus.

Click the **keyboard** icon.

Click the **stylus** option.

Write the text you want to insert.

Continued

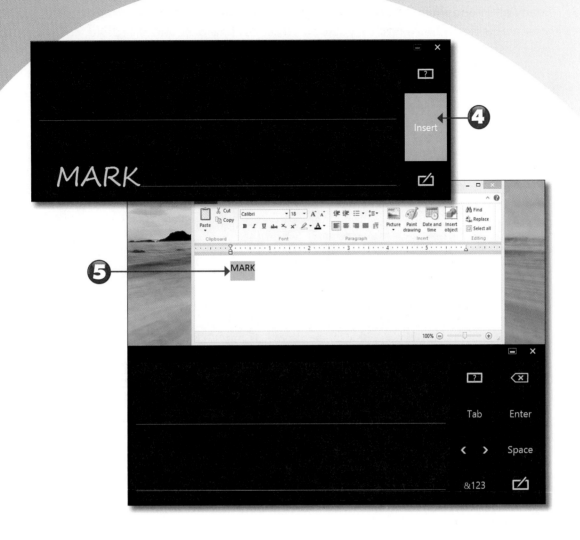

4 Click **Insert** after the text is recognized.

5 The text is inserted into your document.

End

USING YOUR TOUCHSCREEN

If you use Windows on a computer with a touchscreen, such as a tablet, some laptops, and many all-in-one units, you need to know how to open dialog boxes, select text, and copy/paste objects. In this exercise, you open Internet Explorer and WordPad, copy text from IE, and paste it into WordPad.

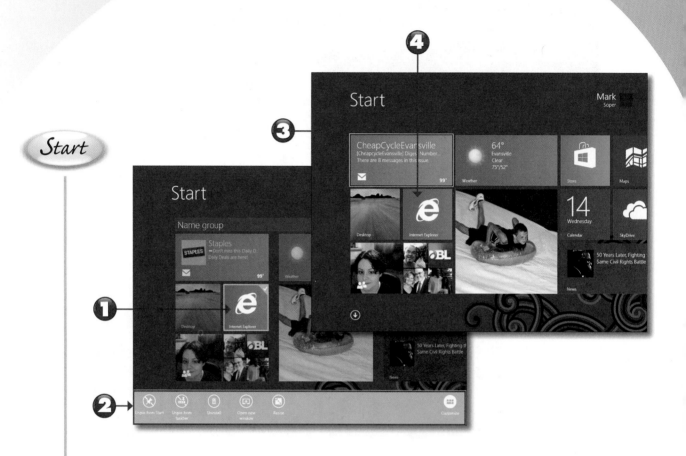

1 Press, hold, and then release the Internet Explorer tile on the Start screen.

2 The App bar appears.

3 Double-tap an empty part of the Start screen to close the menu.

4 Tap the Internet Explorer icon to open the app.

Continued

5 Swipe in from the right to open the Charms bar.

6 Tap **Start** to return to the Start screen.

7 Swipe upward to display the Apps menu.

8 Scroll to the right and tap the **WordPad** icon.

9 Swipe from the middle of the left edge of the screen to reopen Internet Explorer.

Continued

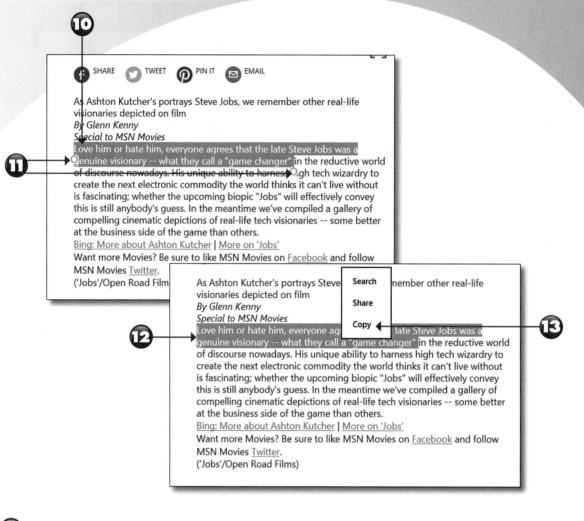

10 To select text, tap and hold a word until it is highlighted.

11 Drag the left and right circles until the words you want to copy are highlighted.

12 Press, hold, and release the highlighted text.

13 Tap **Copy**.

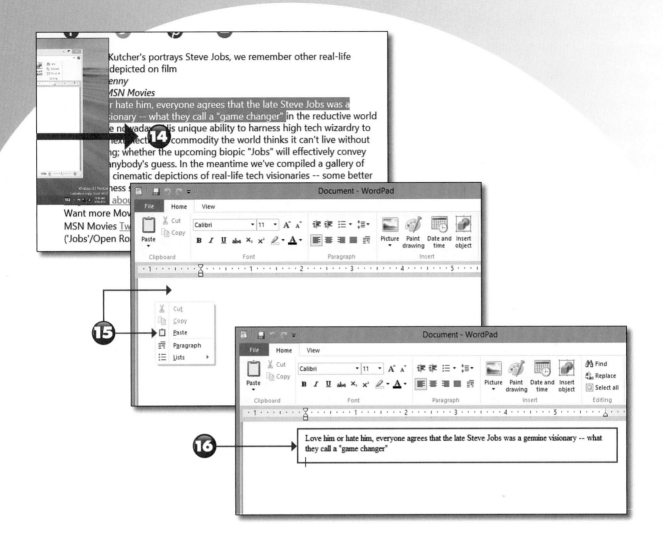

14 Swipe from the middle of the left edge of the screen to reopen WordPad.

15 Press and hold inside the WordPad window and tap **Paste**.

16 The text copied from the web page is pasted into the WordPad window.

Continued

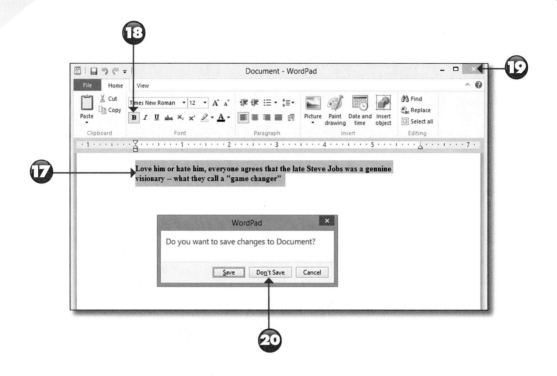

17 Tap and drag across the text to highlight it.

18 Tap the **B** (bold) menu button to activate the command.

19 Tap the **X** (close) button to exit WordPad.

20 Tap **Don't Save**.

Continued

21 Swipe in from the left edge of the screen to reopen Internet Explorer.

22 Drag down the browser window from top to bottom.

23 Continue until the browser window disappears. This action closes Internet Explorer.

End

USING YOUR MOUSE OR INTEGRATED TOUCHPAD

A mouse or integrated touchpad on a Windows computer has two buttons, the left button and the right button. On a touchpad, the lower-left and lower-right corners work like mouse buttons. In this exercise, you open Internet Explorer and WordPad, copy text from IE, and paste it into WordPad.

① Right-click the Internet Explorer tile on the Start screen.

② The App bar appears.

③ Click an empty part of the Start screen to close the customization menu.

④ Click the Internet Explorer icon to open the app.

Continued

TIP

Click and Drag and Right-Clicking *Click and drag* means to press and hold the left mouse button, then move the mouse to select a word, phrase, files, or other objects; release the left button when these items are selected. Right-click is most often used to open menus at the bottom of the Start screen or popup menus in apps or on the Windows desktop. ■

5 Move the mouse until a down-arrow icon appears below the tiles, and click it to see a list of all apps and programs on the computer.

6 Scroll to the right and click the **WordPad** icon.

7 Hover the mouse over the top-left corner of the screen, and click the Internet Explorer thumbnail.

Continued

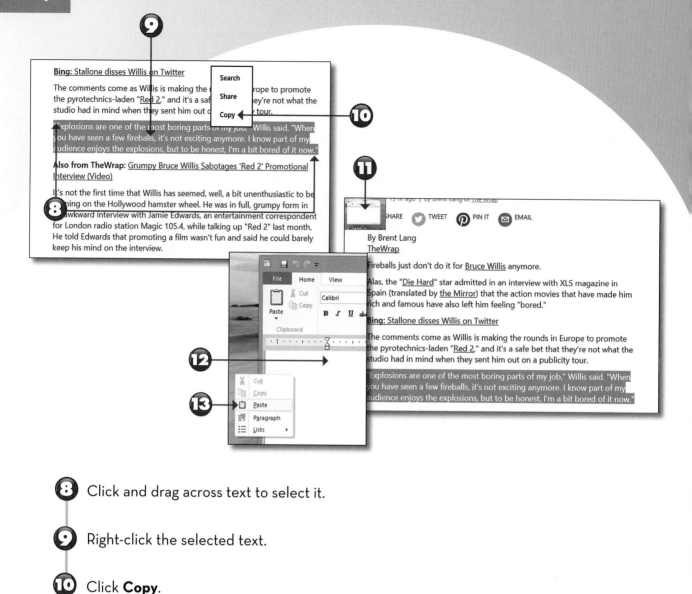

8 Click and drag across text to select it.

9 Right-click the selected text.

10 Click **Copy**.

11 Hover the mouse over the top-left corner of the screen, and click the WordPad thumbnail.

12 Right-click inside the WordPad window.

13 Click **Paste**.

Continued

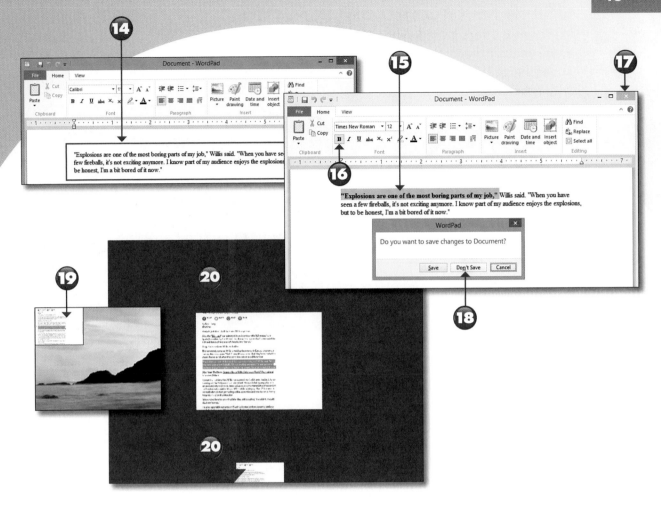

14 The text copied from the web page is pasted into the WordPad window.

15 Click and drag across the text to highlight it.

16 Click the **B** (bold) menu button.

17 Click the **X** (close) button.

18 Click **Don't save**.

19 Hover the mouse over the top-left corner of the screen, and click the Internet Explorer thumbnail.

20 Drag down the browser window from top to bottom. Continue until the browser window disappears.

End

USING KEYBOARD SHORTCUTS

Windows 8 offers more keyboard shortcuts than ever before. As you learn in this lesson, some keyboard shortcuts make working with the Start screen easier, while others supercharge the Windows desktop. These shortcuts use the Windows key in combination with other keys.

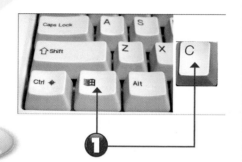

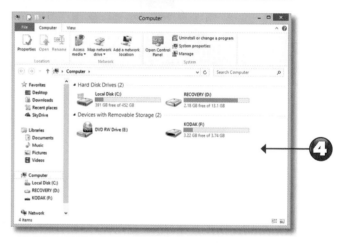

Start

1 Press **Windows key+C**.

2 The Charms bar opens.

3 Press **Windows key+E**.

4 File Explorer opens on the Windows desktop.

Continued

NOTE

More Keyboard and Mouse Shortcuts To find more keyboard and mouse shortcuts, open Help and Support from the Start screen and search for the keyboard shortcut. Look for the "What's new" article. ∎

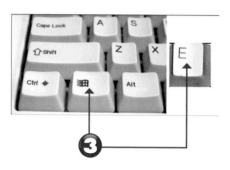

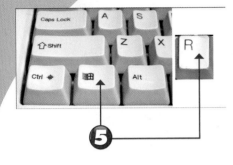

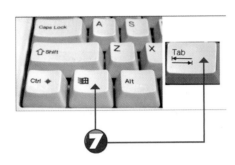

5 Press **Windows key+R**.

6 The Run dialog box opens on the Windows desktop.

7 Press **Windows key+Tab**.

8 Continue to press the **Tab** key—the shortcut toggles through running apps.

End

TIP

Selecting the App to Switch to with Windows key+T When the app you want to use is highlighted, release the keys. The app opens. ■

LOCKING AND UNLOCKING YOUR PC

If you have a password on your account, you can lock your PC when you leave it and unlock it when you return. Once again, the Windows key plays a part in this task.

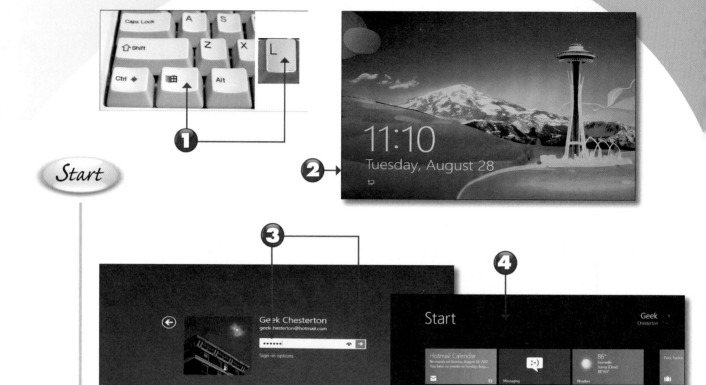

Start

1 Press the **Windows key+L** to lock your computer.

2 Press the **spacebar**, click your mouse, or press the touch keyboard or touchscreen.

3 Enter your password and click the arrow, if applicable.

4 Windows reopens on the screen, where you previously locked it.

End

CHOOSING SLEEP, SHUT DOWN, OR RESTART

When it's time to put away the computer, Windows 8 makes it easy. Want to go back to work (or play) right where you left off? Choose Sleep. Want to start from scratch the next time you start up Windows, or need to put away your PC for more than a few hours? Choose Shut Down. Need to restart the computer? Choose Restart.

Start

1. Move the mouse to either right corner or swipe in from the right.

2. Click **Settings**.

3. Click **Power**.

4. Click one of the options listed.

End

NOTE

Power Options Sleep puts the computer into low-power mode. Shut down turns off the power. Restart restarts the computer. You will need to log in again after choosing any of these options. ■

Chapter 4

USING THE WINDOWS 8.1 START SCREEN

The Windows 8 user interface, or UI for short, is remarkably different from the Windows 7 or previous versions of the operating system you might be used to. By default, the Start screen greets you as soon as you log on to your computer. Before you jump in and start clicking and scrolling, take a few moments to orient yourself to the new interface. Much like learning your way around a new city, navigating Windows 8 has a bit of a learning curve. You must figure out where to find the apps you need and which direction to go to get you where you want to be. Windows 8.1 adds some refinement to the Windows 8 Start screen, and we'll note the differences when they're important.

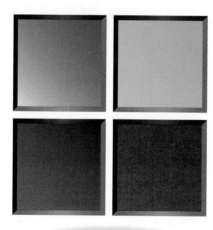

Displaying Apps
by name

Search

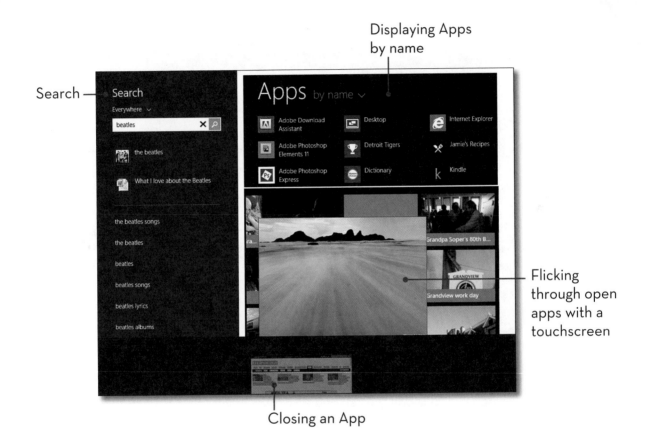

Flicking
through open
apps with a
touchscreen

Closing an App

WORKING WITH THE START SCREEN

By default, the starting point any time you log on to your computer is the Windows 8 Start screen. The Start screen displays the most common app tiles—special icons representing installed apps, short for *applications*. You can also add tiles for desktop programs, such as Microsoft Word, or add shortcuts to web pages, contacts, and more. The Start screen is a jumping-off point for accessing apps, computer settings, and the traditional Windows desktop.

Start

1 Click to switch users or edit your account picture.

2 App tiles appear as square or rectangular boxes, sometimes showing live data (called Live Tiles).

3 Use the scrollbar to navigate through the app tiles.

4 Swipe from the right, or move the mouse to the upper-right or lower-right corner of the screen to display the Charms bar.

5 Opening the Charms bar also displays the current date, time, network, and battery/AC power status.

6 Move the mouse pointer to the bottom-left corner to display the Start button. Click it to switch to toggle between the active app and the Start screen.

End

OPENING AN APP

The app tiles on the Start screen represent applications installed on your computer. You also can add tiles for desktop programs, such as Microsoft Office programs. When you open an app, it fills the screen. The first time you use some apps, you might be prompted to log in to your Microsoft account—just follow the onscreen directions to do so. You can use touch gestures to move around an app, or you can use the mouse and keyboard to interact with the program.

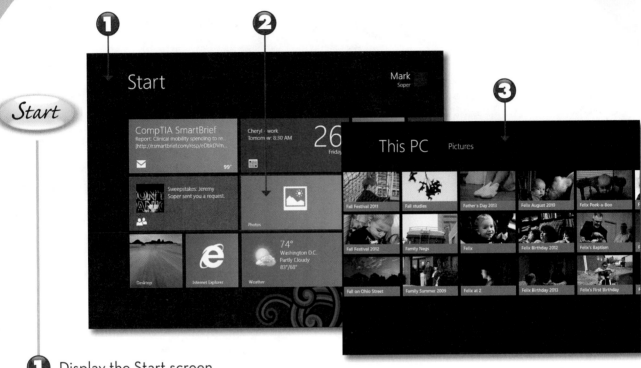

Start

(1) Display the Start screen.

(2) Click the app you want to open.

(3) The app opens in full-screen view. In this example, the Photos app opens.

End

NOTE

Desktop Programs You can still use desktop programs in Windows 8, but they don't use touchscreen capabilities like the Start screen apps do unless they're specifically designed to do so. Regular programs run in their own windows on the traditional Windows desktop and use the same controls found in other desktop software, such as a Ribbon of commands, and Minimize, Maximize, and Restore buttons. ■

SWITCHING BETWEEN APPS

Windows 8 apps do not minimize like traditional program windows. Instead, when you stop working with the app and go on to something else, the app remains suspended in the background ready to pick up where you left off. This makes switching to other apps as easy as a click, swipe, or tap away. You can display a list of open apps on the left side of the screen.

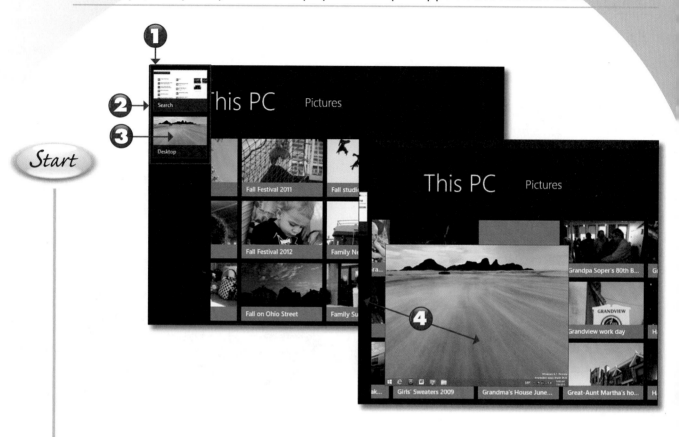

Start

End

1 Swipe from the left side of the screen and back, or hover the mouse pointer in the top-left corner and then move it downward.

2 A list of recently used apps appear as thumbnail images.

3 Select the app you want to open.

4 With a touchscreen, swipe from the left to the middle of the screen to restore a previous task or screen.

TIP

Snapping Apps You can also reopen an app by dragging an app thumbnail from the list of open apps on the left and dropping it in the center of the screen—this is called *snapping*. ■

CLOSING AN APP

Windows 8 Start screen (Modern UI) apps don't use a Close button. If you want to close an app, here's how you do it.

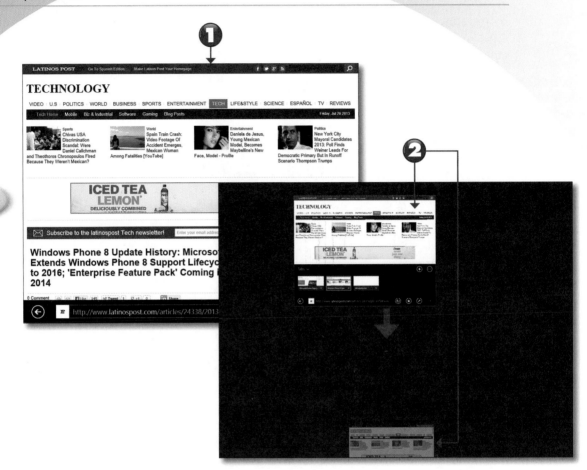

Start

1 Click or tap the top of the app display.

2 Drag it to the bottom of the display until it disappears.

End

NOTE

Confirming You Closed an App To make sure the app is closed, follow the directions in the section "Switching Between Apps." If the app is no longer listed, you successfully closed it. ■

COMPARING MODERN UI APPS AND DESKTOP PROGRAMS

Windows 8's Modern UI apps are designed to respond to touch gestures, use the full screen by default, and do not need window controls (Minimize, Maximize/Restore Down, and Close). Regular desktop programs run in their own resizable windows on the traditional Windows desktop and employ the same controls found in other desktop software. In this example, we compare Windows 8.1 Modern UI (Start screen) Skydrive app with its Windows desktop version.

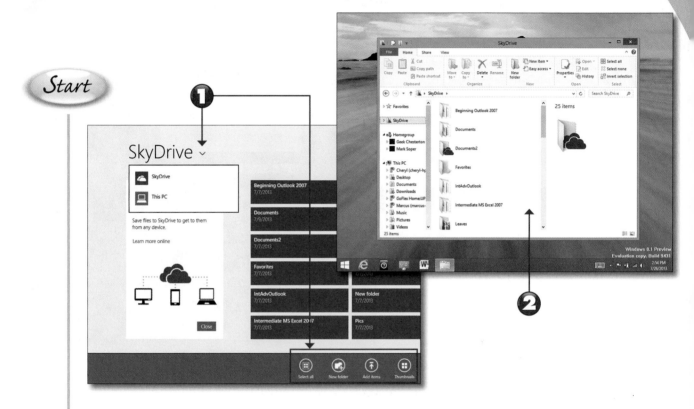

1 A Start screen app fills the whole screen when open, and if you have a touchscreen computer, you can use touch gestures to navigate around the app features.

2 A desktop program opens in its own resizable window on the desktop and features the traditional Ribbon or toolbars, menu bar, and program window controls.

NOTE

No Touchscreen? If your computer does not use a touchscreen, you can still use the traditional methods for navigating around an app using a mouse and keyboard. You can use the mouse to click, drag, scroll, and right-click just as you did with previous versions of Windows. You also can use the keyboard navigation keys and shortcut keys to work with the computer. ■

CONNECTING A DRIVE

When you connect an external drive (USB, FireWire, eSATA) to your computer, Windows gives you a choice of what to do with it.

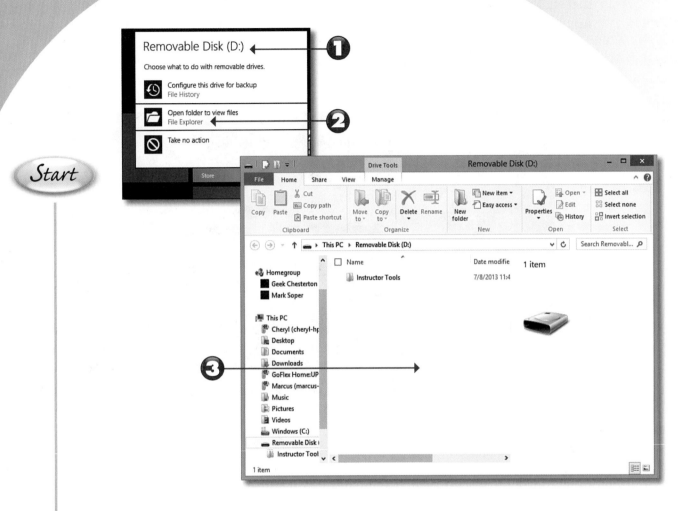

1 Connect a removable drive to your system. The removable disk menu appears.

2 Select an action. In this example, I selected to open File Explorer.

3 File Explorer displays the contents of the drive.

VIEWING AND USING APPS

The default Start screen displays a variety of Windows 8 apps that you can scroll through to view what's available. However, most apps and programs do not appear on the Start screen. To view other apps installed on your computer, including Windows desktop accessories such as Paint and Notepad or Windows system apps such as File Explorer, switch to the Apps screen. The Apps screen lists your apps alphabetically or by other criteria you select.

1. Move your mouse to display the **Apps** (down-arrow) button and click it, or swipe upward from below the program icons (touchscreen).

2. The Apps screen opens; use the scrollbar at the bottom of the screen, or flick the screen to the right or left (touchscreen) to scroll through your apps.

Continued

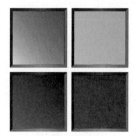

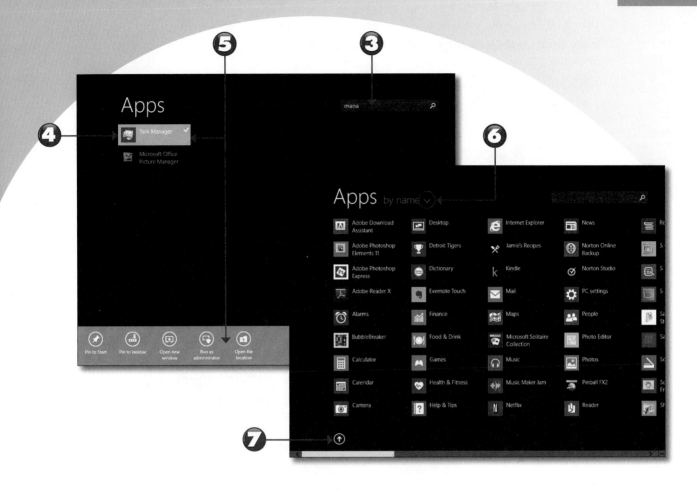

3 To locate a particular app, enter the name.

4 To open an app, click or tap it.

5 To view more controls for an app, right-click (mouse) or press and hold (touchscreen) the app name to open the Apps bar.

6 Open to select other sort options.

7 To return to the Start screen, move the mouse and click the up-arrow button, or flick the screen downward (touchscreen).

End

USING SEARCH TO FIND "EVERYTHING"

Windows 8.1's newly improved Search tool now brings you everything from web pages to local documents and programs with a single search.

Start

1 Type what you're looking for.

2 The Search tool automatically opens and returns matching files and searches.

3 Click a match to learn more.

4 A matching search might include links to additional programs, media, and other information.

5 Scroll to the right to see additional content.

6 Keep scrolling to see more content.

End

USING SEARCH TO FIND SPECIFIC TYPES OF CONTENT

By default, Search looks for matches on the Internet as well as on your local computer. However, if you prefer to limit your search, you can limit it to only specific types of content. Here's how.

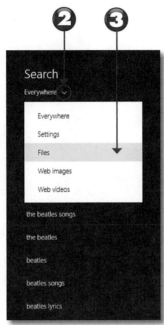

 Enter your search text. The Search box opens.

 Open the Search type menu.

3 Click or tap **Files**.

4 Only files stored on your system or on your SkyDrive are displayed. Click or tap a file to open it in the associated app or program.

End

TIP
Keyboard Shortcut You can quickly summon the Charms bar from the keyboard by pressing Windows key+C. ■

TIP
Using File Explorer You can also search for files using File Explorer. You can access File Explorer from the desktop; press Windows key+X, then select File Explorer. ■

ZOOMING THE START SCREEN

Windows starts you out with several preinstalled apps. As you add more apps and other items to the Start screen, you might need to zoom in and out to view all the app tiles or groups of tiles. You can use the Zoom control on the Start screen to quickly see all your apps at a glance.

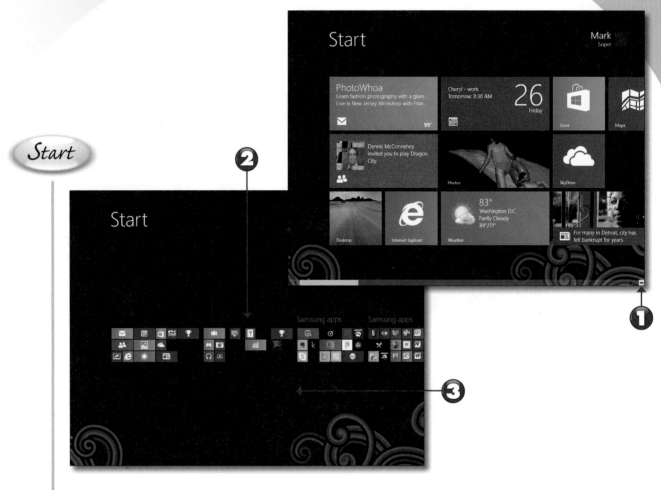

① Tap or click the **Zoom** (minus sign) icon in the lower-right corner of the Start screen.

② The Start screen zooms out.

③ Tap or click an empty area of the screen to return to normal view.

End

TIP

Grouping Apps You can move app tiles around on the Start screen and make groups. For example, you might want all your media apps in one group and all communication apps in another. To learn more, see Chapter 12, "Customizing the Start Screen." ■

BROWSING THE WEB FROM THE MODERN UI

Windows 8 includes Internet Explorer 11 (IE11), the latest version of Microsoft's web browser. You can access IE11 from the Start screen's Modern UI or from the classic Windows desktop. This chapter shows you how to perform basic web-surfing tasks with IE11 from the Start screen.

InPrivate Browsing

Frequently
Used
Websites

Print Preview/
Print Menu

Address Bar, Open Tabs,
and Tools

STARTING INTERNET EXPLORER 11

You can start Internet Explorer 11 from the Start screen. By default, the Internet Explorer tile is visible without scrolling, so you can launch it as soon as you log in to Windows 8.1.

1. Click the Internet Explorer tile on the Start screen.

2. Type the URL for the website you want to visit in the IE11 address bar.

3. Use the IE11 Refresh button to reload the current website.

4. Use the IE11 Favorites button to display favorite sites.

5. Use the IE11 Tools button to find text, view the web page on the Windows desktop, or view downloads.

6. Click the left and right buttons to move to the previous or next web page viewed.

End

ENTERING A WEBSITE ADDRESS (URL)

Internet Explorer 11 includes a feature called AutoComplete. This feature displays the most common websites that match what you type in the address bar.

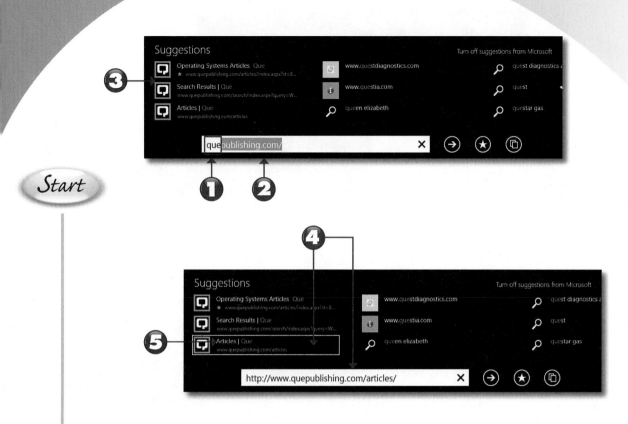

Start

1. Begin typing the name of a website. You do not need to include the "www."

2. If IE11 recognizes the text as part of a website name, it displays the suggested name in the address window.

3. IE11 also displays other websites with matching names online.

4. If you scroll through the list with your keyboard, the selected website is highlighted and placed in the address bar.

5. Click the website you want to open.

End

WORKING WITH TABS IN IE11

You can open a website link in a new tab and easily switch from one tab to another tab in Internet Explorer 11. Here's how to work with tabs in IE11.

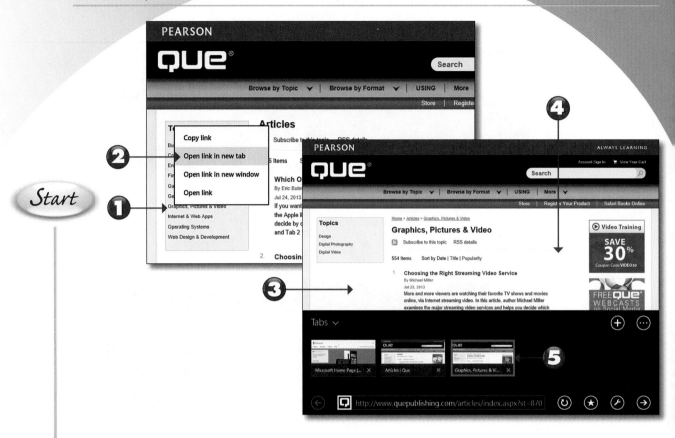

Start

1 Right-click (mouse) or press and hold (touchscreen) a link.

2 Click **Open link in new tab**.

3 The tab appears in the main window.

4 Right-click a blank area in the browser window to see currently open tabs.

5 The current tab is highlighted.

End

NOTE

Tab Switching To switch to a different tab, select the tab after step 5. ■

CREATING A NEW TAB IN IE11

With Internet Explorer 11, you can also create a new tab by using the New Tab button. Here's the process.

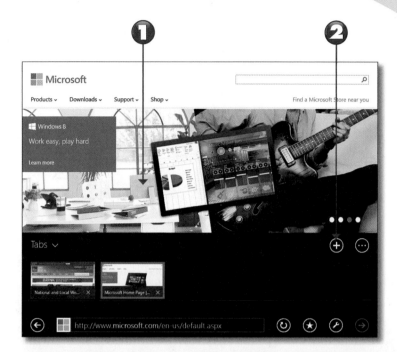

Start

1 Right-click an area without links on the screen.

2 Click the **New Tab** (+) button.

3 Enter a URL or click a thumbnail to open a page in the new tab.

End

TIP

New Tab Keyboard Shortcut You also can press Ctrl+T in Internet Explorer 11 to add a new tab to the browser window. ■

USING INPRIVATE BROWSING

Internet Explorer 11 supports the InPrivate browsing feature that enables you to surf and shop without leaving traces of your web activity behind. Here's how to use it.

1 Right-click a blank area on the screen.

2 Click the **Tab tools** (three dots) button.

3 Click **New InPrivate tab**.

Continued

NOTE

InPrivate Browsing Is a No-Cookie Zone InPrivate browsing does not permit the websites you visit to store cookies (small text files used to store information about your visit). This helps InPrivate browsing to be truly private. ∎

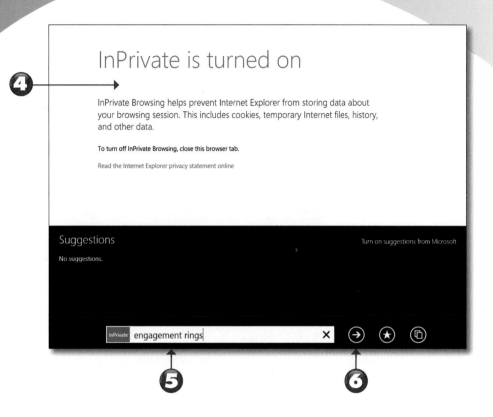

4 The InPrivate tab opens.

5 Enter the desired URL or search term in the address bar.

6 Click **Go**, or press the Enter key to open the URL or search results.

End

NOTE

InPrivate Browsing and Browser History Your browser history does not list any sites you visited while using InPrivate Browsing. ■

REOPENING A FREQUENTLY USED WEB PAGE

Internet Explorer 11 enables you to choose from frequently visited pages right from the browser's address bar. Here's how it works.

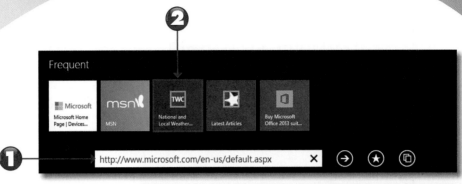

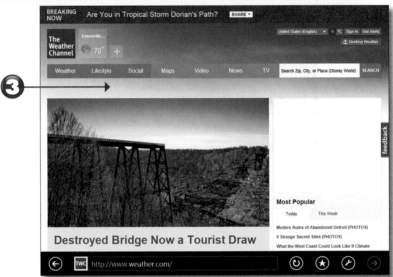

Start

1 Click the address bar.

2 Click an icon.

3 The page opens.

End

NOTE

Building a List of Frequent Entries Microsoft pre-loads some web pages, so the Frequent list includes entries the first time you run IE11 from the Start screen. The pages you visit most often are added to the Frequent list. ■

REMOVING AN ENTRY FROM THE FREQUENT LIST

You can reduce the number of pages displayed in the Frequent list by removing unwanted entries. Here's how to omit entries from the list.

Start

1 Click the address bar.

2 Right-click the entry in the Frequent list that you want to remove.

3 Select **Remove**.

4 The selected item is removed.

End

PINNING A PAGE TO THE START SCREEN

Windows enables you to open your favorite websites with one click thanks to its Pin to Start screen option. Here's how it works.

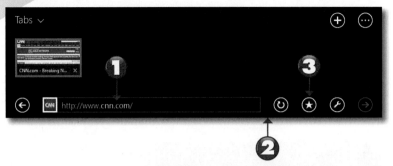

Start

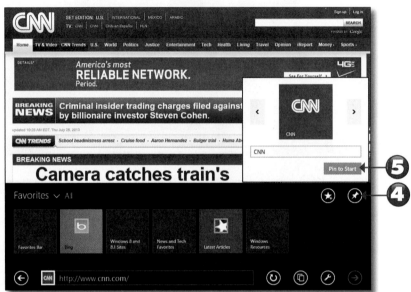

1 Open the website you want to pin.

2 Right-click the bottom of the screen (mouse) or sweep up (touchscreen).

3 Click the **Favorites** button.

4 Click **Pin Site**.

5 Click **Pin to Start**.

Continued

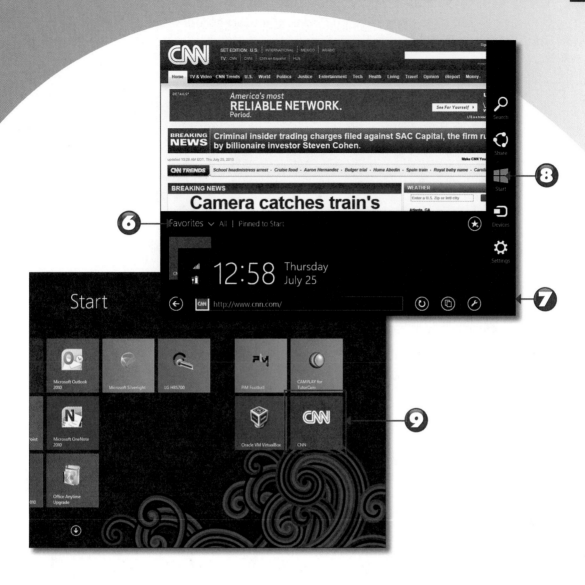

6 The page is added to the Favorites – Pinned to Start list.

7 Open the Charms menu.

8 Click **Start**.

9 The page is also added to the right side of the Start screen.

End

UNPINNING A PAGE FROM THE START SCREEN

Sooner or later, pages you have pinned to the Start screen will no longer be as important to you. Thankfully, they're easy to remove.

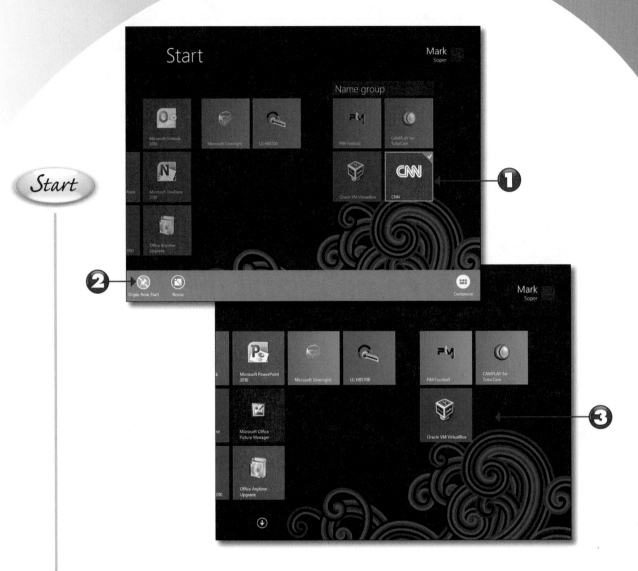

Start

1. Right-click (mouse) or press and hold (touchpad) the page icon on the Start screen.

2. Click **Unpin from Start**.

3. The page is removed from the Start screen.

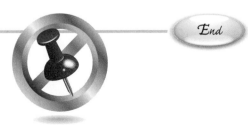

End

CLOSING A TAB IN IE11

After you're finished viewing a tab—including an InPrivate Browsing tab—you can close it in Internet Explorer 11.

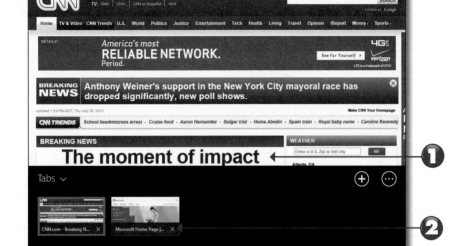

Start

1. Right-click a blank area in the browser window (mouse), or swipe from the bottom (touchscreen).

2. Click the X in the lower-right corner of the tab image.

3. The tab closes.

End

PRINTING A WEB PAGE

Need a printed copy of a web page? Here's how to print it from IE11.

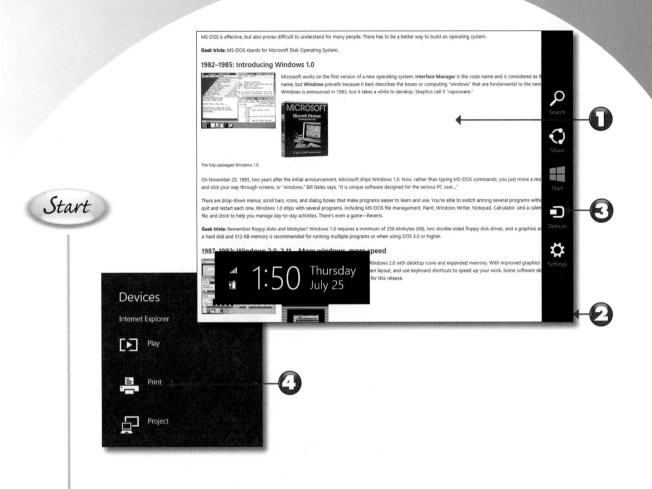

1 Open a website.

2 Open the Charms menu.

3 Click **Devices**.

4 Click **Print**.

Continued

NOTE

More Printing Options in Desktop IE11 To determine ink levels, change print quality, or make other print settings not available from the IE11 Start screen version, open the page in the Desktop version of IE11 and use its Print menu. ■

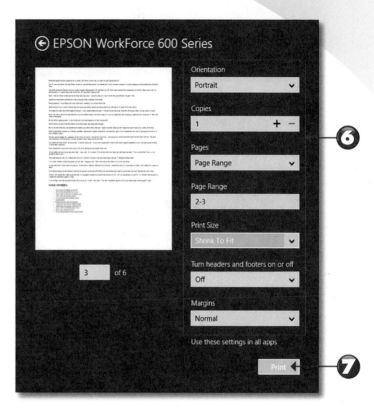

5 Click your printer.

6 Change settings if needed.

7 Click **Print**.

End

NOTE

Print Preview To preview a different page, enter a different number in the pages window below the print preview display. ■

VIEWING A PAGE ON THE WINDOWS DESKTOP

Opening Internet Explorer 11 from the Windows 8 Start screen provides streamlined access to IE11's most common features. However, if you want to set your home page, create a tab group, or manage a tab group, you need to display the web page in the Windows desktop version of IE11.

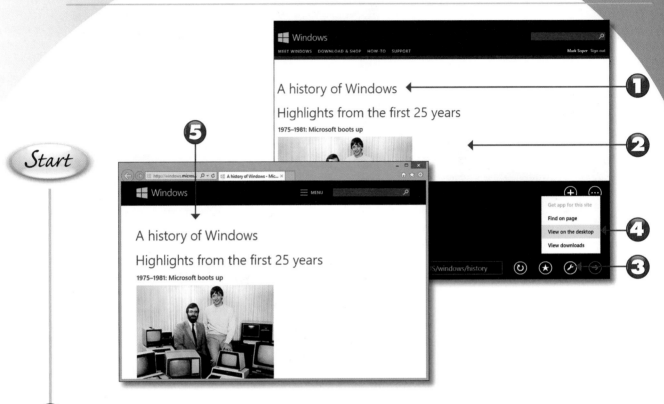

1 Open a website.

2 Right-click the desktop (mouse), or swipe up from the bottom (touchpad).

3 Click the **Tools** button.

4 Click **View on the desktop**.

5 The page opens in IE11 on the Windows desktop.

NOTE

Advanced Features in IE11 To learn about advanced Internet Explorer 11 features available from the classic Windows desktop, see Chapter 20, "Web Browsing from Your Desktop." ■

CLOSING IE11

When you start Internet Explorer 11 from the Start screen, you drag the window to close the browser. Here's how.

Start

 Point to the top of the IE11 window. When the cursor changes to a hand icon, click (mouse) or press (touchpad) and drag downward.

 Drag the IE11 window all the way down to the bottom of the screen until it disappears.

3 The Start screen appears.

End

TIP

Closing IE11 from the Keyboard You also can press Alt+F4 in Internet Explorer 11 to close the browser window. This shortcut closes all open tabs in IE11. ■

Chapter 6

USING ALARMS, CALCULATOR, AND SOUND RECORDER

Windows 8.1 now includes a number of new apps that use the Start screen's Modern UI design. This chapter introduces three of these apps: Alarms, Calculator, and Sound Recorder. You will learn how to start these apps and use them for typical tasks.

Using the Calculator's
Converter function

Creating a
custom alarm
with Alarm

Preparing to edit a sound
file with Sound Recorder

USING ALARMS AS AN ALARM CLOCK

The Alarms app has three functions: alarm clock, timer, and stopwatch. In this section, you learn how to start Alarms and use it to set up alarms.

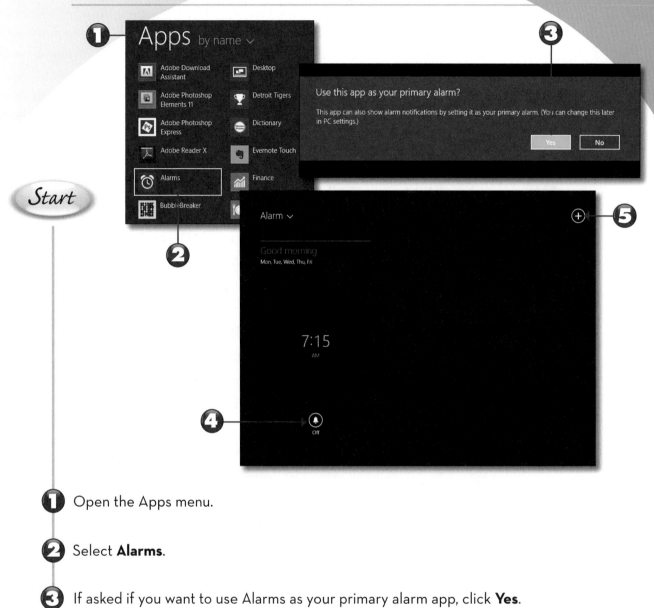

1. Open the Apps menu.

2. Select **Alarms**.

3. If asked if you want to use Alarms as your primary alarm app, click **Yes**.

4. The Good Morning alarm is automatically set up. Click the **Off/On button** to turn it on.

5. Click to set up a new alarm.

Continued

6 Click and type a name for the alarm.

7 Click and drag to set the hour and minute.

8 Click AM or PM.

9 Click **Once** or **Repeats**.

10 Open and select a sound.

Continued

NOTE

Setting Hours and Minutes The hours and minutes settings correspond to clock hand positions. ■

11 Click to save the alarm setting.

12 Click to discard the alarm setting (button visible only after saving the alarm).

13 Click to close.

14 You'll see the new alarm on the Alarm app screen.

15 Click the **Off** icon to turn an alarm on.

16 Click the **On** icon to turn an alarm off.

Continued

NOTE

Notifications Click **Learn More** to find out when notifications appear on your PC. ■

17 When an alarm goes off, its name pops up on the screen.

18 The pop-up also displays the original alarm time.

19 Click to snooze the alarm.

20 Click to shut off the alarm.

End

NOTE

Alarm Displays On Desktop and Start Screen Whether you're working from the Start screen, the Windows desktop, or have any program running, Alarm will wake you up or remind you. ■

USING TIMER

The Alarm app also has a timer feature that you can use for games, cooking, or any other situation in which you need to count down a specific time.

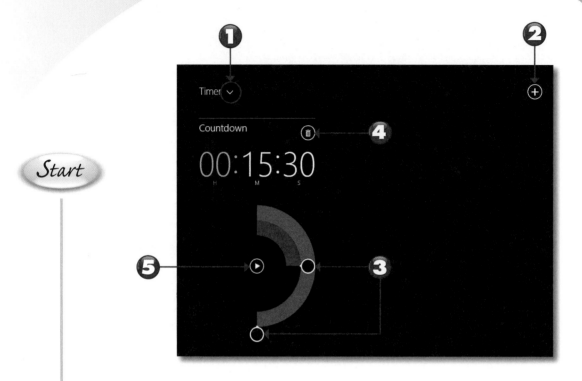

Start

① Open the Alarm app and select **Timer**.

② Click to create a new Timer.

③ Click and drag to adjust the minute or second hands.

④ Click to discard timer.

⑤ Click to start timer.

Continued

 NOTE

Setting Hours To add hours, click hours (currently 00) and drag the new hours ring to set the time desired. ■

6 Click to change the name.

7 Click to pause/continue.

8 Time remaining.

9 Click to restart timer.

10 While counting down, the timer name and duration appear on the screen.
Click to close the timer.

End

USING STOPWATCH

The Stopwatch feature includes support for laps. Here's how to use it.

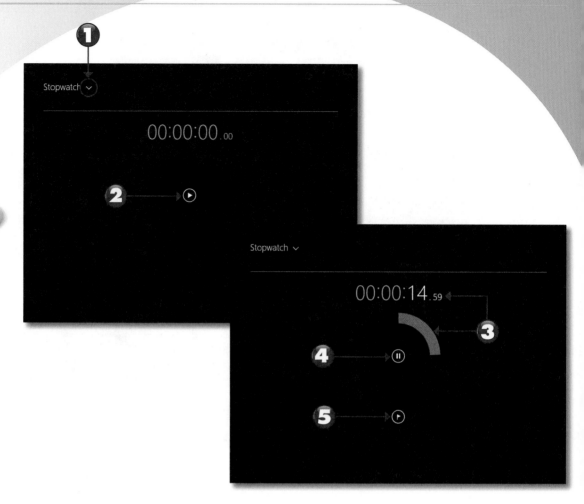

Start

① Open the Alarms app and select **Stopwatch**.

② Click to start timing.

③ When it's running, you can see the elapsed time.

④ Click to pause/continue.

⑤ Click to set lap time.

Continued

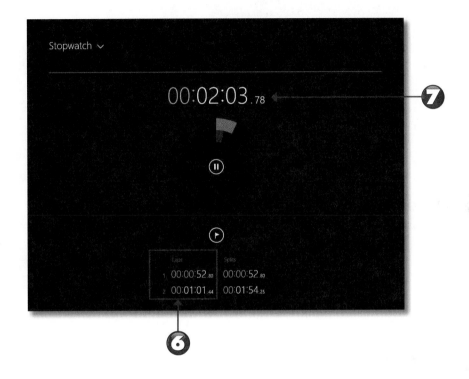

6 You can see your lap times at the bottom of the screen.

7 The elapsed time continues to change at the top of the screen.

End

STARTING CALCULATOR AND SWITCHING MODES

The Windows 8.1 Calculator runs in three modes: Standard, Scientific, and Conversion. Here's how to start it and select the mode you need.

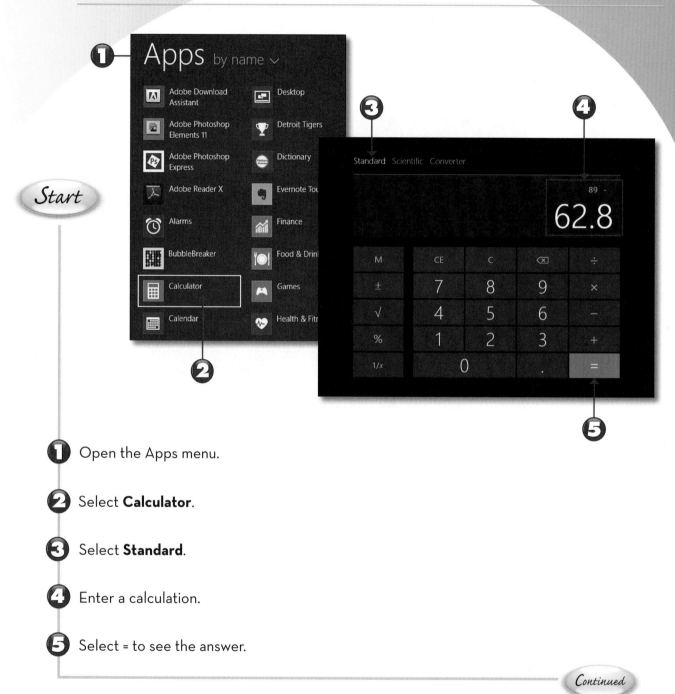

Start

1 Open the Apps menu.

2 Select **Calculator**.

3 Select **Standard**.

4 Enter a calculation.

5 Select = to see the answer.

Continued

NOTE

Clear Versus Clear Entry Click Clear (C) to remove all information in the calculation window; click Clear Entry (CE) to remove the last value. ∎

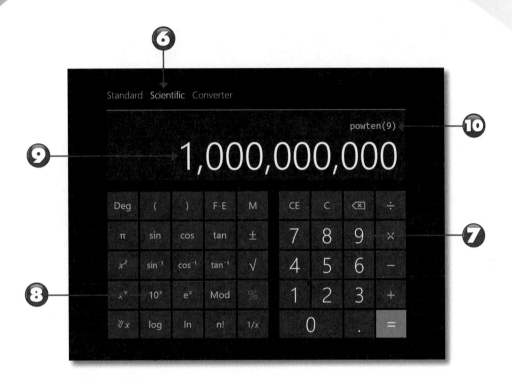

6 Click **Scientific**.

7 Type a number.

8 Click a function.

9 The answer is displayed automatically.

10 The function used is displayed just above the answer.

End

CONVERTING VALUES WITH CALCULATE

You might find the Converter feature in Calculate the handiest of its features. Here's how to use it.

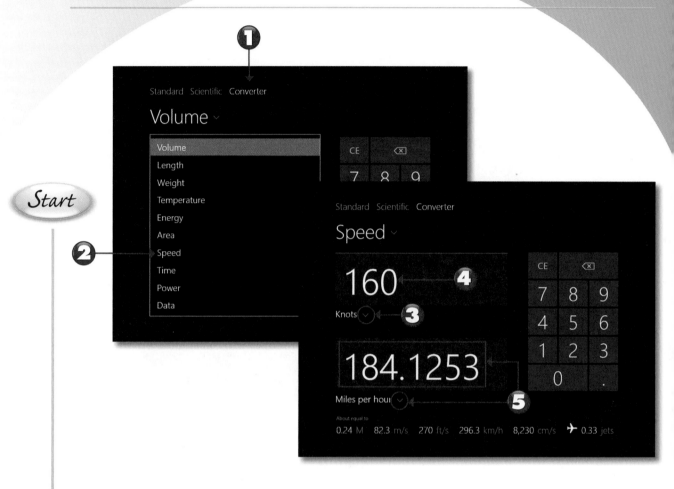

1 Open Calculator from the Start screen and click **Converter**.

2 Select the type of conversion to perform.

3 Select the units from which to convert.

4 Enter the value.

5 Select the units to which to convert, and the answer appears.

Continued

6 Select a different conversion type.

7 Select the unit to convert from.

8 Enter the unit to convert to.

9 Enter the value, and the conversion appears automatically.

10 Calculator also shows you some other common conversions.

End

NOTE

Closing Calculator As with any Modern UI app, drag the Calculator screen down to the bottom edge of your display unit it disappears. ∎

RECORDING AUDIO WITH SOUND RECORDER

You can use your device's built-in or connected microphone to record sounds with Sound Recorder. Here's how to start it and use it.

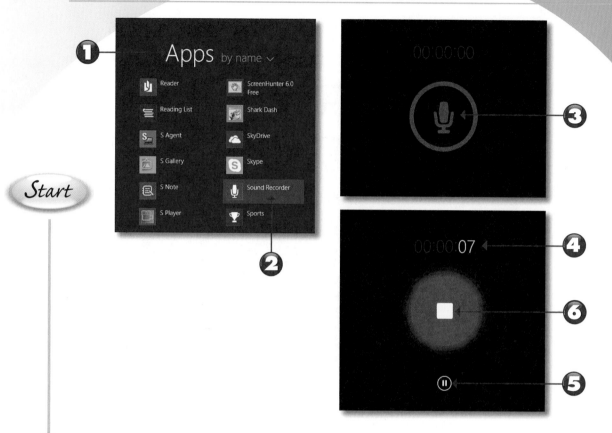

Start

1 Open the Apps menu.

2 Select **Sound Recorder** (if prompted to permit Windows to use your microphone, click **Allow**).

3 Click to begin recording.

4 The elapsed time appears above the play/pause button.

5 Click to pause/continue recording.

6 Click to stop recording.

Continued

7 Click to play the recording.

8 The recording's name, date and time, and duration appear at the top of the screen.

9 Click to rename the recording.

10 Click to delete the recording.

End

NOTE

Alternatives to Sound Recorder If you want to record audio you can use with other programs, use the desktop Sound Recorder located in the Windows Accessories section of the Apps menu, or download other sound recording programs from the Windows Store. The files the Modern UI Sound Recorder creates are stored in a hidden folder and are difficult to access. ■

EDITING RECORDED AUDIO

You can cut out unwanted portions of a recording you make with Sound Recorder and save the results as a new file. Here's how.

Start

1 Select the recording to edit.

2 Click **Trim**.

3 Move the slider to the end of the audio you want to keep.

4 Click **OK**.

Continued

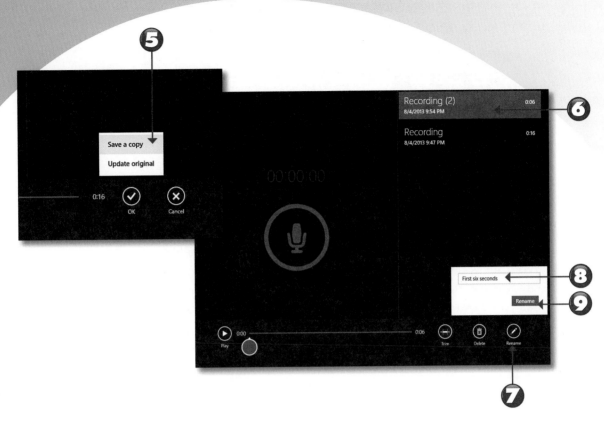

5 Click **Save a copy**.

6 The edited copy of the recording appears in the list. Select it.

7 Click **Rename**.

8 Enter a new name.

9 Click **Rename** to rename the file.

End

NOTE

The Microphone Matters For the highest-quality recording, use a headset microphone. If you use the microphone built in to your laptop, it's likely to pick up extraneous noise. ■

Chapter 7

ENJOYING MUSIC AND VIDEO

The Windows 8 Start screen provides easy access to music and video content. Whether you want to play your own music and video content or discover the latest work from your favorite musicians, actors, and directors, Windows 8 has you covered. This chapter shows you how to tap into the music and video content on your computer and find more content online.

Movie details

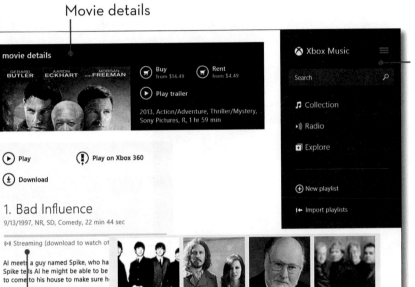

Xbox Music's sidebar

Download and playback options

Radio stations in Xbox music

PLAYING YOUR MUSIC COLLECTION WITH MUSIC

The Music app (also known as Xbox Music) in Windows 8 acts as a one-stop shop for your computer music needs, whether you want to listen to files on your computer or purchase more music online. First, let's learn how to play your own music collection with the Music app.

Start

1. Click the **Music** tile.

2. Click **Collection**.

3. Your music is listed by album.

4. Click an album.

Continued

TIP

Sort Options You can also sort your music by songs, genres, date, and other options. Use the pull-down menus above your collection. ■

5 Click to play the album.

6 The current song is listed in the bottom-left corner.

7 Use the playback controls to control playback.

8 Click to display options including creating a playlist, adding the album to now playing, and others.

9 Click to return to Collections.

End

TIP

Learn More About Your Favorite Artists Use the Search tool shown in step 2 to search online and your computer for music and other information about a particular artist. ■

EXPLORING YOUR MUSIC LIBRARY

If you have set your HomeGroup network to share music from other computers, you can also play those songs through the Music app. Here's how.

1 Right-click, or press and hold **Collection**.

2 Select **Open file**.

3 Click a folder.

4 Hover over a track for more information.

5 Click to play the track.

6 Click to return to Collections.

Start

End

CREATING A RADIO STATION

You can use the Music app as an Internet radio player, playing songs by and related to the artist you choose. Here's how.

1. From the Music main page, click **Radio**.

2. Click **Start a station**.

3. Enter the name of an artist or group, and choose a match from the Radio list.

4. The station is added to the list of stations.

5. Your station begins playing immediately.

6. Click this control to switch between full and compact menus.

End

TIP

One-click Radio Station Creation Sort your collection by artist, and whenever you see the radio station button shown in step 2, click it to create a radio station based on that artist. ■

EXPLORE FEATURED AND TOP MUSIC

Use the Music app to learn more about today's most popular music. Here's how.

Start

1. Click **Explore**.

2. Scroll down to see new albums.

3. Click **View All**.

4. Click to select by genre.

5. Scroll down to see all genres; click a genre.

6. Click the left arrow to return.

End

TIP

Seeing Top Albums To select from top albums, scroll past New Albums in step 2. You can see all genres in the same way as with New Albums. ∎

PLAYING MUSIC FROM EXPLORE

After you find an album or artist with Explore, it's time to enjoy their music. Here's how.

Start

1 Select an album.

2 Click **Play** to play the album.

3 Click to add the album or song to a playlist.

4 Press Windows+Z, or press and hold the playback bar.

5 Click to buy the highlighted song.

6 Click to start a radio station based on the artist.

End

STARTING THE VIDEO APP

You can use the Video app (also known as Xbox Video) to preview, stream, and download video content from the Microsoft store, as well as to view video content from your own camcorder.

Start

1. Click the **Video** tile.

2. Scroll to the left to see all personal videos.

3. Click the arrow to choose videos to play.

4. Scroll to the right to view links to recommended videos, new and featured movies, and new and featured TV shows.

5. Click the Search tool to look for actors, movies, and TV shows.

End

TIP

Preview It As with music selections, you can preview clips and movie trailers for some video content in the online store. Click an item to open it, and then click the Play Trailer button to play a preview clip. To buy the content, click the Buy link. ■

LEARNING MORE ABOUT A HIGHLIGHTED VIDEO

Depending on the item you select in Xbox Video, you might be able to watch a preview, purchase or rent the item, or purchase an entire season. Here's how.

Start

1. Click a video thumbnail.

2. Click to play a trailer.

3. Select a purchase or rental option.

4. Click the reviews for details.

5. User rankings.

6. Click to return.

End

TIP

Reviews on Split Screen If Internet Explorer is your default browser and you click on a review, the screen splits and Internet Explorer opens the review on the right side of the screen. Click the boundary and drag it to the left to make the browser use full-screen. Videos is still running, and you can switch back to it. ■

BUYING MUSIC AND VIDEOS

You can shop for music and videos online from within the Music and Video apps. Both apps access albums, movies, and television shows. Using your Microsoft account, you can purchase items for downloading or streaming. In this example, we'll buy a TV show episode.

Display the item you want to buy.

Click the **Buy** button.

Enter your Microsoft account password.

Click **OK**.

Review the playback options (choose one if more than one is listed).

Click **Next**.

Continued

Confirm Purchase

Buy $1.99 plus tax

Mark E Soper
**** ****
Expires on:

Change Payment Options

This transaction is subject to the **Xbox LIVE Terms of Use**. You will be charged at this time. No Refunds. The content might not be available for re-download in the future.

Confirm   Cancel

The Weird Al Show
Season: 1
Episode 1 "Bad Influence"
1997
Rating: NR
Audio: English
SD Download and Stream
255.93 MB

e" from The Weird Al Show, Season 1

The Weird Al Show
Season: 1
Episode 1 "Bad Influence"
1997
Rating: NR
Audio: English
SD Download and Stream
255.93 MB

Done

7 Review purchase details.

8 Click **Confirm**.

9 Click **Done**.

End

NOTE

Microsoft Account and Your Payment Information If you did not set up payment information when you set up your Microsoft account or have never purchased anything from Microsoft, you will be prompted to provide a form of payment before you can complete your purchase. ■

SEARCHING FOR TV SHOWS AND MOVIES

If you're a classic film buff, or are just looking for a TV show or movie that wasn't released in the past few months, use the Search tool to track down your favorites.

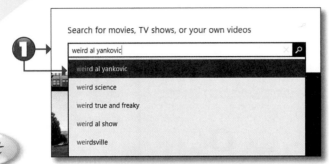

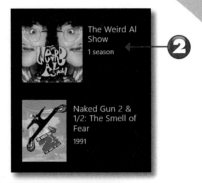

Start

1. After clicking the search tool, enter your search terms. Click the best match.

2. Click a link.

3. Click to buy a season.

4. Click an episode to see information about buying/renting the episode.

End

NOTE

Searching for Movie Moments If you use Movie Moments to create videos (see Chapter 8, "Using Movie Moments"), keep in mind that Video only searches the Videos folder or library. Copy the Movie Moments folder from Pictures to Videos if you want its contents to show up when you search for videos. ■

PLAYING AND DOWNLOADING YOUR PURCHASE

After you buy a song or video, you might have options to download it as well as play it. If you download the item, you can play it whenever you want. Here's how.

Start

1 Click **Play** to play the item from the cloud (online).

2 Click **Download** to store the item on your device.

3 After the item is downloaded, it's listed as one of your personal files (My TV, My Movies, or Collection).

4 This icon indicates streaming content.

5 Click to resume playing a video you have in progress.

End

Chapter 8

USING MOVIE MOMENTS

Windows 8.1 features a new video editor for editing short videos (60 seconds or less) by adding music, titles, and captions. In this chapter, you learn how to start Movie Moments and go through the process of using it to edit and share a short video.

Selecting a title
style (Classic)

Choosing music

Sharing
options

Modern title
style

Chroma title style

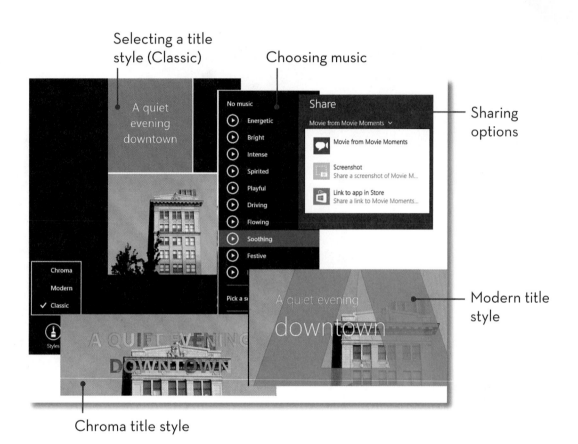

STARTING MOVIE MOMENTS

Movie Moments is listed in the Apps menu. Here's how to locate it, start it, and select a
video to work with.

Start

1 Open the Apps menu.

2 Click or tap **Movie Moments**.

3 Click to pick a video.

Continued

NOTE

Take a Video If you choose Take a Video in step 3,
you must click **Allow** when prompted to permit Movie
Moments to use your webcam and microphone. ■

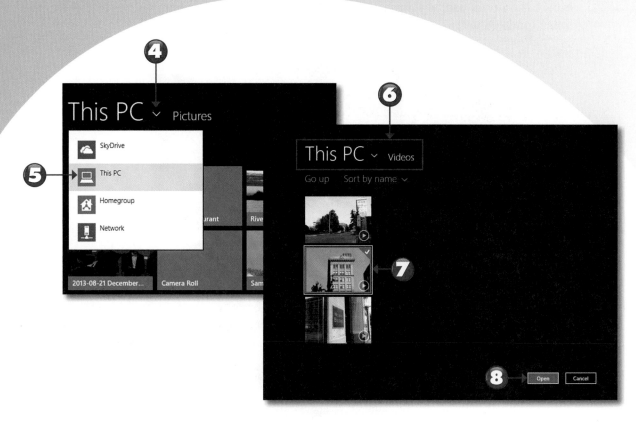

4 Open the This PC (or Libraries) menu.

5 Navigate to the location where your videos are stored.

6 Select the folder or library containing your videos.

7 Click a video.

8 Click **Open**.

End

MOVIE MOMENTS' BASIC CONTROLS

Movie Moments uses a simple set of controls along the bottom edge of your video. Here's a quick guide to what you'll find.

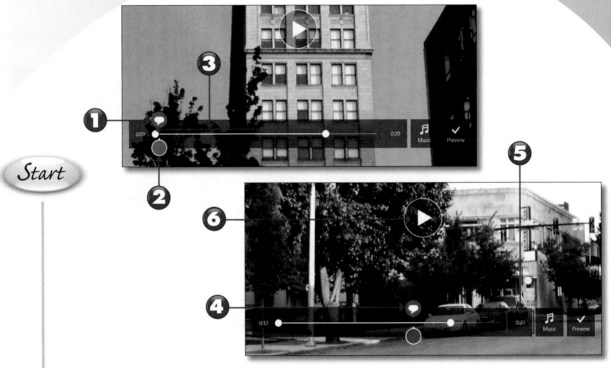

Start

1 Click to add a title to your video.

2 Drag to the desired position in the video.

3 Drag to trim the video's beginning or ending.

4 Click to add a caption.

5 Total length of video.

6 Click to play video.

End

NOTE

The Timeline View of Title and Captions When you view your video timeline after adding a title and/or captions, you will see purple marks along the timeline. Each of these represents a title (if at the beginning of the video) or a caption (later in the video). For examples, see the figures in "Adding Music," p. 120, later in this chapter. ■

TRIMMING AND SPLITTING YOUR VIDEO

Before you do anything else with your video, take advantage of the Movie Moments trim and split tools to cut your video down to size. Here's how.

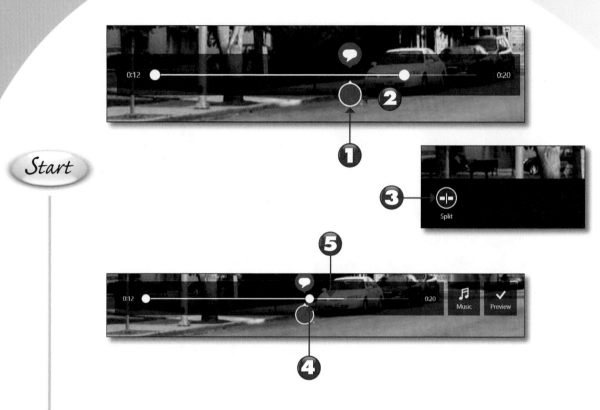

① Drag to the desired position for the split.

② Right-click, or tap and hold the editing tool.

③ Click **Split**.

④ The new end of the video.

⑤ The discarded section.

NOTE

Seeing the Actual Duration After you click Play or Preview, Movie Moments displays the new duration of the video. ■

CREATING A TITLE

It's easy to start your video clip out with style: Just click the Title bubble at the beginning of the video (refer to step 1 in "Movie Moments' Basic Controls," p. 116, earlier in this chapter) to get started. Here's what happens next.

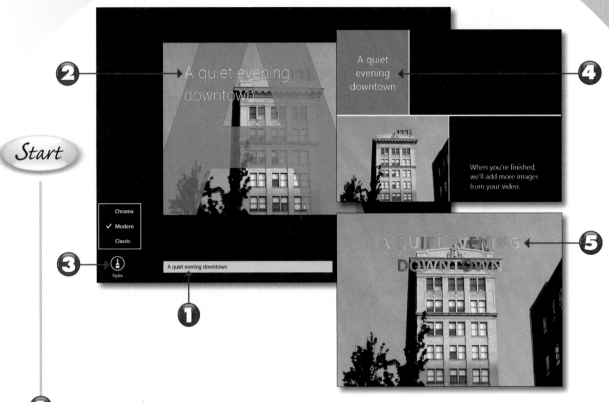

Start

1 Enter a title for your video.

2 The title appears on the frame in the default Modern title style.

3 Click **Style** and select a different style.

4 This title is in Classic style.

5 This title is in Chroma style.

End

NOTE

Adding Captions To add a caption to your video, drag the video position tool to the desired location, click the title/captions button, and enter the caption. ■

EMPHASIZING SELECTED TEXT
Tweak your title design by selecting text to emphasize (enlarge). Here's how.

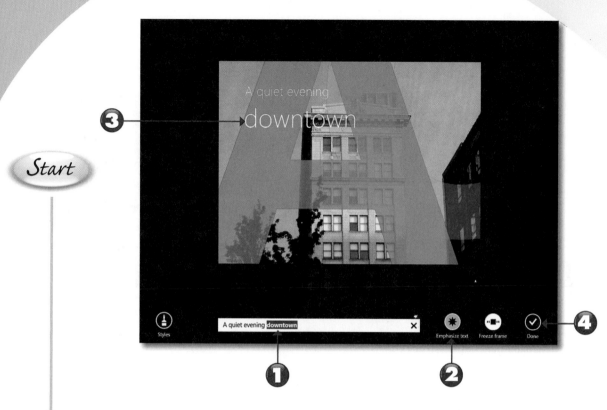

Start

End

1 Highlight some of the text in your title.

2 Click **Emphasize text**.

3 This is the Modern style after emphasizing the word *downtown*.

4 Click **Done** to continue.

NOTE

Freeze Frame, Your Choice Titles and captions use freeze-frame by default. However, if you don't like freeze-frame, click the Freeze frame button next to Emphasize Text to disable this feature for the current title or caption. ∎

ADDING MUSIC

You can use either Movie Moments' own library of audio tracks and music or audio tracks from your Music folder. You can use music alongside existing audio in your video, or you can mute your video and use its audio only. It's your choice.

Start

1 The first time you click **Music**, click **Download recommended songs**.

2 Click a song track to add it to the video.

3 Click if you want to mute audio in the video.

4 Click to choose a song from your music collection.

End

NOTE

One Song Per Video Movie Moments creates short videos, so only one song per video is allowed. ■

PREVIEWING AND SAVING YOUR VIDEO

Ready, set, preview! Let Movie Moments do the work while you enjoy it. Then, you can make more edits or save the results.

Start

1 Click **Preview** to play the edited video.

2 Click **Edit** if you need to make changes.

3 Click **Save** to save your completed video.

4 Click **Share** to share your video.

End

NOTE

Where to Find Your Video Oddly enough, Movie Moments saves your video to your Pictures folder or library into a subfolder called Movie Moments. It automatically names each movie, but you can rename the files in File Explorer. Movie Moments creates MP4 files, which is a very popular video file format. ■

SHARING YOUR VIDEO

You can share your video via email. As long as the file isn't too big, it's easy. After you click Share in the previous lesson, here's how.

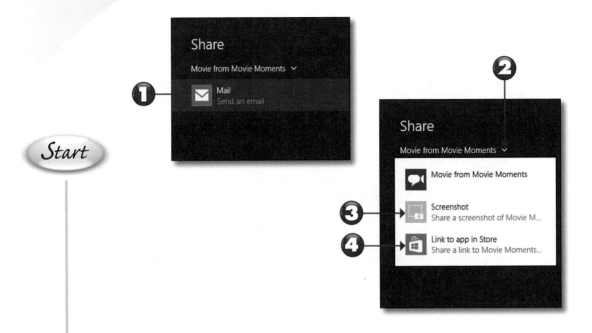

Start

1 Click **Mail** to email your movie.

2 To see other options, open the Share menu.

3 Click to send a screenshot.

4 Click to send a link to Movie Moments in the Windows app Store.

Continued

5 Select your contact or enter their email address.

6 Click to add a message.

7 Click to send.

End

NOTE

Checking Your Movie's File Size Although Movie Moments creates short movies, HD video files can be very large. If you are wondering how large your movie is, go to the Movie Moments folder and hover over the movie icon to see how large it is in megabytes (MB). Some email services cannot send a file that's more than 10MB in size. To send a larger movie, copy your movie to SkyDrive and send your recipient a link to it.

Chapter 9

VIEWING AND TAKING PHOTOS WITH PHOTOS AND CAMERA

Windows 8.1 helps you take digital photos with your device's webcam or rear-facing camera, edit them, and view them. In this chapter you learn how to use Camera and how to edit your photos in Camera Roll or Photos.

A photo edited in
Camera Roll

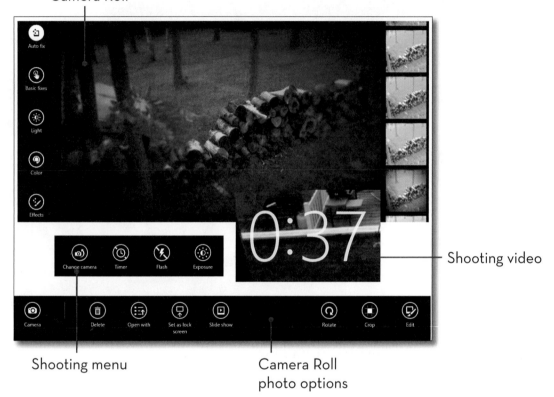

Shooting video

Shooting menu

Camera Roll
photo options

SHOOTING PHOTOS WITH CAMERA

The Camera app is listed in the Apps menu. It requires a built-in camera (rear-facing and/ or webcam). The photos in this chapter were shot with the rear-facing camera and webcam built in to my Samsung Windows 8 tablet. Here's how to use Camera to shoot still images.

Start

1 Open the Apps menu from the Start screen.

2 Click or tap **Camera**.

3 Click **Allow**.

4 Click to take a still photo.

5 Click to shoot a video.

Continued

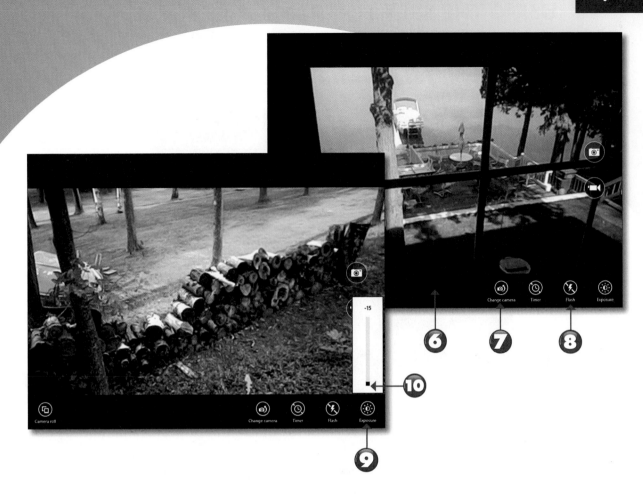

(6) Swipe up and to the right, or right-click to open the app bar.

(7) If your device has multiple cameras, click to switch between rear-facing and front-facing (webcam) cameras.

(8) Click to select flash settings (if your device has a flash).

(9) Click **Exposure**.

(10) Adjust the slider up to lighten or down to darken the photo or video you shoot.

End

NOTE

Flash Settings Typical flash settings include No flash, Auto flash, and Flash (which fires each time you shoot). ■

USING THE SELF TIMER

The Camera app includes a dual-setting (3 seconds/10 seconds) self-timer. Use it to get into your own photos.

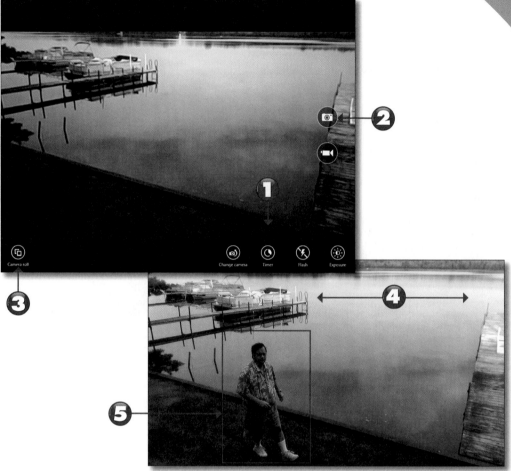

Start

1 Click the self-timer.

2 Click the still camera button and move into position.

3 Click the **Camera Roll** button to view your photos.

4 Scroll through your photos.

5 The self-timer enables you to get into the photo.

End

USING VIDEO MODE

When you select Video mode, you can shoot MPEG4 video files with your device. Here's how to use this feature.

Start

End

1 Click to shoot video.

2 Elapsed recording time.

3 Click to stop the recording.

NOTE

Camera Roll for Photos and Videos, Too To view your videos without leaving Camera, select Camera Roll. You can also trim your videos in Camera Roll. ■

NOTE

Changing Exposure When Shooting Video To change exposure while shooting video, open the App bar. Click the Exposure button and adjust the slider. ■

VIEW YOUR PHOTOS WITH CAMERA ROLL

You can view your photos with Photos, This PC, or Camera Roll. Here's how to view your photos with Camera Roll.

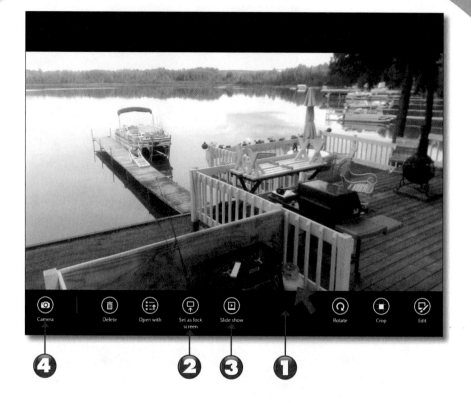

Start

1 After opening Camera Roll, right-click or swipe up and to the left to open the Camera Roll menu.

2 Click to set this photo as your lock screen photo.

3 Click to view your photos as a slide show.

4 Click to switch back to Camera mode.

End

NOTE

Viewing and Editing Your Photos with the Photos App To view and edit photos from your device's camera or a digital camera, open the Photos app from the Start screen. The steps in the following sections work the same way from either Camera Roll or the Photos app. ■

CROP YOUR PHOTOS

You can edit your photos from Camera Roll or Photos. The process works the same way in either case. Your device probably shoots widescreen photos, but if you want traditional print sizes, you should crop your photo to the correct print size. Here's how.

1. After opening a picture in Camera Roll or Photos, open the App bar and click **Crop**.

2. Open the **Aspect ratio** menu.

3. Click the print size or use desired.

4. Drag the frame and adjust the corners as needed.

5. Click **Apply**.

6. Click **Save a copy**. Your original remains unchanged.

End

MAKING AND SAVING OTHER CHANGES

Camera Roll and Photos also enable you to change colors and brightness and add effects to your photos.

Start

1 From the app bar, click **Edit**.

2 Select an editing type.

3 Click and turn an item to adjust it.

4 The control displays the amount of adjustment.

Continued

NOTE

Edits You Can Make Auto Fix provides a series of preset adjustments. Basic fixes include Crop, Red-eye, Rotate, and Retouch. Light fixes include Brightness, Contrast, Highlights, and Shadows. Color fixes include Temperature (warms/cools photos), Tint, (color) Saturation, and Color enhance. Effects include Vignette and Selective focus. ■

5 Here's the photo after applying vignette, selective focus, and color adjustments.

6 Click to apply a black-and-white auto fix effect.

7 Here is the photo after applying black-and-white auto fix plus previous adjustments.

8 Open the menu.

9 Click to save a copy of the photo including all changes. (If you don't want to save changes, click Undo instead.)

End

Chapter 10

WORKING WITH FILES

Windows 8.1 provides SkyDrive access directly from the Start screen. SkyDrive is cloud-based storage, enabling you to access files from anywhere you can connect to the Internet with a Microsoft account. To make it even better, you can also view files stored on your computer (This PC) without going to the Windows desktop.

Creating a new
folder on SkyDrive

Selecting a different
app with Open With

This PC's
thumbnail
view

Copying
files to
SkyDrive

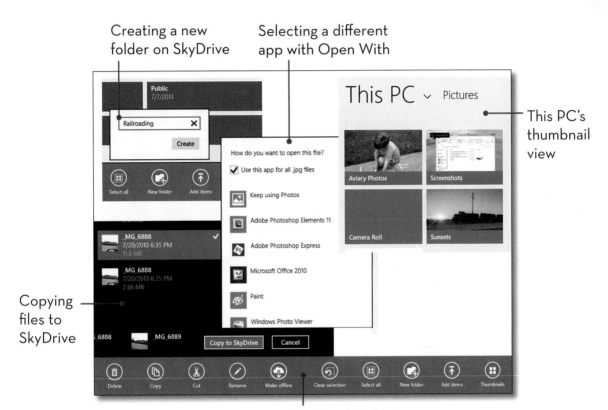

SkyDrive's folder menu

VIEWING FILES ON SKYDRIVE

Microsoft provides SkyDrive cloud-based storage to everyone with a Microsoft account. If you've been using Windows-based computers for a while, you might already have some files on SkyDrive. Or, it might be a brand-new feature for you. Here's how to see what's on your SkyDrive.

Start

1. Click or tap the **SkyDrive** tile.

2. Hover the mouse over a folder to see details.

3. Folder details.

4. Click to close the help box if you don't need to learn more.

5. Click to open a folder.

Continued

NOTE

New to SkyDrive? Click the Learn more online link to open a web page with more information about SkyDrive. ■

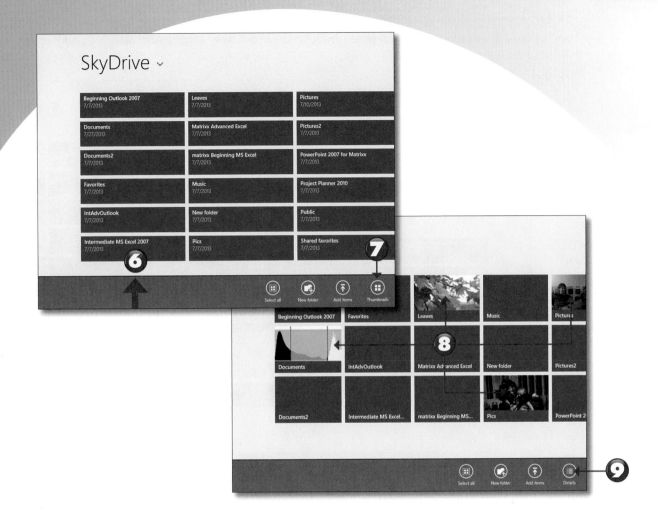

6 Right-click the bottom of the screen or swipe up from the bottom to open SkyDrive's app bar.

7 Click **Thumbnails**.

8 Thumbnails are displayed for folders that include supported picture types.

9 Click **Details** to return to the default view.

End

CREATING FOLDERS AND ADDING FILES IN SKYDRIVE

SkyDrive makes it easy to add files to an existing or new folder from your computer so you can access them everywhere. Here's how to create a new folder and add files to it.

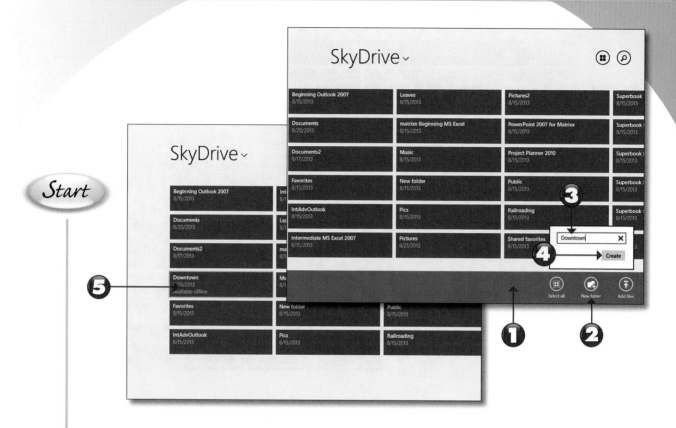

1 In SkyDrive, right-click the bottom of the screen, or swipe up from the bottom to open the app bar.

2 Click **New Folder**.

3 Enter the name of the folder.

4 Click **Create**.

5 Click the new folder.

Continued

NOTE

Copying to an Existing Folder To copy files to an existing folder, start with step 5. ■

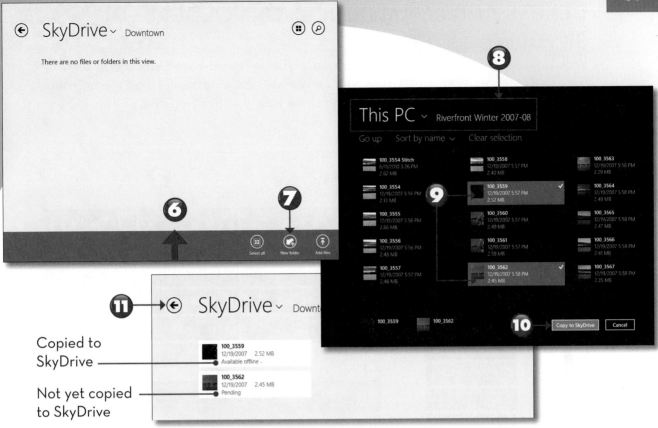

Copied to
SkyDrive

Not yet copied
to SkyDrive

6 Open the folder menu (right-click or drag up from the bottom of the screen).

7 Click **Add items**.

8 Navigate to a folder.

9 Click or tap some files.

10 Click **Copy to SkyDrive**.

11 When all files have been copied, click the left-arrow button to return to
the SkyDrive main menu.

End

NOTE

Selecting All Files or Most Files To select all files in a folder, click **Select all**
in step 9. If you want most of the files, click **Select all**, and then click or tap the
files you don't want. Checked files will be uploaded to SkyDrive. ∎

DELETE AND RENAME FILES OR FOLDERS ON SKYDRIVE AND THIS PC

With a single click, you can switch between SkyDrive (cloud-based storage) and This PC (local file storage). With either view, you can delete, copy, paste, cut, and rename files and folders. The tasks in this section work the same way in either SkyDrive or This PC except as noted.

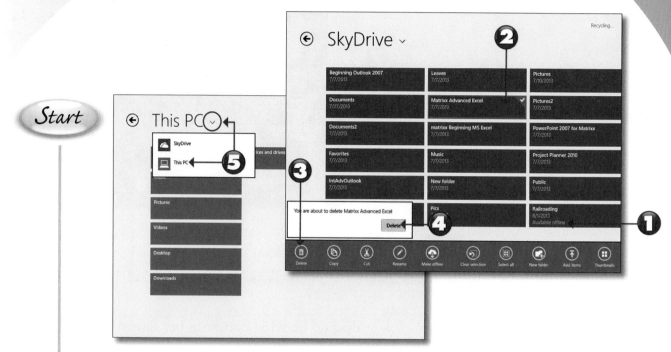

1 Files available on This PC as well as SkyDrive.

2 Select a file or folder: tap and hold until the checkmark appears, and then release (touch screen) or right-click it.

3 Click the **Delete** button to remove it.

4 Click **Delete** to confirm deletion.

5 Select **This PC** to see This PC's default folders.

Continued

NOTE

Can't Delete Default Folders in This PC You can delete any folder or file in the SkyDrive view, and you can delete any file in This PC except for the default This PC folders (refer to step 6). ■

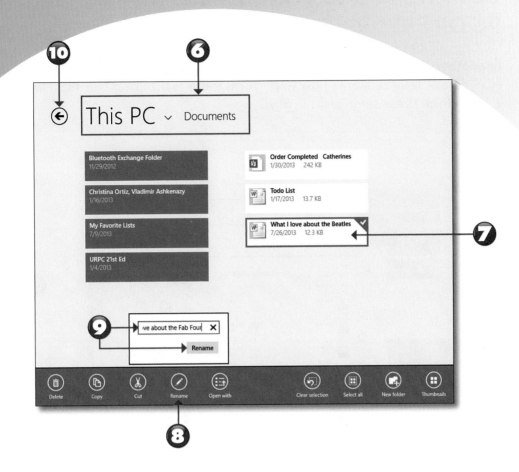

6 Navigate to a file or subfolder.

7 Select it.

8 Click **Rename**.

9 Enter the new name and click **Rename**.

10 Click the back arrow to return to the previous view.

End

NOTE

Make Offline **Make offline** is available from the SkyDrive Folder menu only. Choose this option when you want to download a file or folder from SkyDrive to the corresponding location on This PC. ∎

CUTTING AND PASTING FILES AND FOLDERS IN THIS PC OR SKYDRIVE

Cutting and pasting files and folders enable you to move files or folders from one location to another. You can cut and paste any files or folders in SkyDrive or This PC except for This PC's default folders. Here's how to perform these tasks using This PC. However, you can also perform these same tasks in SkyDrive.

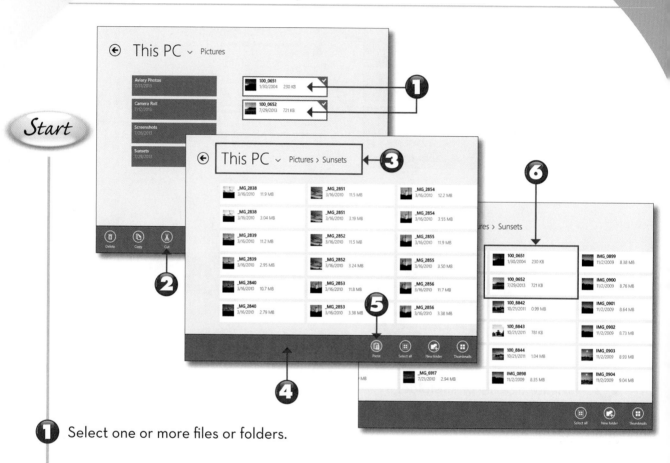

1. Select one or more files or folders.

2. Click **Cut**.

3. Navigate to the desired location.

4. Open the folder menu.

5. Click **Paste**.

6. The files or folders in their new location.

Start

End

COPYING AND PASTING FILES IN THE SAME FOLDER

Copy and paste is similar to cut and paste, except that the same files or folders stay in their original locations and a copy is in another location. To copy to a different location, follow the steps in the previous exercise but choose Copy instead of Cut in step 2. In this exercise, you learn how to make copies of files in the same location.

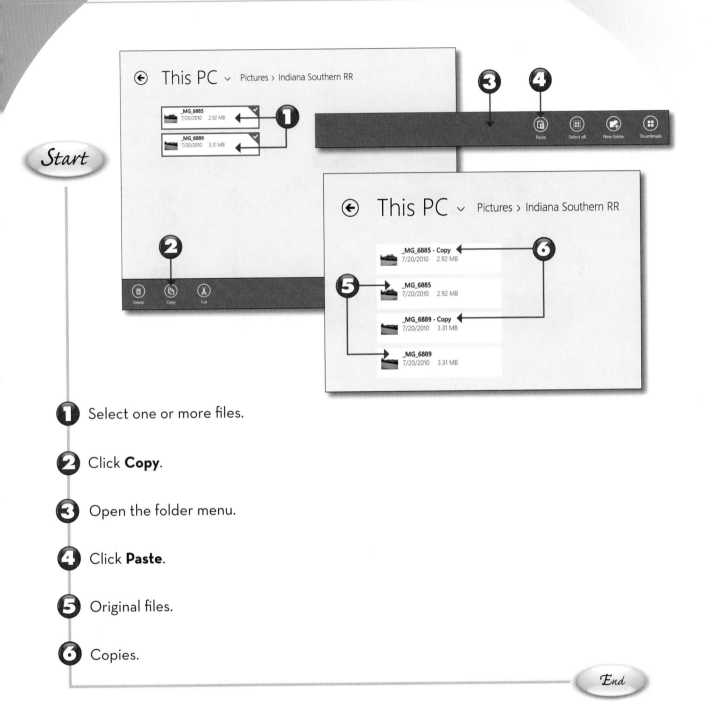

Start

1. Select one or more files.

2. Click **Copy**.

3. Open the folder menu.

4. Click **Paste**.

5. Original files.

6. Copies.

End

USING OPEN WITH

If you install more than one app designed to open a particular type of file, such as an MP3 audio file or a JPEG photo file, the most recent app you install will be used to open that file. However, if you have more than one app installed that works with the same type of file, Open With lets you choose the app you prefer. Here's how.

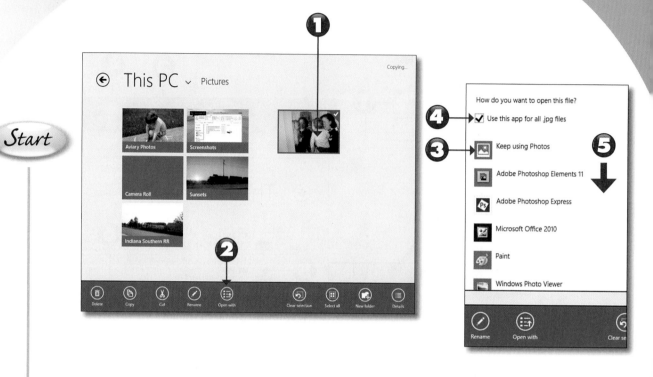

Start

1 Select a file.

2 Click **Open with**.

3 Current default.

4 The app you select will be used for this file type from now on when this box is checked.

5 Scroll down to see all listed apps.

Continued

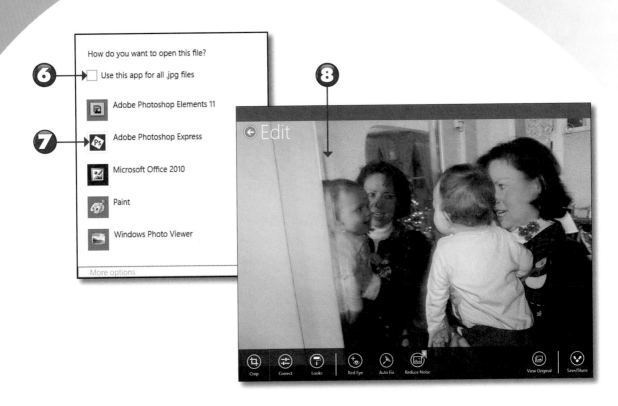

6 When this checkbox is cleared, regardless of which app you select right now, the default app will still be used the next time you open this type of file.

7 Click or tap an app.

8 The file opens in the selected app.

End

NOTE

Using More Options Use More Options if you want to use an installed app that doesn't show up on the list. It's up to you to navigate to the correct folder and app file you want to use. It is usually easier to start an unlisted app and use its own Open option to open a file than to use More Options. ∎

Chapter 11

MAIL, SKYPE, AND INFORMATION SERVICES

Windows 8.1 adds Skype and several new Bing-powered information services to improved versions of Mail, Maps, Calendar, People, and Finance apps. Whether you're looking for finance, messages, travel guidance, or nutrition and exercise advice, Windows has you covered.

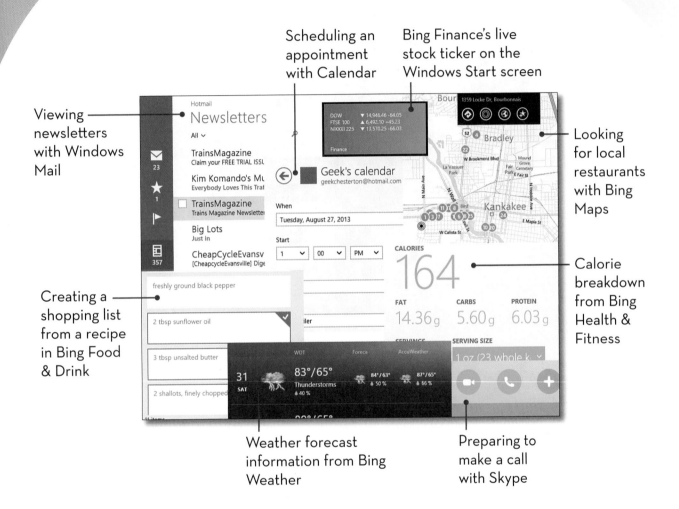

Scheduling an appointment with Calendar

Bing Finance's live stock ticker on the Windows Start screen

Viewing newsletters with Windows Mail

Looking for local restaurants with Bing Maps

Creating a shopping list from a recipe in Bing Food & Drink

Calorie breakdown from Bing Health & Fitness

Weather forecast information from Bing Weather

Preparing to make a call with Skype

STARTING MAIL

Windows Mail works with Microsoft's web-based email service (formerly Hotmail, now Outlook.com) and with some other email services, including Gmail (Google Mail), Yahoo! Mail, and most others that use the IMAP email protocol (POP3 email services are not supported). It's easy to start and to add supported third-party email services during startup (the email accounts associated with your Microsoft account, such as Hotmail and Outlook.com, are automatically added to Windows Mail).

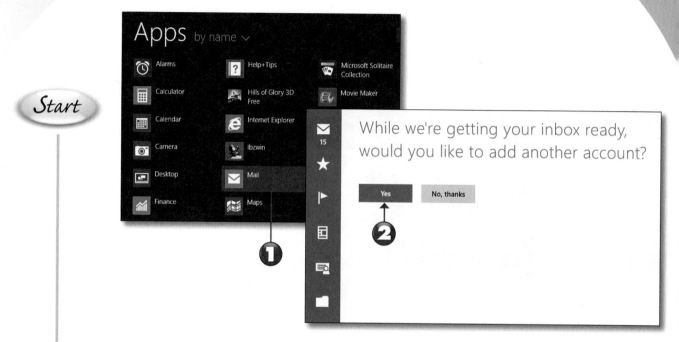

Start

1 From the Apps screen, click **Mail**.

2 Windows Mail automatically loads your Microsoft email account. To add another account, click **Yes**. (To skip this step, click **No, thanks**.)

Continued

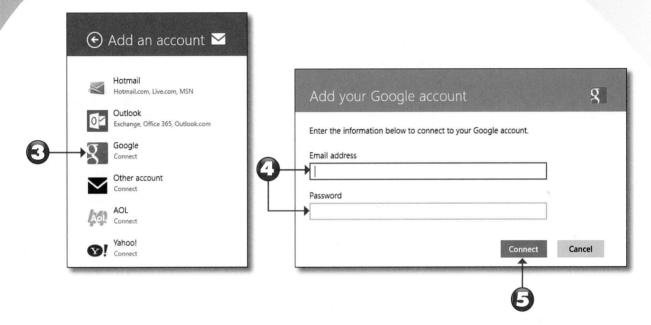

3 Choose an email account to add.

4 Enter the email address and password for your account.

5 Click **Connect** to add your account.

End

NOTE

Adding Email Accounts To add an email account at any time, start Mail, open the Settings charm, and click Accounts. Follow the prompts to add an account. ■

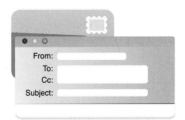

READING A MESSAGE IN MAIL

Windows Mail provides a streamlined menu that puts commands on the left side and provides plenty of room for you to read your messages.

Start

1. Click to view your inbox (shown).

2. Click to view Favorites (people).

3. Click to see only flagged messages.

4. Click to view newsletters.

5. Click to view social updates (emails from Twitter, Facebook friends, and so on).

6. Click to view folders.

Continued

NOTE

Switching Accounts If you have two or more email accounts in Windows Mail, you will see an envelope icon on the bottom of the menu pane. Click the envelope, and select the account to view. ■

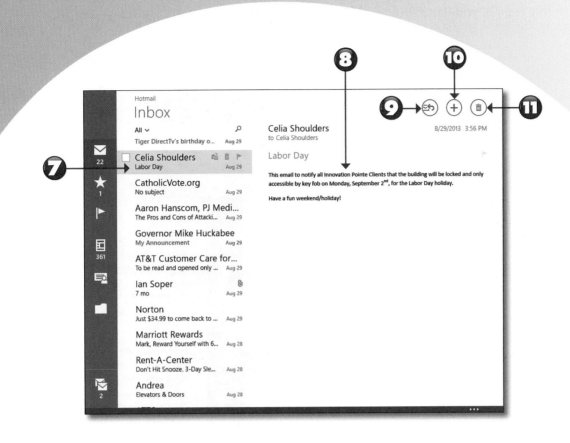

7 Click a message.

8 The message appears in the reading pane.

9 Click to reply.

10 Click to create a new message.

11 Click to discard the message.

End

MARKING A MESSAGE AS JUNK

In this lesson, you use Windows Mail's Junk mail feature to get rid of unwanted email.

1 Click a message you don't want, and click the checkbox when it appears.

2 Click **Junk**.

3 The message is removed.

Start

End

NOTE

Your App Bar May Vary The buttons in the app bar vary by email service and by activity. ∎

VIEWING A NEWSLETTER

If you have a Microsoft email account (Hotmail or Outlook.com), Windows Mail helps keep your inbox uncluttered by automatically sending newsletters to a Newsletter mailbox. The app bar commands shown here work with all types of messages.

Start

1 Click the Newsletter icon.

2 Right-click a newsletter or click its checkbox to view it and open the app bar.

3 Click to file it in a folder. Select from the folders that appear when you click this option.

4 Click to flag it.

5 Click to mark it as unread.

6 Click to open it in a new email window.

End

WRITING AND SENDING A MESSAGE

Windows Mail makes it easy to send a message and add attachments. Here's how.

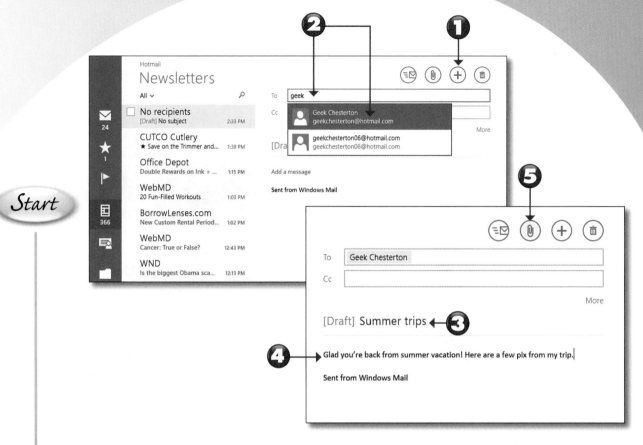

Start

1. Click the **New** button.

2. Enter the name of the recipient, and click the matching entry from your People (contact) list. Otherwise, enter the recipient's email address.

3. Enter the subject.

4. Enter your text.

5. Click to attach a picture or other file.

Continued

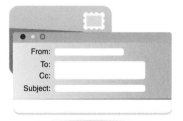

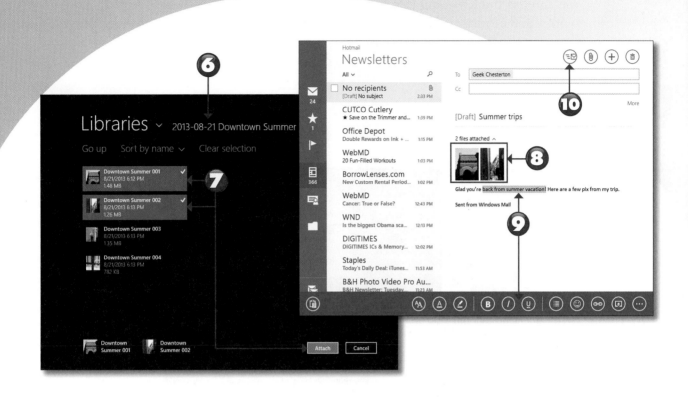

6 Navigate to the file's location.

7 Select the file(s) you want to attach and click **Attach**.

8 Attached files appear in the email body.

9 Highlight text to display the app bar, and select an option to format your text.

10 Click the **Send** button when your message is finished.

End

NOTE

Highlight Text for Enhancements and More The app bar shown in step 9 has buttons for font, font size, font color, bold, italic, underline, lists, emoticons, and hyperlinks. Click Lists, and choose from numbered or bulleted lists. Click the Clipboard icon at the left end of the app bar to copy your selected text for pasting elsewhere. ■

STARTING AND USING CALENDAR

You can use the Calendar app to keep track of your schedule, including daily appointments, events, and other special occasions. You can switch between five different views of your calendar: What's Next (default), Month, Work Week, Week, and Day. The view you select when you close Calendar becomes the default the next time you open this app.

Start

1 Click the **Calendar** tile.

2 The What's Next view highlights upcoming events.

3 Right-click, swipe up, or press Windows key+Z to display the Apps bars.

4 Scroll the top bar to the right and click **Month** .

Continued

5 In month view, click the arrows to move from month to month.

6 Right-click, swipe up, or press Windows key+Z.

7 Click **Week** to display your calendar by week.

8 Click the down arrow to open the selected month's calendar.

9 To view the current day, click **Today**.

End

TIP

Calendar Options You can change the colors displayed for birthdays and holidays on your calendar. With the Calendar app open, press Windows key+C to display the Charms bar, click Settings, and then click Options. ■

SCHEDULING APPOINTMENTS WITH CALENDAR

Here's how to schedule an appointment with Calendar.

Start

1. Click the appointment date and time.

2. Type a title for the appointment.

3. Optionally, type any message text you want to include.

4. Open the details menu and click **Add details**.

5. Click and type additional information.

6. Click **Show more** for additional settings.

Continued

TIP

Select a Calendar You can also select a calendar in step 4 if you use more than one calendar. ■

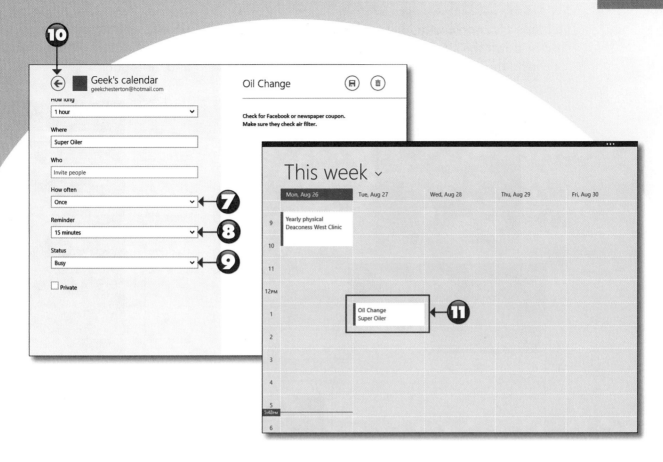

7 To make the appointment a recurring appointment, click here and make a selection.

8 To add a reminder alarm, click here and set a time.

9 To show a status setting on your shared calendar, click here and make your selection.

10 Click to return to the Calendar.

11 The appointment appears on the calendar.

End

TIP

Editing Appointments To edit an appointment, select it on the calendar and make changes to the appointment form page. To remove an appointment, click the Delete (trashcan) button on the form page. ∎

GETTING DIRECTIONS WITH MAPS

The Maps app works with Microsoft's Bing website to help you find locations around the world or down the street. You can find directions, look up an address, or view your current location. In this task, you learn how to look up a location and find directions.

Current location

New location

Start

1 Click the **Maps** tile.

2 Type the Zip code or name of a city (Windows opens the Search pane). Click **Search**.

3 Press Windows key+Z, or swipe up to display the Apps bar.

4 Click **Directions**.

Continued

NOTE

Location Services The first time you use the Maps app, you might be prompted to turn on location services. Click **Allow** if you want Maps to start with your location, or **Block** if not. ∎

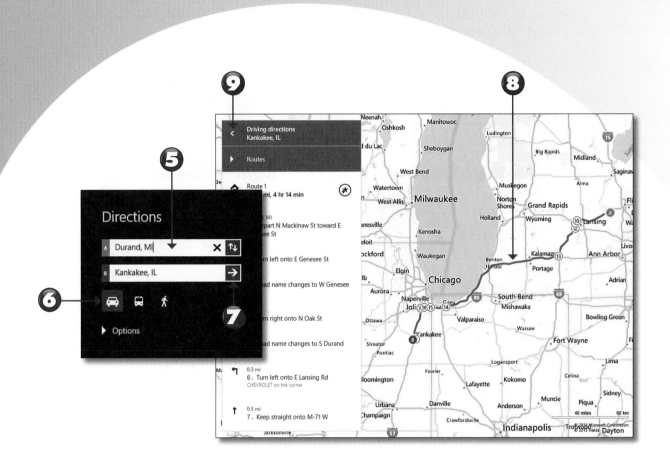

5 Fill in the starting point (Maps fills in the current location as the destination).

6 Click the car icon for driving directions (the others are for transit and walking directions).

7 Click to calculate directions.

8 Maps displays a suggested route to the specified location with turn-by-turn directions.

9 Click to return to your specified location.

End

TIP

Zooming Your View You can use the Zoom buttons (the plus and minus buttons that appear when you click on the map) to zoom your map view in or out. ■

TIP

Printing Your Map Open the Charms bar (swipe from right, mouse to the lower- or upper-right corners, or press Windows key + C), select **Devices**, and select **Print** to print your directions. ■

TRIP PLANNING WITH MAPS

Traveling to a destination isn't the end of a trip: it's the beginning of one. Use Maps' Nearby feature to find out where to eat, where to stay, and much more.

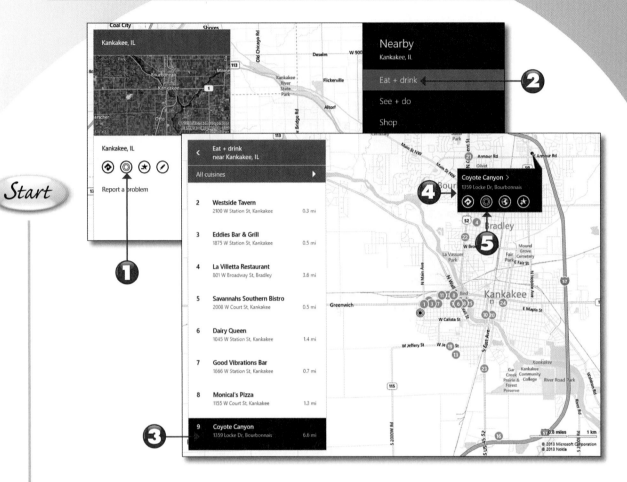

1. While viewing a location in Maps, click the **Nearby** button.

2. Select **Eat + Drink**.

3. Click a listing.

4. The listing you selected is highlighted on the map.

5. Click its **Nearby** button.

Continued

6 Select **Hotels**.

7 Click a location.

8 Click to open the location's website.

9 Press Win+Z, or swipe up to open the apps bars.

10 Select from other options, such as adding a location as a favorite or changing the style of the map view.

End

TIP
Changing the Map View You can switch the map between Road view and Aerial view by clicking the Map style button on the Apps bar. ■

USING THE PEOPLE APP

The People app is handy for compiling and maintaining a list of contacts. Acting like a digital address book, the People app keeps a list of people you contact the most, including Facebook friends, email contacts, and more. To view a contact, simply click it. You can add new contacts as needed.

1. Click or tap the **People** app.

2. Click to see notifications, photos, and contacts.

3. Swipe or press Win+Z to open the app bar.

4. Click **New contact**.

5. Fill out the contact form with as many details as needed.

6. Click **Save**.

Continued

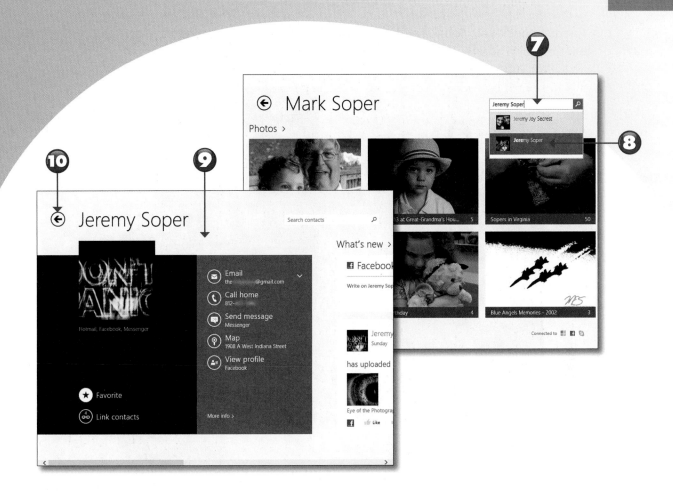

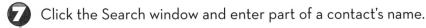

7 Click the Search window and enter part of a contact's name.

8 Click the contact's name.

9 The contact's page appears.

10 Click to return to the previous page.

End

NOTE

First-Time People App Startup The first time you start this app, you might be prompted to add friends from Facebook or other social networking sites you use. Click **Connect** when prompted, and log in to your Microsoft account when prompted to finish the process. ■

NOTE

Changing Views You can use the People app to view social notifications from accounts such as Facebook, favorite people, and an alphabetized listing of all your contacts. The What's New button (step 3) opens the latest social account postings. The All contacts button (step 3) lists all contacts in alphabetical order. ■

CHECKING WEATHER WITH THE WEATHER APP

You can check your local weather report using the Weather app. You can specify favorite locations and see the latest forecast.

1 Click the **Weather** tile.

2 Press Windows key+Z to display the Apps bar.

3 Click **Places**.

4 Click **Add**.

Continued

NOTE

Weather Options Click Current Location to view local weather. Click Refresh for the latest weather. Open the Weather Maps menu to select weather maps by world region. Click Ski Resorts to see weather at nearby ski resorts. ∎

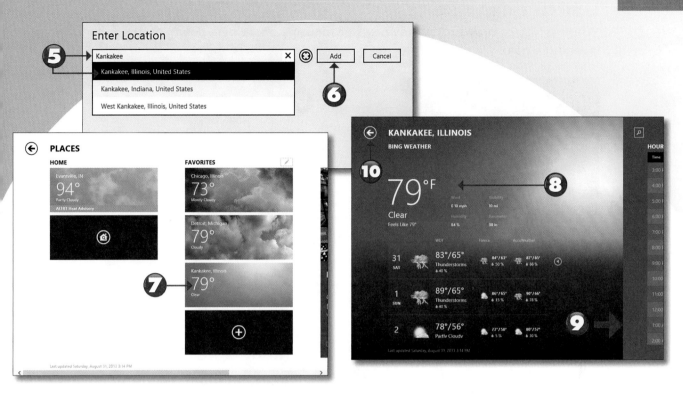

5 Type a location and select the correct match.

6 Click **Add**.

7 Click the new location.

8 The Weather app displays the information.

9 Scroll to the right for hourly forecasts, radar and other weather maps, and historical weather data.

10 Click to return to the previous location.

End

NOTE

Activate It The first time you use the Weather app, you might be prompted to turn on your current city to retrieve the latest data pertaining to your location. ■

TIP

Changing Default Locations To create a new default location that appears as soon as you open the Weather app, press Windows key+Z to display the Apps bar, and click the **Change Home** button. Select the location to use, or click **Add a new location**. ■

USING FINANCE

Whether you're browsing money news or focusing on a single company, the Finance app is ready to help.

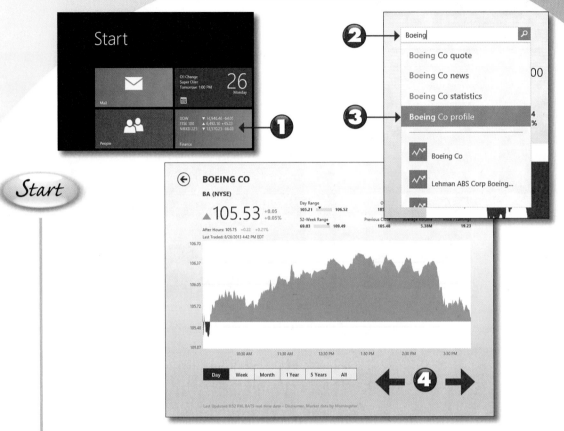

 Start

1 Click the **Finance** tile.

2 Click the Search box and enter a stock symbol, company name, or index name.

3 Click the item desired.

4 Scroll to the left or right for more information about the selected item.

Continued

TIP

Getting Started The first time you run the Finance app, the right pane includes a guide. Click the X to close it.

You can use the top-level apps bar menu to jump directly to a section, or scroll right to browse the app. Browsing helps you find mortgage, time value of money, and other calculators. ■

5 Press Windows key+ Z, swipe from the bottom, or right-click the screen to open the app bar.

6 To pin a specific stock to your Start screen, click **Pin to Start**.

7 Click **Pin to Start**.

8 The tile is placed on the right end of the Start screen.

End

CREATING A SHOPPING LIST FROM A RECIPE WITH FOOD & DRINK

Windows 8.1 introduces two lifestyle-based apps: Bing Food & Drink and Bing Health & Fitness. Here's how to use Bing Food and Drink to build a shopping list from a recipe.

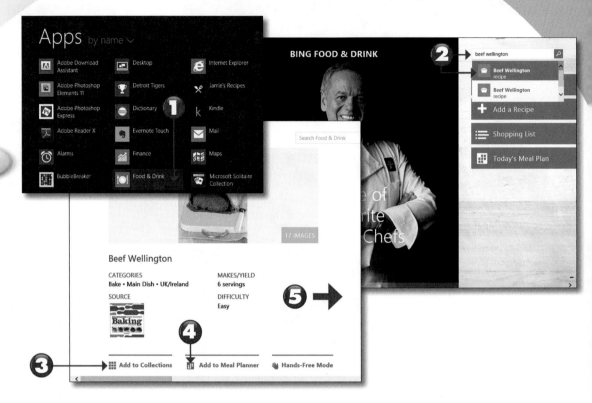

Start

① From the Apps screen, click the **Food & Drink** tile.

② Search for a recipe and click a match.

③ Click to add the recipe to your collections.

④ Click to add the recipe to your meal planner.

⑤ Scroll to the right to view the ingredient list.

Continued

TIP

Getting Started with Bing Food & Drink The first time you run this app, you might be prompted to note that recipes and collections are shared with other users. Click **Accept** to continue. ■

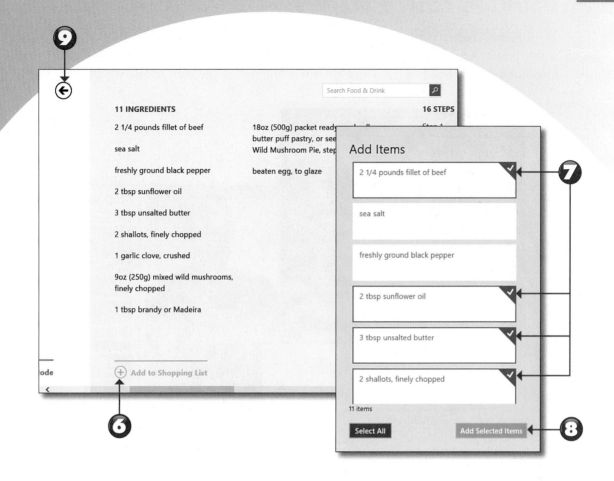

6 Click to add the ingredient list to your shopping list.

7 Click each ingredient you need to buy.

8 Click to add selected ingredients to your shopping list.

9 Click to return to the home page.

End

TIP

Exploring Food & Drink To learn more about Food & Drink's features, press Windows key+Z to open its app bar. You can go to Recipes, Tips & Techniques, Wines, Cocktails, Food Planner, and Collections. Scroll right from the main menu to browse tips from favorite chefs and articles on food culture. ■

USING HEALTH & FITNESS FOR NUTRITIONAL INFORMATION

Bing Health & Fitness provides one-stop access to diet, exercise, and health information. Here's how to check the nutrition information in your favorite foods.

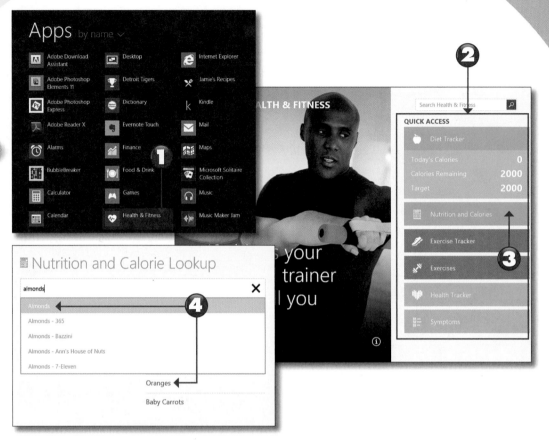

① From the Apps screen, click the **Health & Fitness** tile.

② Access all sections from the Quick Access menu.

③ Click **Nutrition and Calories**.

④ Enter a food item, or click a matching item from the Recent Searches or Common Food Items lists.

Continued

TIP

First-Time Startup and Search Tips To see the Quick Access menu the first time you start Bing Health & Fitness, close the guide in the right pane.

If you search for a food item, matching products are listed. Choose one. ■

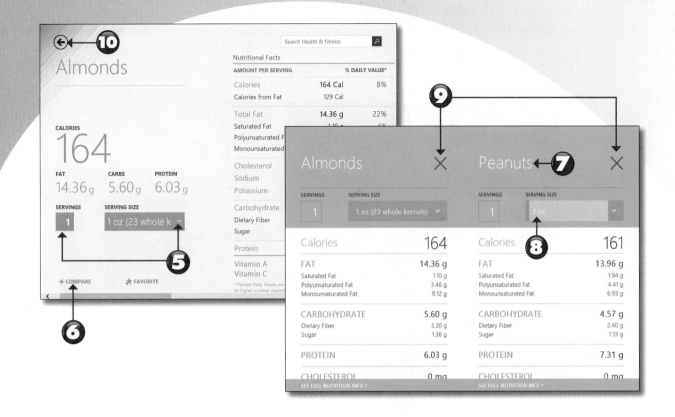

5 Select the serving size and number of servings to display information.

6 Click to compare.

7 Search for an item.

8 Select a serving size to see nutrition information.

9 Click to close the comparison.

10 Click to return to the app's home screen.

End

TIP

Scroll for More Information To see calorie breakdowns, percentage of daily calorie target, and typical activities to burn off the calories in the serving size you select, scroll to the right. ■

STARTING AND JOINING SKYPE

Microsoft has replaced its former instant messaging programs with Skype, enabling you to make free voice and video calls and text chats to any other Skype users and place low-cost voice calls to telephone numbers worldwide. Because Skype is also available to other platforms, you must sign up for the service if you're new to Skype. Here's how.

Start

1 From the Apps screen, click the **Skype** tile.

2 If prompted, click **Allow** to let Skype access your webcam or microphone.

3 If you want Skype to work whether you're in the app or not, click **Allow** to let it run in the background.

Continued

TIP

Skype in the Background? Your Choice Letting Skype run in the background enables your device to notify you of status and notifications from the lock screen as well as while you use your device. If you prefer to use Skype on an as-needed basis, click **Don't allow** in step 3. ■

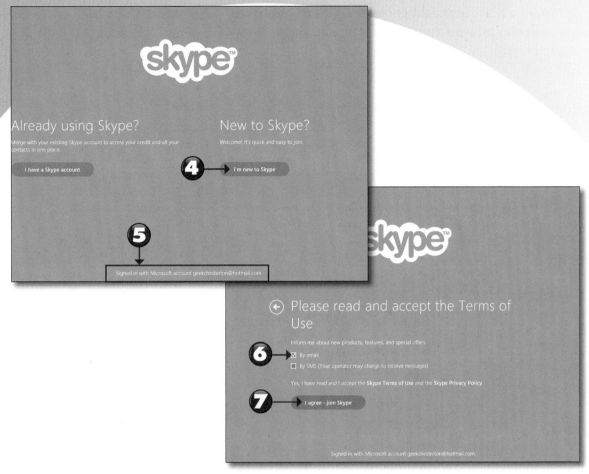

4 Click to set up a Skype account.   *walameda@msn.com*

5 Your Microsoft account will be used to sign in to Skype.

6 Click one or both boxes to be informed about new products, features, and special offers (optional).

7 Click to join Skype.

End

TIP

Starting Skype for Existing Skype Users If you already have a Skype account, select that option in step 4. Follow the prompts to merge your existing Skype account with your Microsoft account. When you use Skype in the future on any device, use your Microsoft account information as your Skype login. ■

SELECTING FAVORITES

Your contact list might contain hundreds of people, but you probably stay in close contact with only a few of them. Here's how to select favorites from your contact (People) list in Skype.

1 After starting Skype, click the **favorites** button.

2 Click a contact.

3 Click **Add**.

4 Scroll left to return to the main Skype dialog after selecting all favorites.

5 Your Favorites are displayed next to all people.

RECEIVING A CALL WITH SKYPE

If you accept the default (normal) settings when you start using Skype, you can accept a Skype call whenever your system is on. Here's how to receive a call.

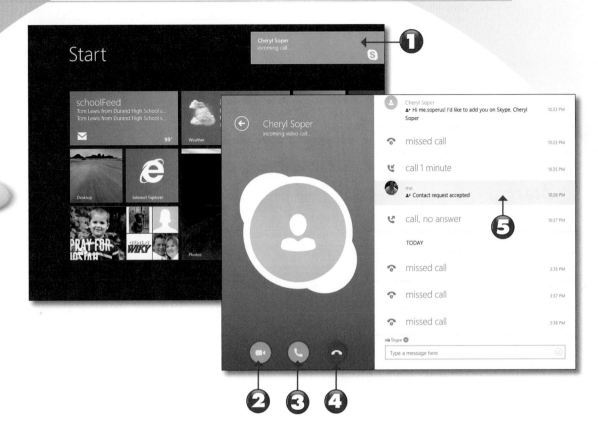

Start

1 When the Skype notification message appears, click it.

2 Click to accept using video and audio.

3 Click to accept using audio only.

4 Click to reject the call. (This icon also hangs up on a call after you've accepted.)

5 The call log records information about the call and caller.

End

TIP

Chatting with Skype To see what happens after you accept a call in step 2, see step 4 and beyond in the next lesson. ■

PLACING A CALL WITH SKYPE

Whether you place a call or receive a call with Skype, the options available are the same after the call is accepted. In this lesson, you learn how to place a call with Skype and use its video chat feature.

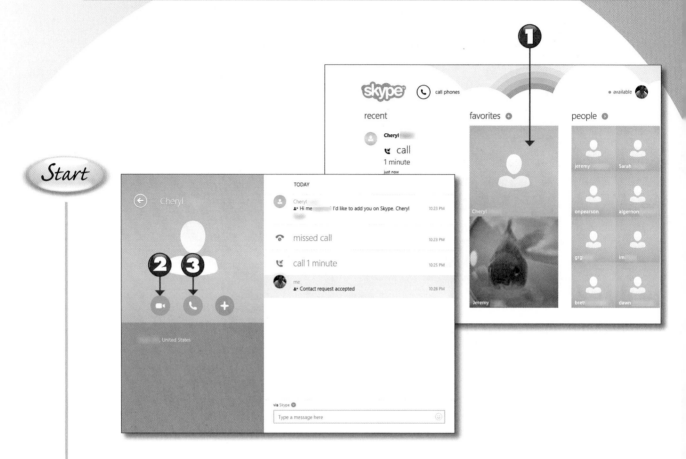

Start

1 From Skype, click the contact you want to call.

2 Click to make a video call.

3 Click to make a voice call.

Continued

4 Click to toggle video off or on.

5 Click to toggle your microphone off or on.

6 Click to view options related to the call.

7 Click to hang up.

8 The caller and call duration are listed at the top.

9 Click to return to the previous screen.

End

TIP

Call Options Options available when you click the options button in step 6 include instant message (text messaging), dial pad (for telephone calling), and send (receive) files. ∎

TEXT MESSAGING WITH SKYPE

Although Skype is best known for video and voice chatting, its instant messaging feature enables you to send and receive texts via Skype or via cell phone SMS. Here's how to use it.

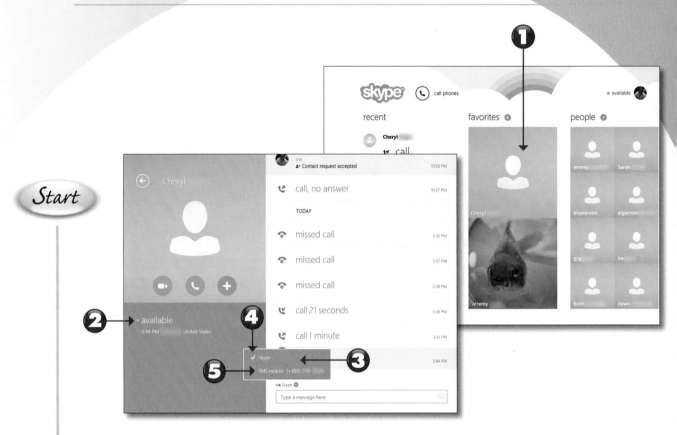

Start

1 From Skype, click the contact you want to chat with.

2 The contact is available.

3 Click to change how the message will be sent.

4 The checkmark indicates the current setting.

5 Click to use SMS.

Continued

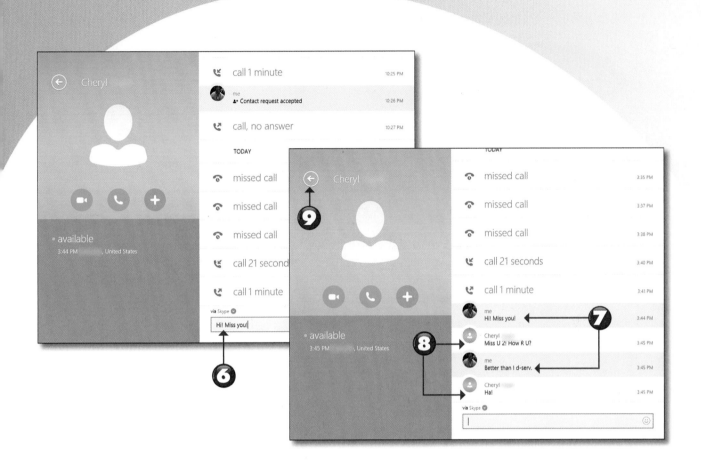

6 Type text and press the **Enter** key to send your message.

7 Your messages.

8 Their replies.

9 Click to return to the previous screen.

End

Chapter 12

CUSTOMIZING THE START SCREEN

The Windows Start screen and its default appearance provide fast, easy access to Windows 8 apps. However, you can customize what's on the Start screen and make it your own by changing its appearance and settings. This chapter shows you how to customize the Start screen.

The Start screen
Personalize menu

Rearranging tiles on
the Start screen

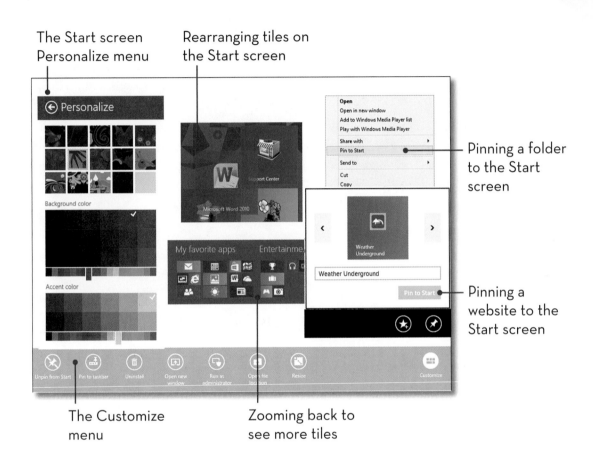

Pinning a folder
to the Start
screen

Pinning a
website to the
Start screen

The Customize
menu

Zooming back to
see more tiles

RELOCATING TILES ON THE START SCREEN

You can rearrange the tiles on the Start screen by dragging them to the location you want.
Use this technique to place the tiles you use most on the left side of the Start screen, so
they appear first.

1 Click and hold the tile you want to move.

2 Drag the tile to the preferred location.

3 Release the mouse button to drop the tile.

End

SETTING UP NAME GROUPS

Windows 8.1 includes the new Name Group feature. Use Name Groups to assign a name to groups of related tiles after you arrange them how you want.

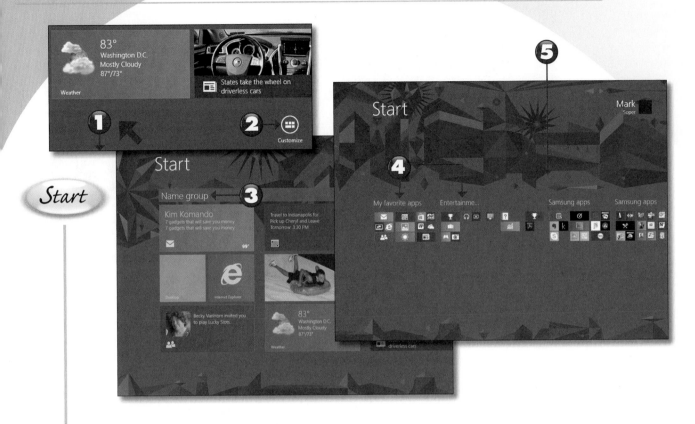

Start

1. Swipe from the bottom edge of the screen up and to the left (touch screen), or right-click the bottom of the screen to display the Customize icon.

2. Click **Customize**.

3. Find the first **Name group** field you want to change, click it, and enter the name desired.

4. Repeat as needed until you have named each name group you wanted to name.

5. Zoom back to see more groups at a time.

End

NOTE

Zooming Back With a touch screen, press two fingers to the screen and move them apart. With a mouse, move the mouse to the lower-right corner of the screen and click the minus sign (–). To restore the screen, tap or click it. ■

PINNING AN APP TO THE START SCREEN

The Start screen lists only a few of the apps installed on your system. In this section, you learn how to pin an app from the Apps screen to the Start screen so you can open it faster.

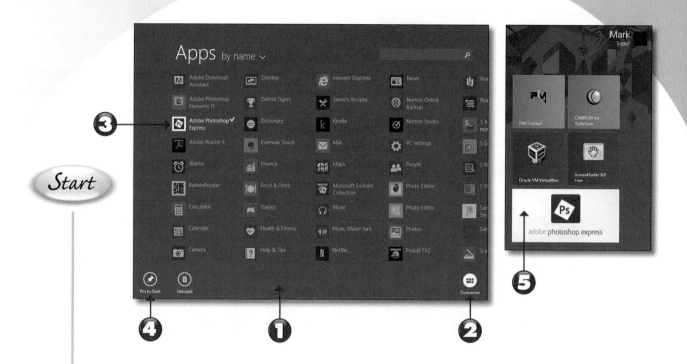

Start

① From the Apps screen, swipe from the bottom edge of the screen up and to the left (touch screen), or right-click the bottom of the screen to display the Customize menu.

② Click **Customize**.

③ Click the app you want to pin.

④ Click **Pin to Start**.

⑤ The app is added to the right side of the Start screen.

End

NOTE

Desktop Apps on the Start Screen To learn how to add desktop apps to the Start screen, see Chapter 16, "Running Desktop Apps." ■

UNPINNING AN OBJECT FROM THE START SCREEN

If you decide you don't need a particular item on the Start screen, removing it is easy. Apps you unpin from the Start screen can still be started from the Apps screen.

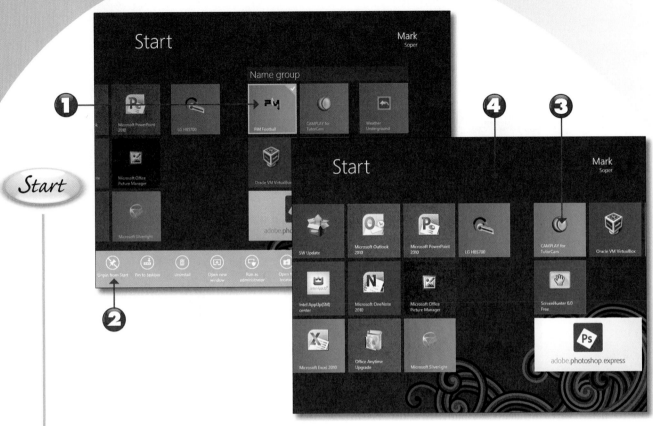

1 Right-click or press and hold (touch screen) the tile you want to remove.

2 Click **Unpin from Start**.

3 The tile disappears and nearby objects realign automatically.

4 Tap or click the screen to complete the process.

End

NOTE

Starting an App After You Remove It from the Start Screen To use apps you unpin from the Start screen, switch to the Apps screen and start them from there. ■

NOTE

Uninstalling an App If Uninstall is listed as an option when you right-click a tile, you can remove the app from your system. Keep in mind that if you uninstall an app, you can't use it again until you reinstall it. You might not be able to use another program to open data you created with that app. ■

PINNING A FOLDER TO THE START SCREEN

Just as you might want fast access to a particular website directly from the Start screen, you might also want one-click access to a folder that you use frequently. Here's how to add a folder to your Start screen.

1. Click **Desktop**.

2. Click **File Explorer**.

3. Navigate until the folder you want to pin is visible.

4. Right-click or tap and hold (touch screen) to open the folder's properties sheet.

5. Select **Pin to Start**.

6. The folder is added to the right side of the Start screen.

End

TIP

Pin, Pin, and Pin Again You can also pin Favorites such as Downloads, Desktop, and Computer to the Windows 8/8.1 Start screen, using the same steps outlined here. ■

PERSONALIZING THE START SCREEN

Windows offers thousands of possible combinations of colors and patterns for its Start screen, including some new ones in Windows 8.1 that weren't available before. Here's how to choose your favorites when you open the Settings charm from the Start screen.

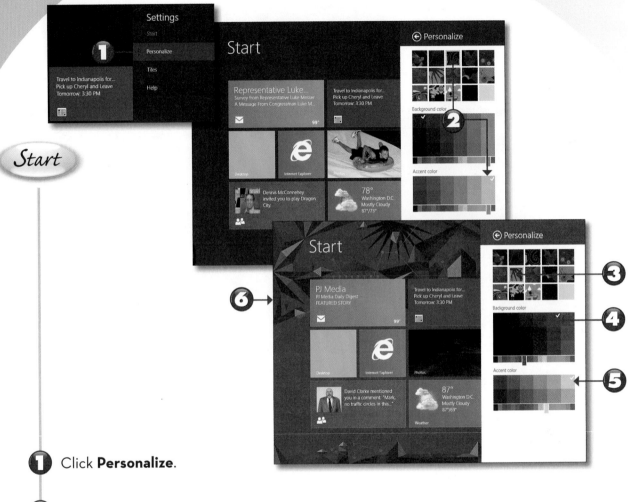

Start

1. Click **Personalize**.

2. The current background design and color settings.

3. Select a different background design.

4. Select a different background color.

5. Select a different accent color.

6. The Start screen preview changes to reflect your new settings.

End

ADJUSTING THE SIZE OF START SCREEN TILES

Windows uses four different sizes of tiles on the Start screen, including two that are new to Windows 8.1. If you want to change the default size settings for some tiles, here's how to do it.

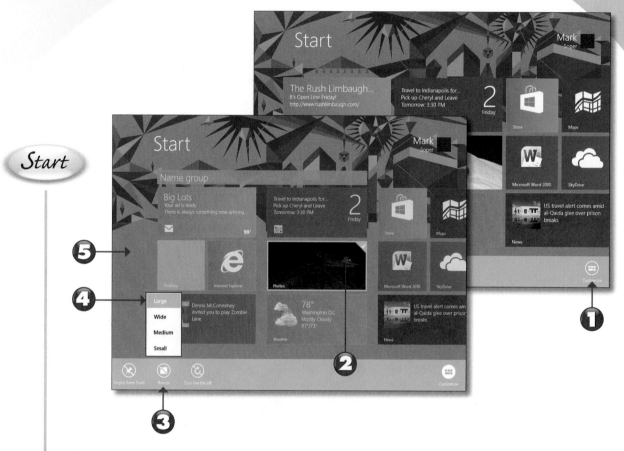

Start

1. Open the App bar and click **Customize**.

2. Select the **Photos** tile (or tile of your choice).

3. Click **Resize**.

4. Select the size you want.

5. Click or tap the screen to exit Customize mode.

Continued

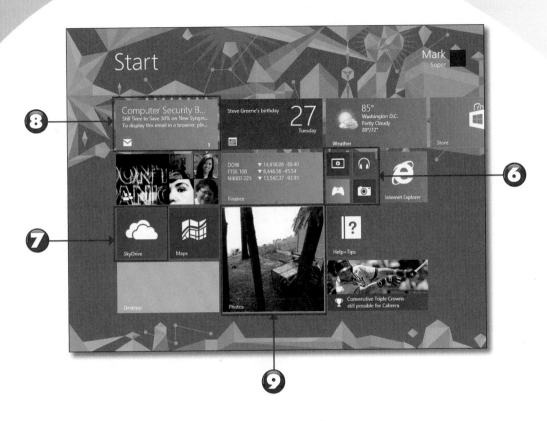

6 Small tiles appear as small square boxes.

7 Medium tiles are twice the size of small tiles.

8 Wide tiles are the same height as medium tiles but take up two columns.

9 Large tiles are twice the size of medium tiles.

End

NOTE

Small Tiles Pros and Cons Follow the steps above but select Small if you want to put a lot of tiles on a screen. However, keep in mind that Small tiles are 1/4 the size of medium tiles and can't display live updates. ■

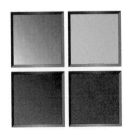

TURNING LIVE TILES OFF AND ON

Tiles such as Photos, Weather, Sports, News, and others are live tiles—Photos provides a live slide show of your photos, while others provide real-time updates of information and social network updates. If you prefer not to see real-time updates, you can disable the live tile feature for any tiles you prefer. In this tutorial, we disable the live tile for Weather (at its normal size) and then restore the live tile.

Start

1. Open the Customize menu and click **Customize**.

2. Click the Weather tile.

3. Click **Turn live tile off**.

4. The tile now displays static content instead of live content.

5. Tap or click the screen to close the Customize menu.

Continued

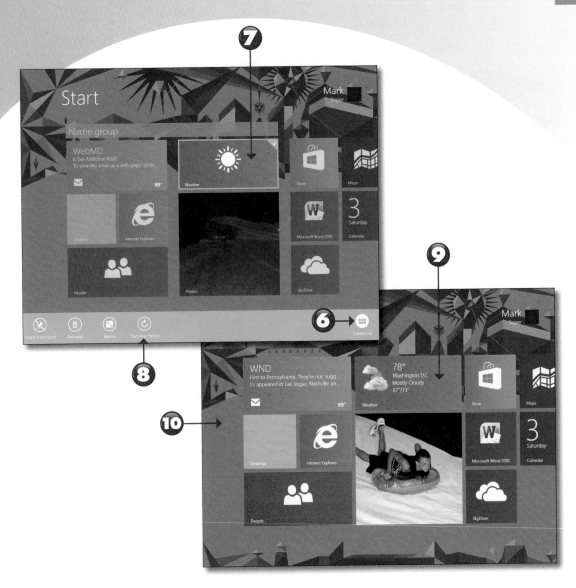

6 Open the Customize menu and click **Customize**.

7 Click the Weather tile.

8 Click **Turn live tile on**.

9 The tile provides live content again.

10 Tap or click the screen to close the Customize menu.

End

Chapter 13

MANAGING WINDOWS WITH PC SETTINGS

With Windows 8.1, PC settings configures many more settings than in Windows 8. The end result is that you can spend less time flipping between Desktop's Control Panel and the Start screen and more time working (or playing) with Start screen apps.

Adjusting volume

Configuring an additional display

The PC settings main menu

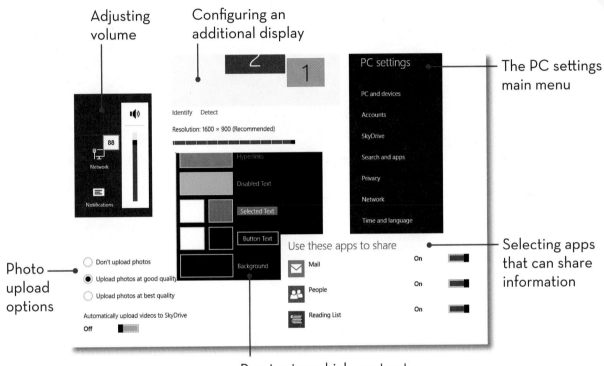

Photo upload options

Selecting apps that can share information

Previewing a high-contrast color scheme

ADJUSTING SYSTEM VOLUME

Although you can control the volume for most computers via the PC's speakers, you can also adjust system volume from the Settings menu. Here's how.

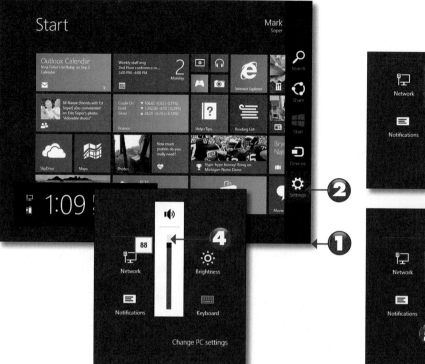

Start

1. Swipe from the right, move your mouse into the lower-right or upper-right corner, or press Windows key+C to open the Charms menu.

2. Click **Settings**.

3. Click **Volume**. (The number beneath the icon indicates its current loudness setting.)

4. Slide the control up (louder) or down (softer). Notice that the loudness number rises and falls with the slider.

5. When you click away from the slider, the new volume setting appears in the Settings charm.

End

TIP

Muting System Audio To mute audio, click the speaker icon in step 4. If you mute system audio in step 4, the speaker icon in step 5 is marked with an X. To unmute audio, repeat steps 3–4. ■

CHANGING SCREEN BRIGHTNESS AND NOTIFICATIONS

You can adjust screen brightness (on laptops) and temporarily hide notifications (on all devices) when you don't want to be disturbed. Here's how.

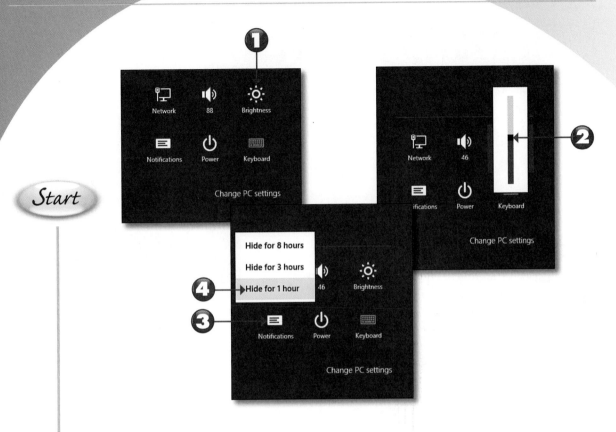

Start

1 From the Settings charm, click **Brightness**.

2 Adjust the slider to the desired screen brightness, and release it.

3 Back in the Settings charm, click **Notifications**.

4 Select the desired amount of time to hide notifications.

End

NOTE

Tiles Options You can also change settings for Tiles from the Settings menu. Options include displaying administrative controls and clearing personal information from tiles. However, if you don't want to have live personal information displayed on tiles such as Mail, Weather, and so on, I recommend you disable each live tile instead. You can reset the tiles you select to display live information later, but clearing tiles of personal information is not reversible. ∎

PC SETTINGS OVERVIEW

The PC Settings dialog provides a useful way to access the settings you're most likely to change. Here's how to open it.

① Swipe from the right, move your mouse into the lower-right or upper-right corner, or press Windows key+C to open the Charms menu.

② Click **Settings**.

③ Click **Change PC settings**.

④ The PC settings main menu. Select a setting to see what options you can change.

⑤ Click to see the most recently used settings.

End

CUSTOMIZE THE LOCK SCREEN

The PC and devices screen includes some of the most common settings to change, including display, power and sleep, AutoPlay, lock screen, and various types of devices. The lock screen is the screen that greets you when you turn on your device or need to unlock it. In this lesson, you learn how to adjust its settings.

Your Current Lock Screen Photo

1 From the PC settings screen, click **PC and devices**.

2 Click **Lock screen**.

3 Click a new lock screen picture.

4 The new picture appears.

5 Turn on the **Play a slide show** option to use pictures from your Pictures folder on your lock screen instead of the selected picture.

End

SETTING DISPLAY RESOLUTION

PC and devices also includes display settings such as resolution and support for multiple displays. Here's how to set your display as needed.

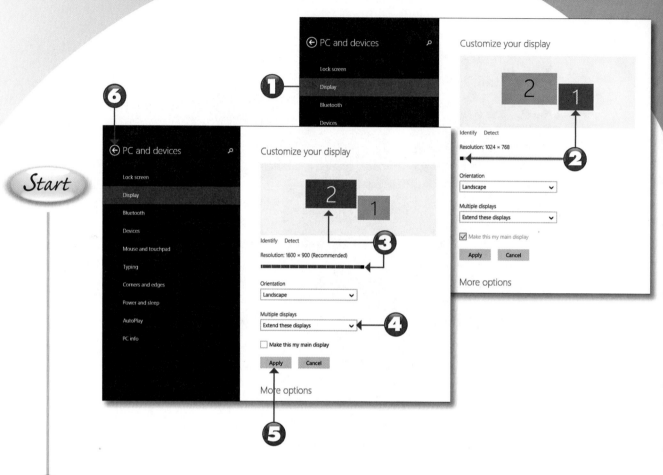

Start

1. From PC and devices, click **Display**.

2. Click display 1 and adjust resolution and other settings as needed.

3. Click display 2 and adjust resolution as needed.

4. To use a second display as part of the first display's desktop, select **Extend these displays**.

5. Click **Apply** to accept changes.

6. Click to return to PC settings.

End

ADJUSTING MOUSE AND TOUCHPAD SETTINGS

The Mouse and touchpad dialog enables you to switch mouse buttons, adjust mouse wheel, and solve problems with accidental touchpad swiping.

Start

1 From PC and devices, click **Mouse and touchpad**.

2 To adjust how many lines the mouse will scroll, click and drag the slider.

3 If you have problems with accidentally touching the touchpad while you type, select a different delay from the Touchpad menu.

End

NOTE

Other Mouse Options To enable a mouse to be used with the left hand, change the primary button from Left to Right. If you prefer to have the scroll wheel move a screen at a time, select that option from the **Roll the mouse wheel to scroll** menu. ■

CHANGING AUTOPLAY SETTINGS

The AutoPlay feature can display the contents of a removable-media drive, memory card, or digital camera/camcorder; import media; or ask you what to do. Use the AutoPlay option in PC and devices to adjust settings as desired.

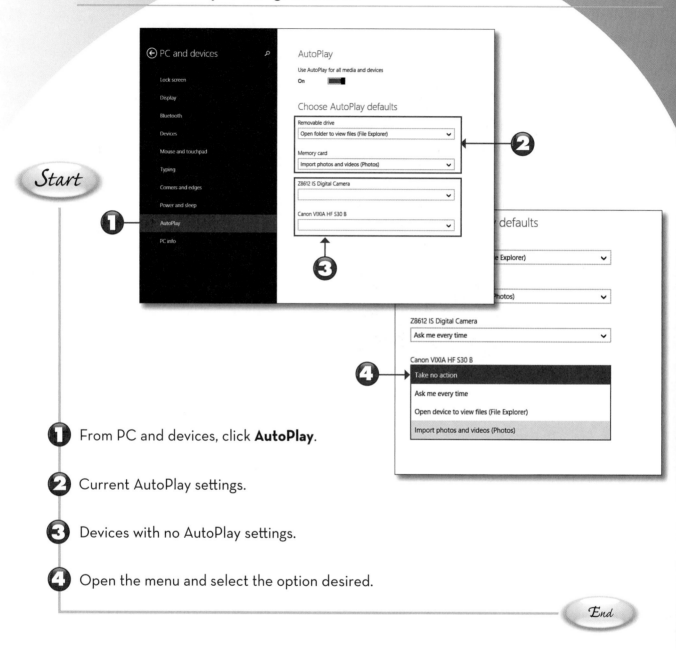

Start

 From PC and devices, click **AutoPlay**.

2 Current AutoPlay settings.

3 Devices with no AutoPlay settings.

4 Open the menu and select the option desired.

End

NOTE

Disabling AutoPlay If you prefer to disable AutoPlay, turn off the **Use AutoPlay** slider at the top of the dialog. ■

VIEWING PC INFO

Sometimes, you need to know the "inside story" of your device's name, processor, RAM, and so on. PC Info brings it to you.

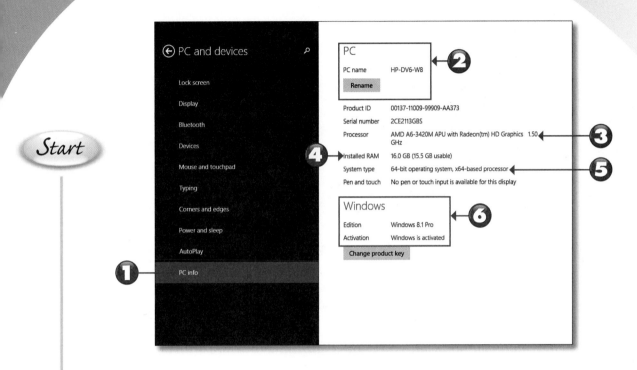

Start

1. From PC and devices, click **PC info**.

2. Your PC's name (as seen by Network).

3. Processor model and clock speed.

4. Memory (RAM) size.

5. Identifies 32-bit or 64-bit Windows version.

6. Windows edition and activation details.

End

MANAGING SKYDRIVE STORAGE SETTINGS

To manage local and cloud-based storage settings, click **SkyDrive** from the PC settings menu and select the options desired. Here's how.

Start

1. From PC settings, click **SkyDrive**.

2. Current cloud-based storage capacity and amount used.

3. Click to buy more storage space.

4. To turn off automatic copying of files to cloud-based storage, slide to **Off**.

5. Click to see files on SkyDrive.

Continued

NOTE

Turning Off Save to SkyDrive If your network is already set up to enable remote access to your files, consider turning off the **Save documents to SkyDrive** setting. You can always copy files to SkyDrive manually. ■

6 Your SkyDrive folders appear in split screen.

7 Click to return to the SkyDrive menu.

8 Drag to the left to view SkyDrive folders in full screen.

End

NOTE

SkyDrive to Become...? Microsoft has decided to change the name SkyDrive after losing a trademark infringement lawsuit brought by UK's BSkyB broadcast service. The new name for Microsoft's cloud-based storage was not yet known as this book went to press. ∎

SETTING CAMERA ROLL OPTIONS

The pictures and videos you shoot with your device's onboard webcam and/or rear-facing cameras are stored in a folder called Camera Roll (the Camera Roll is a folder within your Pictures folder). Use the Camera Roll SkyDrive setting to determine whether to upload them and whether to adjust quality during upload. Here's how.

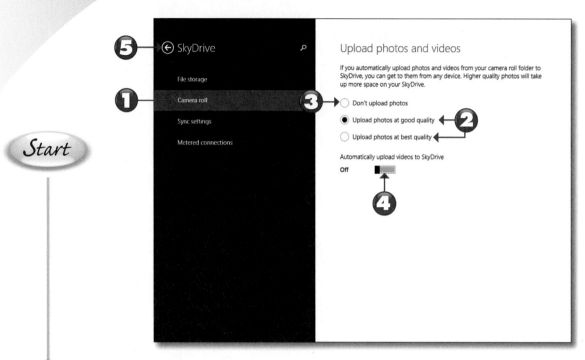

Start

1 From the **SkyDrive** pane, click **Camera Roll**.

2 Select an upload quality setting between good or best.

3 Click to discontinue automatic photo uploading.

4 To upload videos automatically, slide to **On**.

5 Click to return to PC settings.

End

NOTE

Best Quality, Video Uploading and SkyDrive Capacity The default settings for Camera Roll are designed to help you share pictures via SkyDrive without using up your SkyDrive capacity too quickly. Switching from Good quality to Best quality for photo uploads and enabling automatic uploads of your videos will use up your 7GB of SkyDrive capacity quickly. If you want to use these options, consider buying more space on SkyDrive. ■

SYNC SETTINGS

Windows 8 enables you to use the same settings on each of your Windows 8 computers. This feature, known as synchronization or synching, is controlled through SkyDrive's Sync settings dialog. Here's a closer look.

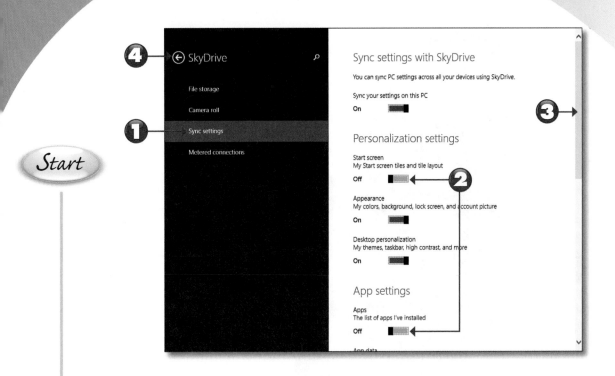

Start

1 From the **SkyDrive** pane, click **Sync settings**.

2 By default, Start screen and app list sync are turned off.

3 Scroll down to see and change additional settings.

4 Click to return to PC settings.

End

NOTE

Sync Settings and Your Devices If you use two or more devices that have the same apps installed, consider enabling the disabled settings. Otherwise, I recommend leaving the settings at the defaults. ■

METERED CONNECTIONS

Many tablets and laptops come equipped with 4G cellular connections for wireless data access. However, most data plans limit the amount of data you can transfer during a month, and roving connections can be both data-limited and expensive. The Metered connections dialog enables you to fine-tune how your device works with this type of connection.

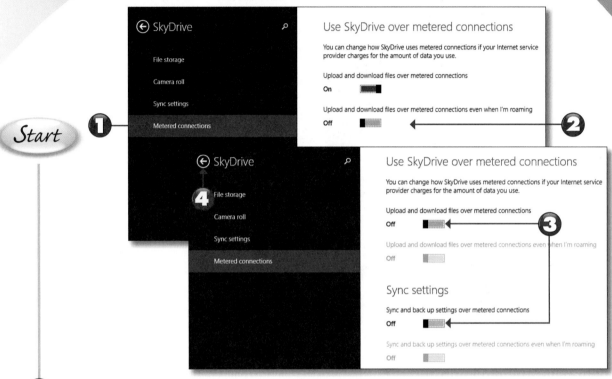

1 From the SkyDrive pane, click **Metered connections**.

2 The default settings prevent data use if you're roaming out of your home area.

3 If you prefer to use only Wi-Fi connections for file upload/download and sync instead of 4G, turn off both options.

4 Click to return to PC settings.

End

NOTE

More Metered Connection Settings There are two more settings governing metered connections; however, they are found in the Search and Apps settings. These options enable you to limit Bing's search capabilities when on a metered connection or when roaming. ◼

SETTING SEARCH OPTIONS

Windows uses Microsoft's own Bing search engine. Use the Search pane in the Search and Apps section of PC settings to customize how Bing works.

1 From PC settings, click **Search and apps**.

2 Click **Search**.

3 Click to clear search history.

4 Slide to turn off Bing search.

5 Select the level to which you want Bing to have access to personal data in generating search results.

6 Use the Safe Search controls to filter out adult content from search results.

Start

End

SETTING APP SHARE OPTIONS

Many of the apps included with Windows 8 are designed to share information by means of the Share charm. The Share dialog enables you to configure app sharing settings.

Start

1 From Search and apps, click **Share**.

2 To adjust the number of apps shown in the Share list in Charms, select a number.

3 To clear the list of items you share most often, click **Clear list**.

4 To turn off an app's sharing feature, use its slider.

End

NOTE

Using the Share Charm If you want to share a web page or article with others, press Windows key + C, swipe from the right, or move your mouse into the upper- or lower-right corners to open the Charms menu. Then, click the Share button. Select the app to use for sharing. ∎

GENERAL NOTIFICATION SETTINGS

Your computer can be a very annoying device when it bombards you with notifications from calls, apps, and messages. Use the Notifications section of Search and apps to find some peace and quiet.

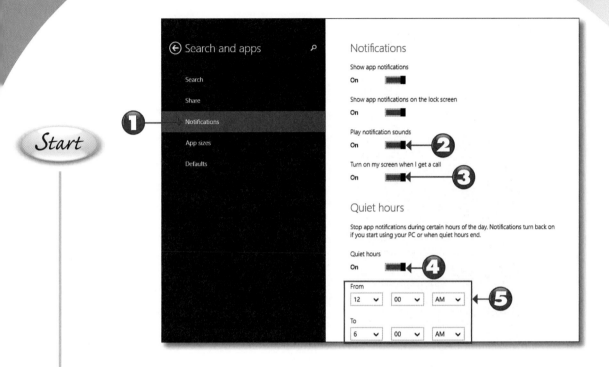

Start

① From Search and apps, click **Notifications**.

② Slide to off to turn off notification sounds.

③ Slide to off to leave your device's screen off when receiving calls.

④ Leave on to enforce quiet hours.

⑤ Sets quiet hours start/ending times.

End

NOTE

Tailoring Quiet Hours to Your Schedule If you work second or third shift and don't want your device annoying you when you're trying to get some sleep, adjust the quiet hours accordingly. ∎

APP-SPECIFIC NOTIFICATION SETTINGS

Many Windows 8 apps include notification features. Scroll down the Notifications section to the Show notifications section to make changes.

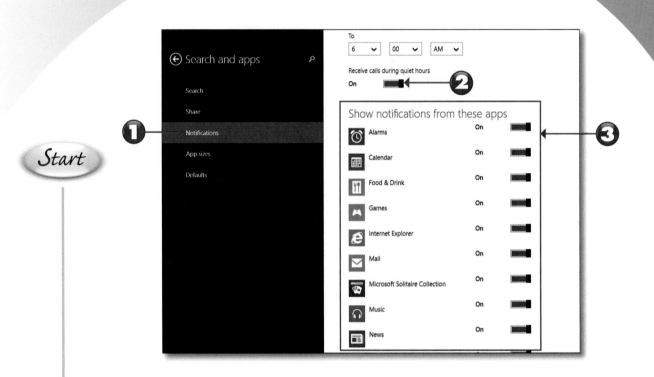

Start

1 From Search and apps, click **Notifications**.

2 Slide to off to block calls during quiet hours.

3 Notification is turned on for all apps by default. Scroll down and disable notifications for specific apps as desired.

End

APP SIZES AND UNINSTALL OPTIONS

Particularly with Ultrabooks and tablets, both of which use small-capacity SSD storage, knowing how much space an app uses can be very helpful, especially if you also have the ability to uninstall Start screen apps that you don't need anymore. The App sizes dialog provides you with both features.

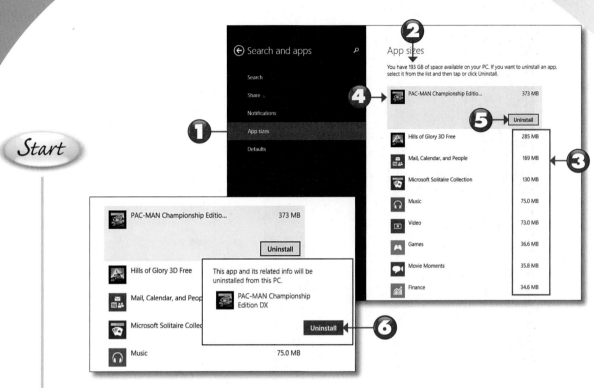

Start

1 From Search and apps, click **App sizes**.

2 The total amount of available space.

3 Apps are listed in order from largest to smallest.

4 Click an app if you want to uninstall it.

5 To remove an app, click **Uninstall**.

6 Click **Uninstall** to remove it.

End

GENERAL PRIVACY SETTINGS

Getting ads and information tailored to you can be convenient, but the reason it happens is because of your system's privacy settings. To get back some control over your privacy, use the Privacy section of PC settings. Here's how to adjust general privacy options.

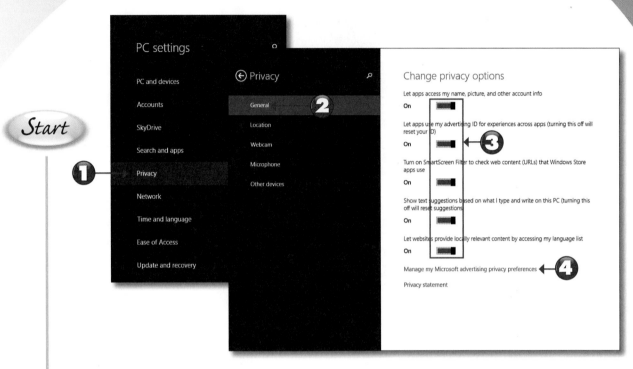

Start

From PC settings, click **Privacy**.

Click **General**.

To improve privacy, slide any or all settings desired to off.

To change your Microsoft personalized ad settings, click the **Manage my Microsoft advertising** link. The screen will split, displaying the appropriate Microsoft website on the right side.

End

NOTE

Privacy Versus Convenience Before you adjust privacy options, read the description for each one carefully. If you're not sure of a setting's impact on your computer use, turn one setting off, use your computer as you do normally, and decide whether turning off that setting caused you any significant difficulty. Continue with the next setting until you have the right balance of settings for you. ■

CONFIGURING LOCATION SETTINGS

Many Start screen apps are designed to use your location to provide you with more relevant information. If you need to change these settings, use the Location dialog in the Privacy section of PC settings.

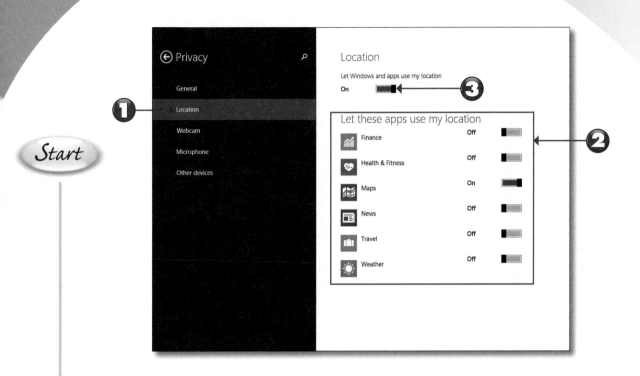

1 From the Privacy category of PC Settings, click **Location**.

2 Adjust location usage for each app listed as desired.

3 To disable all location settings, drag this switch to **Off**.

End

NOTE

Benefits of Enabling Location Settings By enabling location settings for listed apps, you can find items that apply to your location more quickly. ■

CONFIGURING WEBCAM USAGE

Most computers today either include built-in webcams or use webcams attached via USB ports. Windows 8.1's Webcams dialog enables you to specify the Start screen apps that can use your webcam.

1 From the Privacy category of PC Settings, click **Webcam**.

2 Apps that can be configured to use your webcam.

3 Move to Off to block all webcam use by your apps.

NOTE

Privacy and Webcams Even if you block listed apps from using your webcam, it's possible for malware to use your webcam. If you're concerned about this potential privacy risk, unplug your USB webcam when you're not using it or cover up the lens of your device's built-in webcam. ■

CONFIGURING MICROPHONE USAGE

If your computer has a webcam (either built-in or USB-based), it also has a microphone. You might also have a headset or dedicated microphone connected via a USB or mini-jack. You can determine which Start screen apps can use the microphone.

Start

1 From the Privacy category of PC settings, click **Microphone**.

2 Apps that can be configured to use your microphone.

3 Move to Off to block all microphone usage by your apps.

End

NOTE

Privacy and Microphones Even if you block listed apps from using your microphone, it's possible for malware to use your microphone. If you're concerned about this potential privacy risk, unplug it when you're not using it. ∎

CONFIGURING TIME ZONE

New computers and tablets are often set to the wrong time zone for your area when you first receive them. Fixing the problem is easy with PC settings' Time and language's settings.

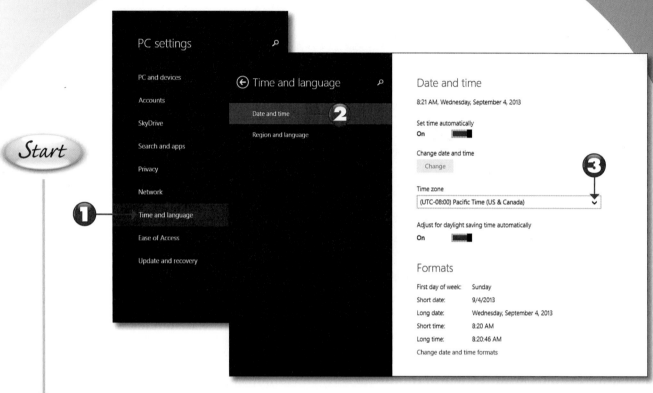

Start

① From PC settings, click **Time and language**.

② Click **Date and time**.

③ If the time zone shown is incorrect, click to open the time zone menu.

Continued

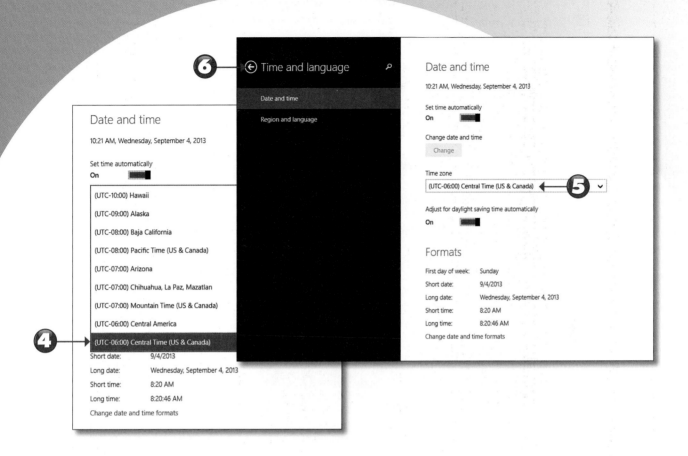

4 Select the correct time zone.

5 The correct time zone is now listed.

6 Click to return to PC settings.

End

NOTE

Check Time as Well as Time Zone After changing the time zone, look at the current time (shown under Formats in step 5). If the time shown is incorrect, turn off Set Time Automatically, click the Change button, and enter the correct time. ∎

CONFIGURING EASE OF ACCESS

If you need to customize Windows to be easier to use for someone with physical limitations, PC settings' Ease of Access menu is where to start. Here are some of its major features.

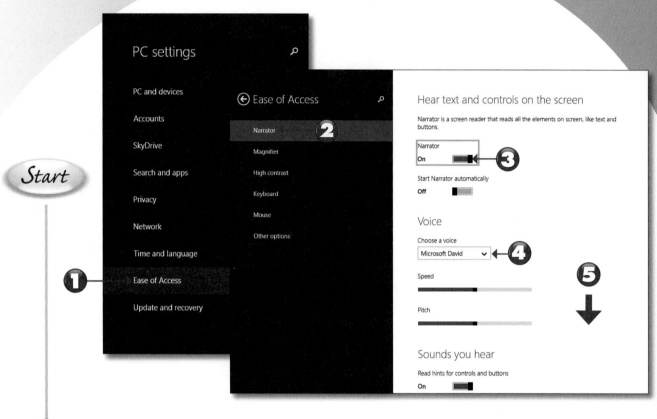

Start

1 From PC settings, click **Ease of access**.

2 Click **Narrator** if you want to enable the Narrator screen reader.

3 Enables/disables Narrator.

4 Select a voice.

5 Scroll down for other settings.

Continued

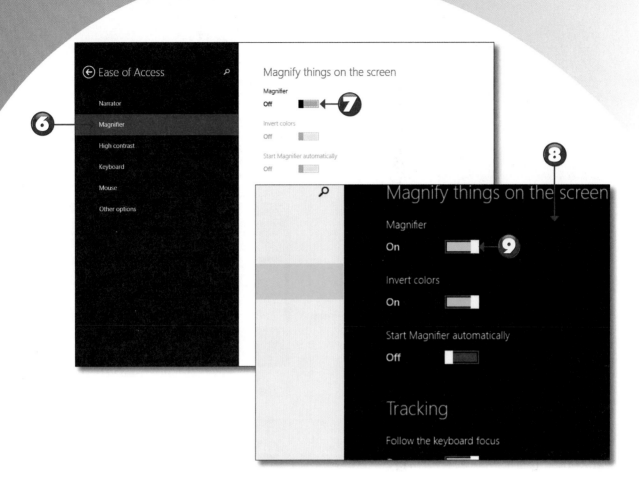

6 Click **Magnifier** if you want to enlarge the screen image.

7 Enables/disables Magnifier.

8 Magnifier and Invert Colors turned on.

9 Drag to turn off Magnifier and related features.

Continued

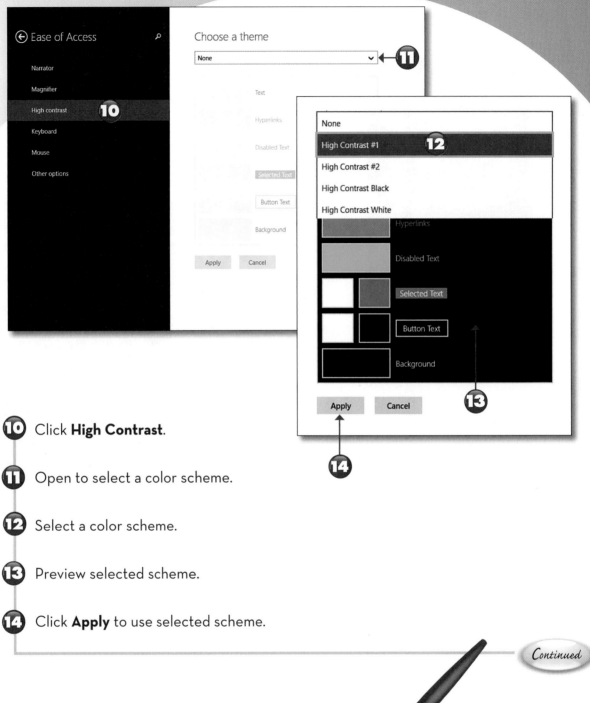

10 Click **High Contrast**.

11 Open to select a color scheme.

12 Select a color scheme.

13 Preview selected scheme.

14 Click **Apply** to use selected scheme.

Continued

NOTE

Back to the Regular Color Scheme To return to the regular Windows 8 color scheme, select **None** (see step 12) and click **Apply**. ■

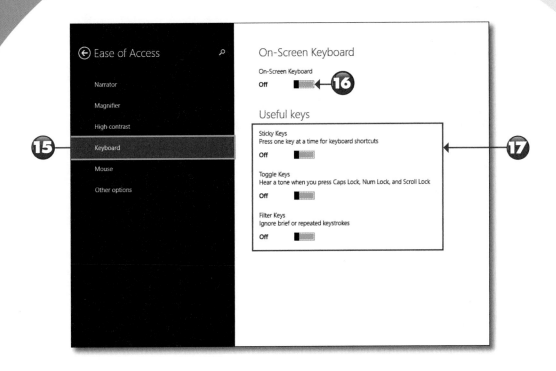

15 Click **Keyboard**.

16 Slide to On to enable the on-screen keyboard.

17 Turn on other settings as desired.

Continued

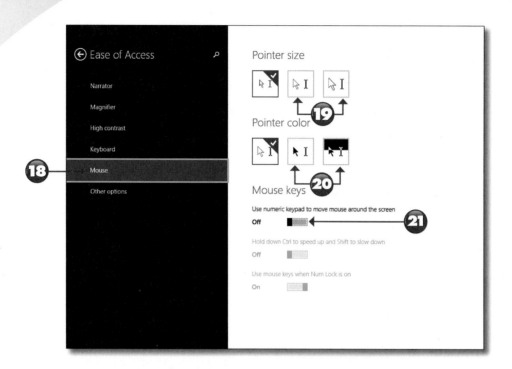

18 Click **Mouse**.

19 Click to select a new pointer size.

20 Click to select a different pointer color.

21 Slide to on to use numeric keypad as mouse (mouse keys).

Continued

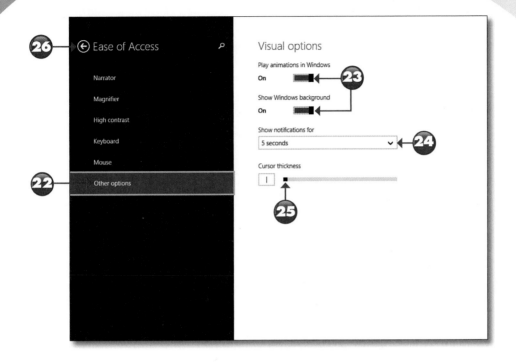

22 Click **Other options** to adjust visual options.

23 Drag to turn off these features.

24 Open to select a longer notification time (7 seconds to 5 minutes).

25 Drag to adjust cursor thickness.

26 Click to return to PC settings.

End

THE RECENT SETTINGS PANE

If you recently made a change with PC settings but want to change it again, use the Recent settings pane to save time and effort.

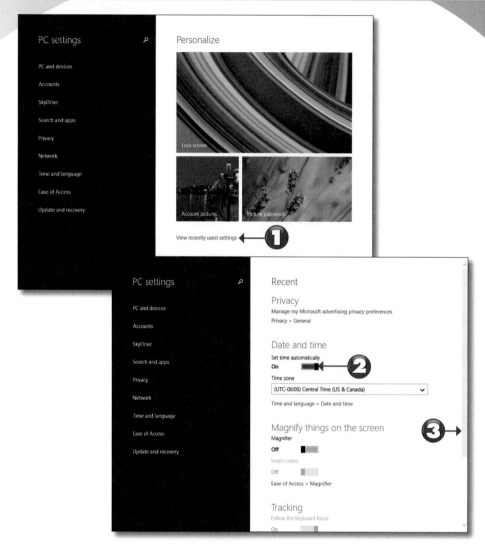

Start

1. From PC settings, click **View recently used settings**.

2. Choose a setting to reverse.

3. Scroll down to see more recent settings.

Continued

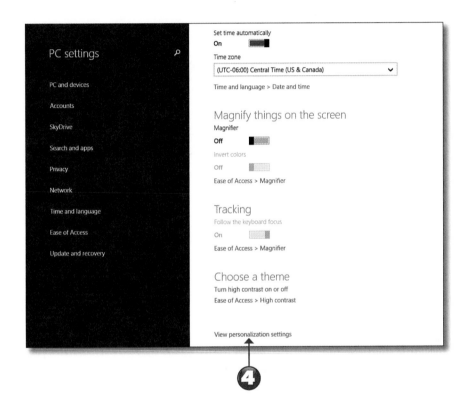

4 Click **View personalization settings** to return to the Personalization pane shown in step 1.

End

USING THE WINDOWS STORE

You can use the Windows Store app to shop online for more apps and commercial programs. The Windows Store features a variety of apps for a variety of uses, and it has been streamlined in Windows 8.1. You can find plenty of free apps, paid apps, and trial versions in the Store using the Search or the Categories view. In this chapter, you learn how to navigate the Store to find just the right apps for you and your device.

Sorting apps   App description

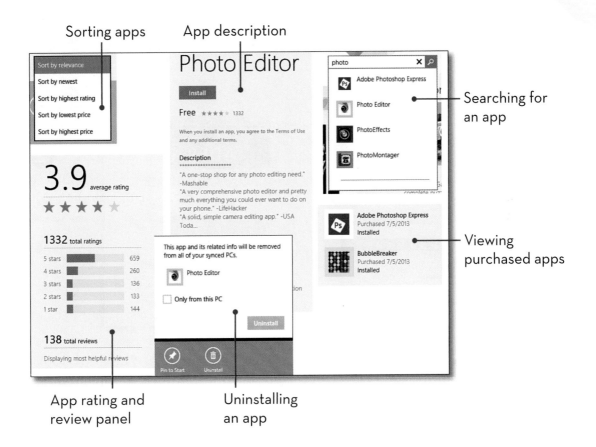

Searching for
an app

Viewing
purchased apps

App rating and
review panel

Uninstalling
an app

GOING TO THE STORE

When you first open the Store app, the first screen displays a currently featured app and links to the most popular apps and new releases. As you scroll through the Store, you can find apps suggested for you, new apps, and the most popular paid and free apps.

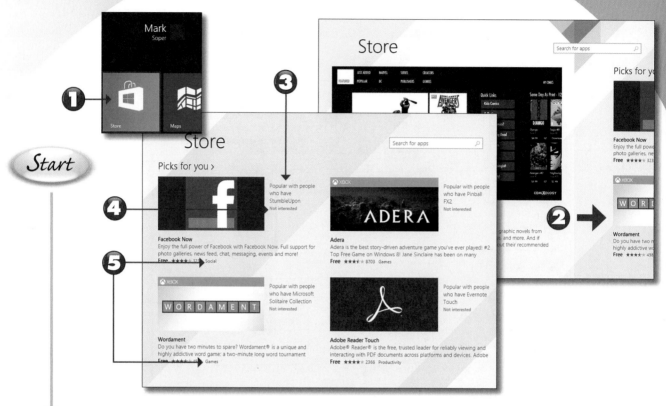

Start

1 Click or tap the **Store** tile.

2 After viewing the current featured app, scroll to the right to view app categories.

3 Why the app is suggested for you.

4 Click if you're not interested in this app (optional).

5 Click a category name to see more apps in the category..

End

NOTE

App Categories in the Scrolling Menu Scroll to the right to see these additional categories: Popular now, New Releases, Top paid, and Top free. ■

SEARCHING FOR APPS BY NAME

You can use the Windows Store Search window to search the Store for a specific app or
type of app. Here's how to search for your favorite app.

1 Click the **Search** field.

2 Type the search text.

3 Apps with partial name matches.

4 Click an app to go to that app's page.

5 Scroll down to see matching keywords.

NOTE

Don't Like the Name Matches? Search by Keyword See
"Searching for Apps by Keyword Phrase," later in this chapter,
p. 236, to track down the apps you want and need. ■

BROWSING FOR APPS BY CATEGORY

The Windows Store also enables you to browse by category. Here's how to open the category view.

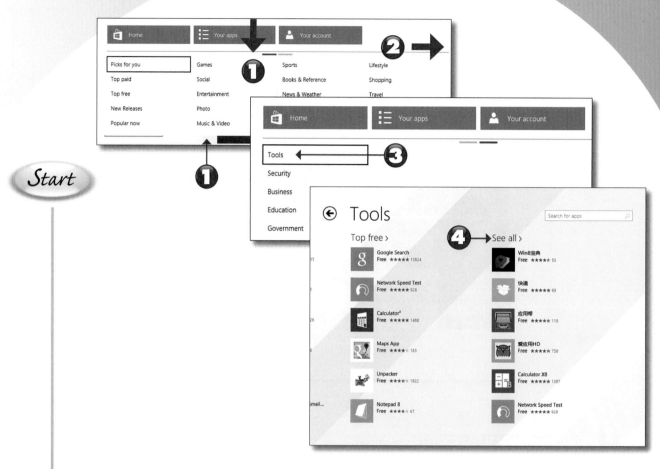

Start

1. Open the Store's App bar by pressing Windows key+Z, swiping from the top, or right-clicking an empty part of the page.

2. Scroll through the categories.

3. Click or tap a category.

4. Scroll to **See all** and click to see all matching apps.

Continued

TIP
Returning Home You can click the Home link in the Store's Apps bar to return to the opening screen.

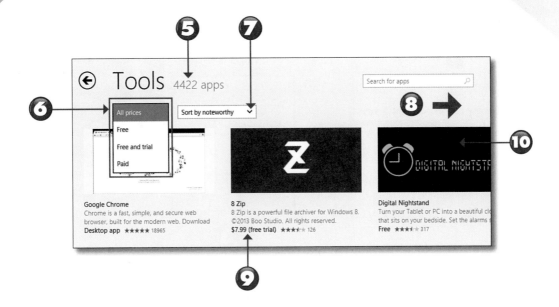

5 The number of apps in this category.

6 Select by price.

7 Open to select your preferred sort.

8 Scroll to see more matches.

9 The app's price.

10 Click an app to learn more.

End

LEARNING MORE ABOUT AN APP

Before you install an app from the Windows Store, take a few minutes to learn more about it. Here's how.

1. Click the app you want to learn more about.

2. Review the description and features.

3. Click **Show more** to learn more about the app.

4. Additional information about the app.

5. Review the category, app size, and other information about the app.

Continued

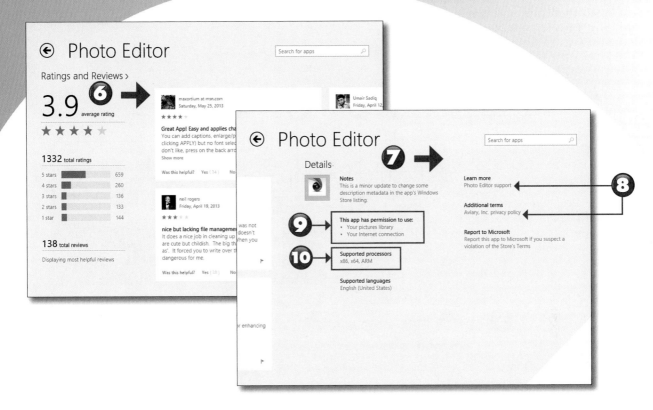

6 Scroll to see ratings and reviews.

7 Scroll to read details.

8 Click for more information about the app's support policies, privacy, and so on.

9 What the app uses on your device.

10 The PC types with which the app works. ARM works on Windows RT devices, such as Microsoft Surface; x86 and x64 work on PCs and devices with Intel or AMD processors.

End

NOTE

Getting Ready to Buy Apps If you have not yet created a Microsoft account, you will need one to buy apps. See "Getting a Microsoft Account," Chapter 2, p. 19, for details. To learn more about adding payment methods to your account, see the task, "Adding a Payment Method to Your Account," at the end of this chapter. ■

SEARCHING FOR APPS BY KEYWORD PHRASE

If the Windows Store Search doesn't show you a name match or you don't like the name matches, you can still find what you want by searching by keyword phrase.

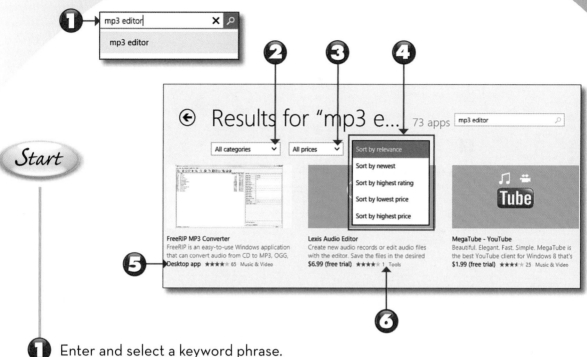

Start

1 Enter and select a keyword phrase.

2 Open to view matches by category.

3 Open to view matches by price.

4 Sorting by preferred criteria.

5 Desktop apps.

6 Ratings and category.

End

NOTE

Start Screen Apps Versus Desktop Apps Some content available in the Microsoft Store includes desktop apps, which run exclusively on the Windows desktop. This means the programs run in their own windows, not integrated with the Start screen. You can pin a desktop app to the Start screen for easy startup. Learn more about desktop apps in Chapter 16, "Running Desktop Apps." ■

INSTALLING AN APP

When you find an app you want, you can easily install it in just a few clicks. Windows does most of the hard work for you. When you install an app, a tile representing the app is added to the Windows Apps screen.

1 From the page for the app you want to download, click **Install**.

2 After installation, the app page lists the date you installed it or last updated it.

3 Open the Charms bar.

4 Click **Start**.

5 Open the Apps menu to see your new app.

Start

End

NOTE

Installing Paid Apps When you install a paid app, Windows directs you to a login screen where you can log in to your Microsoft account and choose a payment method. Windows might also prompt you to log in to your Microsoft account before continuing with the download. ■

RATING AN APP

The Windows Store includes user reviews. This information is helpful when you're deciding whether you want to try an app. By rating an app, you help other potential users know how it worked for you.

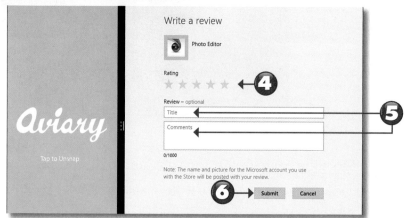

Start

1. Open the app.

2. Display the Charms bar and click **Settings**.

3. Click **Rate and review**.

4. Drag across the stars to rate the app.

5. Type a title and review text.

6. Click **Submit**.

End

UNINSTALLING AN APP FROM THE START SCREEN

You can easily remove an app you no longer use or want. Uninstalling an app removes it from your computer and deletes the app tile from your Start screen.

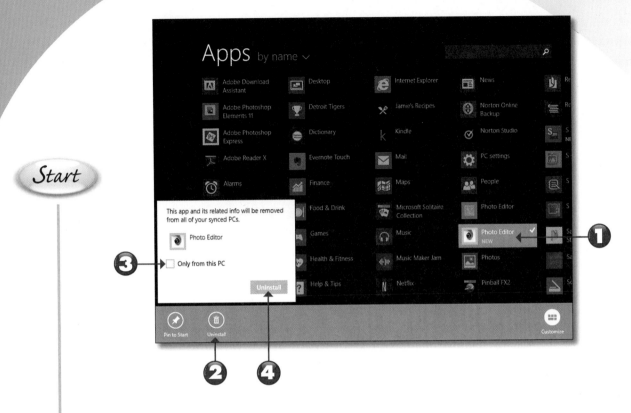

Right-click, or press and hold (touch screen) the app you want to uninstall.

Click **Uninstall**.

Click to uninstall the app from this PC only if you want to keep it installed on other Windows 8 devices you have.

Click **Uninstall**, and the app is removed.

End

TIP

Reinstalling Store Apps The Your Apps page in the Microsoft Store keeps track of apps you downloaded and uninstalled. You can revisit the list and reinstall an app at any time. ■

ADDING A PAYMENT METHOD TO YOUR ACCOUNT

You must specify a payment method to use along with your Microsoft account before you can buy apps through the Windows Store. Here's how.

Start

① From within the Store app, display the Charms bar and click **Settings**.

② Click **Your account**.

③ Click **Add payment method**.

Continued

NOTE

Security Step One option found on the Your Account page is a security option requiring you to enter your password any time an app is purchased. Leave this setting on if you share your computer with other users. If you are the only user, you can turn this setting off and bypass the account verification and sign-on procedure. ■

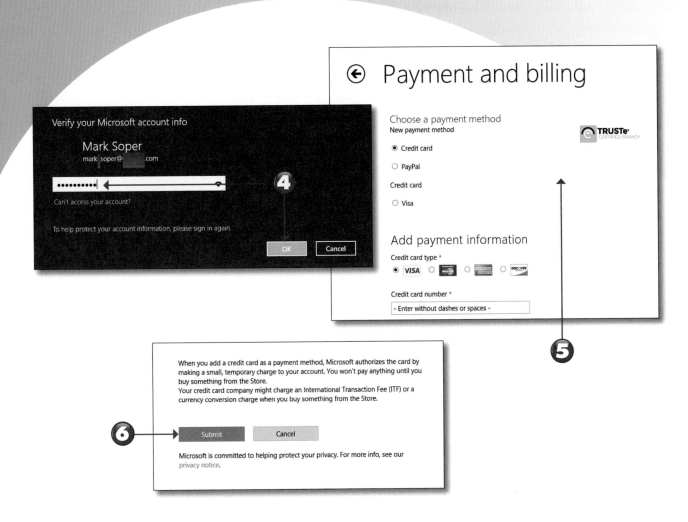

Verify your Microsoft account info

Mark Soper
mark_soper@_____.com

••••••••••

Can't access your account?

To help protect your account information, please sign in again.

OK   Cancel

Payment and billing

Choose a payment method
New payment method

● Credit card
○ PayPal

Credit card

○ Visa

Add payment information

Credit card type *
● VISA   ○   ○   ○ DISCOVER

Credit card number *
- Enter without dashes or spaces -

When you add a credit card as a payment method, Microsoft authorizes the card by making a small, temporary charge to your account. You won't pay anything until you buy something from the Store.
Your credit card company might charge an International Transaction Fee (ITF) or a currency conversion charge when you buy something from the Store.

Submit   Cancel

Microsoft is committed to helping protect your privacy. For more info, see our privacy notice.

4 Log in as prompted, and click **OK**.

5 Fill out your payment details, including billing address information and credit card information.

6 Click **Submit** at the bottom of the page.

End

TIP

Editing Your Account Anytime you need to make changes to your payment method, you can revisit the Your Account page and add other payment methods. ■

VIEWING YOUR APPS

You can see your installed apps any time you visit the Windows Store. Here's how.

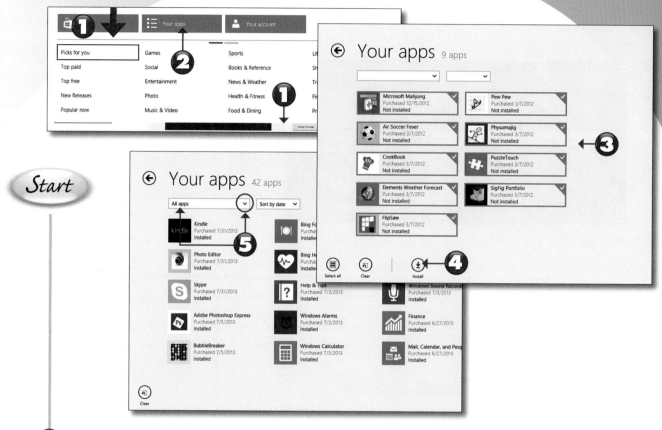

Start

1. Open the Store's App bar by pressing Windows key+Z, swiping from the top, or right-clicking an empty part of the page.

2. Click **Your apps**.

3. The default view shows apps not installed on this device.

4. Select the apps you want to install, and click to Install.

5. Select **All apps** to see all apps you have downloaded.

End

TIP

Purchased and Downloaded The Windows Store uses the term "purchased" for both apps you purchased and for free apps (including trial apps). ■

PLAYING GAMES

With Windows 8, Microsoft changed how PC gaming works. Whether you want to while away a break with a quick hand of solitaire, play some chess, or race against rivals, it's up to you to choose the games you want: Windows no longer includes built-in games. However, scores of games of all types are just a couple of clicks away in the Windows Store. In this chapter, you learn how to select your favorite free or paid games, install them, and play them.

Family games available
on Xbox Games

Managing your
gamer profile

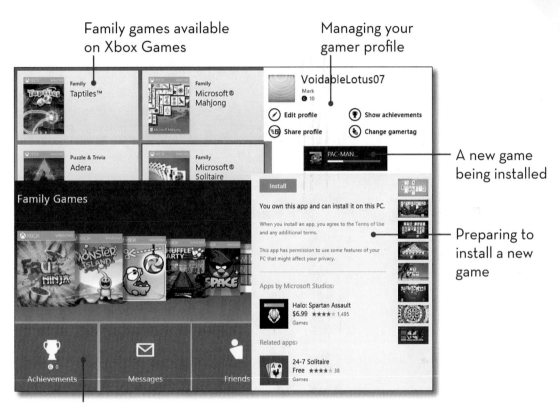

A new game
being installed

Preparing to
install a new
game

Accessing achievements,
messages, and friends on
Xbox Games

SHOPPING FOR GAMES

You can shop online to access the Xbox Games and Windows Store online offerings. You can find a wide variety of games for every kind of player of every age. Some games are available free, while others must be purchased (but many offer a free trial). You can use the Games app to peruse game offerings, as demonstrated in this task.

Start

1 Click the **Games** tile.

2 Scroll right to view games available for free or purchase.

3 Click a title to learn more.

Continued

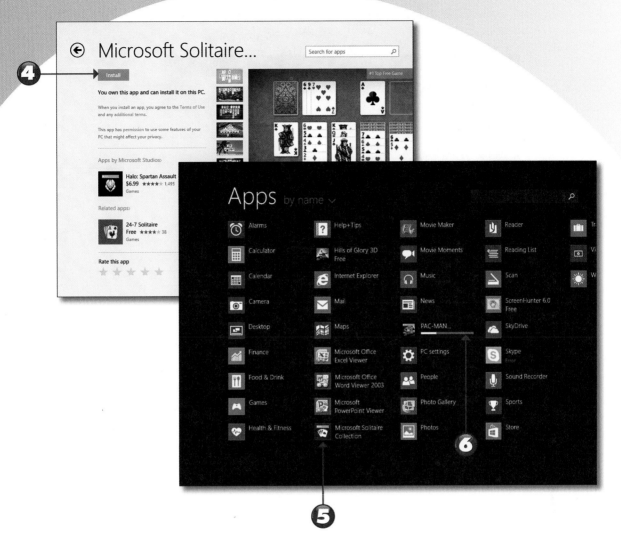

4 Click the **Install** button to download and install the app. (This is a Buy button if the game isn't free.)

5 The game creates an icon on the Apps screen.

6 Another game being downloaded and installed from the Xbox Games.

End

NOTE

Additional Preview Features Some games offer additional information, such as a game trailer. To access the download screen for such games, click the **Show More** link on their introductory screen. ∎

MANAGING YOUR ONLINE GAMING EXPERIENCE

You also can use the Games app to manage your Xbox avatar and view gaming friends online.

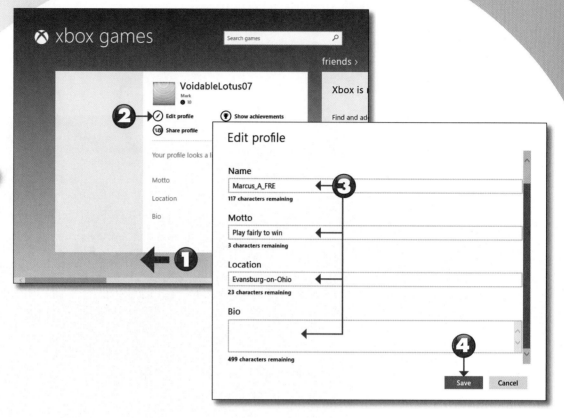

1 Scroll to the far left of the Games app to view your gamer information.

2 Click to edit your gaming profile.

3 Enter as much detail as you prefer to share.

4 Click **Save**.

Continued

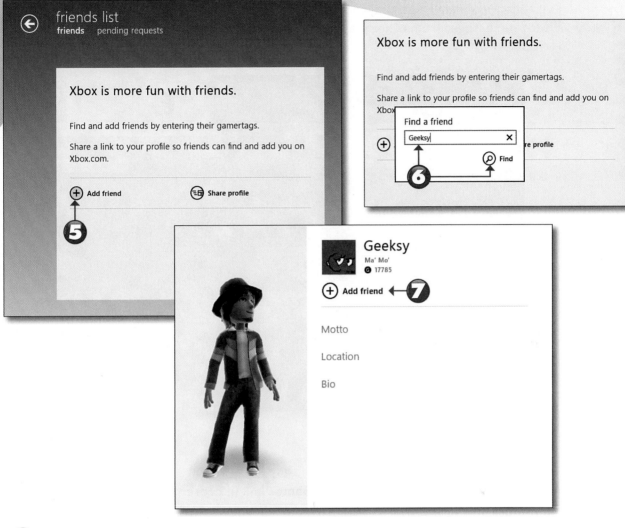

friends list
friends   pending requests

Xbox is more fun with friends.

Find and add friends by entering their gamertags.

Share a link to your profile so friends can find and add you on Xbox.com.

⊕ Add friend   ⊟ Share profile

5

Xbox is more fun with friends.

Find and add friends by entering their gamertags.

Share a link to your profile so friends can find and add you on Xbox

Find a friend

Geeksy   ✕

⊕   re profile

🔍 Find

6

Geeksy
Ma' Mo'
⬢ 17785
⊕ Add friend ← **7**

Motto

Location

Bio

5 Scroll to the right to the friends list and click to add a friend.

6 Enter a friend's gamertag and click **Find**.

7 Click **Add friend**.

End

REVISITING THE XBOX GAMES PAGE FOR YOUR GAME

Even after you install a game, you should revisit the Xbox Games page for the game to discover messages from other players, achievements, and friends who also play the game. Here's how.

Start

1 After starting the game, click the **Xbox Games** link (if present).

2 The Xbox Games page for the game opens in split screen.

3 Click **Achievements** to see in-game achievements.

4 Click **Messages** to see messages from other players.

5 Click **Friends** to return to the Friends page.

6 Drag the divider to the left to make Xbox Games run in full screen.

Continued

 Move the mouse into the upper-left corner, and click the game thumbnail to switch back to your game.

End

TIP

Game Help Most games offer some help with gameplay. Look for a Help link or button. With some games, you can also display the Charms bar and click **Settings** to find links to rules and game options. ∎

Chapter 16

RUNNING DESKTOP APPS

Windows 8 includes two interfaces—the Modern UI tile interface on the Start screen, and the familiar Windows desktop. Every program—whether it's designed for the new Windows 8 UI or for the Windows desktop—can be run from the Start screen. In this chapter, you learn how to find desktop programs, how to add your favorite apps to the Start screen, and how to add programs to the Windows 8 desktop. You also learn how to use some of the Windows desktop apps included in Windows 8.

Sorting apps
by category

Using Clipping Tool

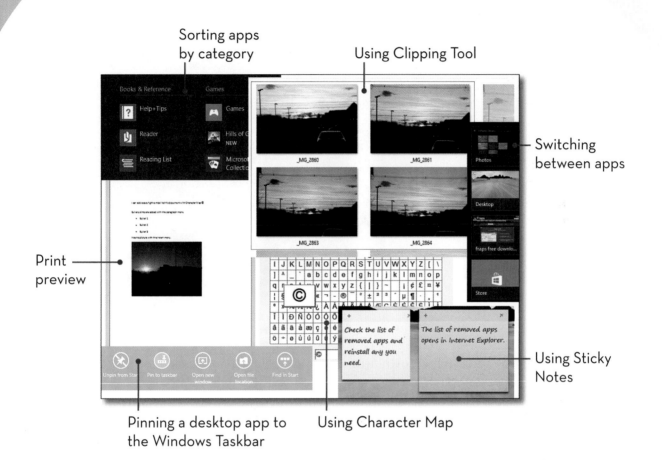

Switching
between apps

Print
preview

Using Sticky
Notes

Pinning a desktop app to
the Windows Taskbar

Using Character Map

OPENING THE APPS SCREEN

The Start screen lists only Windows 8 UI apps. However, another screen in Windows 8—called the Apps screen—displays both new UI and Windows desktop apps, including third-party apps that you have installed. Here's how to display the Apps screen.

1 Move the mouse until the down-arrow icon is displayed and click it, or flick up with a touchscreen.

2 Scroll to the right to see desktop apps included in Windows 8.

3 Desktop apps are listed in alphabetical order by vendor or category.

4 Click the up-arrow icon, or flick downward to return to the Start screen.

End

TIP
Can't Find an App? If you can't find the app you want to open, use the Search method described in the next section, "Searching for 'Hidden' Apps." ■

NOTE
Where Desktop Apps Appear Some desktop apps that you install yourself might be intermingled with Start screen apps on the Apps screen. ■

SEARCHING FOR "HIDDEN" APPS

Despite the name, the Apps screen might not always show you every app on your system, especially if you have downloaded and installed apps not found in the Windows Store. It's also easy to overlook a particular app. You can use the Search tool from the Start screen to find so-called "hidden" apps.

1 Move your mouse or pointer to the lower-right corner of the screen.

2 Click **Search**.

3 Enter the name of the app.

4 An app that matches your search.

5 Online matches.

NOTE

Search the Same Way Anywhere These steps work exactly the same regardless of whether you're on the Start screen, the Apps screen, or the desktop. ■

USING SORT OPTIONS TO FIND AN APP

The Apps screen normally displays apps listed by name; however, you can choose other sort options as well. Here's how.

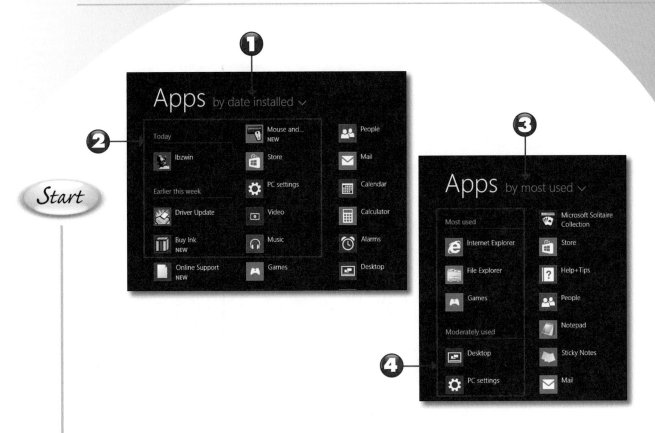

Start

① Open the Apps sort menu and select **by date installed**.

② Apps are listed from the most recently installed to the oldest.

③ Open the Apps sort menu again and select **by most used**.

④ Apps are listed from most used to never used.

Continued

NOTE

More About By Date Installed The categories used include Today, Earlier This week, and Older. ■

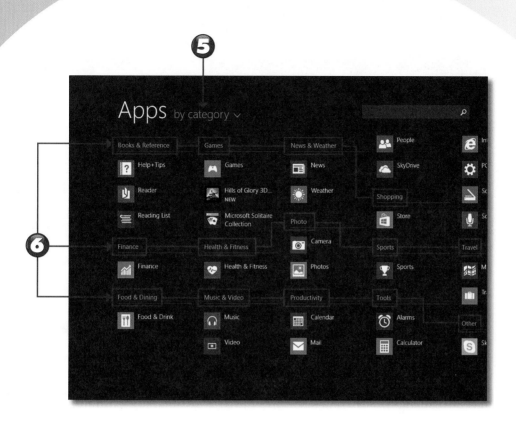

5 Open the Apps sort menu again and select **by category**.

6 Apps not otherwise listed in categories are placed in categories such as Games, Productivity, and so on.

End

NOTE

Searching for Apps As an alternative to changing sort settings to find an app, you can use the Search window at the top of the Apps screen. Note that this search window searches only the Apps screen. ■

STARTING A DESKTOP APP FROM THE APPS SCREEN

When you locate the app you want to start on the Apps screen, launching it is easy. And if it's a desktop app, the Windows desktop opens at the same time.

Start

1 Click the app's icon.

2 The app opens on the Windows 8 desktop.

3 To adjust the window size, click the lower-right corner and drag. Release the mouse button when you're finished.

Continued

Taskbar icon for Windows
Media Player

4 To use the entire screen for the app, click **Maximize**.

5 To hide an app from the screen but keep it running, click Minimize.

6 To go back to a window, click **Restore Down**.

7 To close the app, click **Close**.

End

TIP

Restoring a Minimized App All open apps have an icon
on the taskbar. To return a minimized app to the screen,
click its icon. ■

PINNING A DESKTOP APP TO THE START SCREEN

Finding an app in Apps takes a few steps, so why not pin your favorite desktop apps to the Start screen for easier access? Here's how to add it, and how to make its tile a different size.

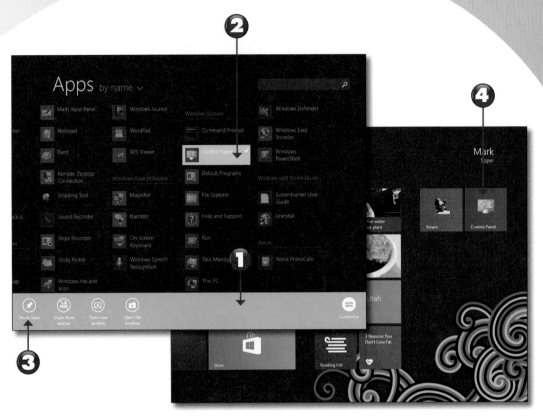

Start

 Open the App bar (right-click with your mouse, press Windows key+Z, or press and hold with a touchscreen).

2 Select the app you want to pin.

3 Click **Pin to Start**.

4 The app is now listed on the right end of the Start screen.

End

NOTE

Run as Administrator If you need to run an app as an administrator (also called "with elevated privileges"), select the Run as Administrator option from the bar shown in step 2. Some apps, usually older ones, don't work correctly if you don't choose this option. ■

ADDING AN APP TO THE DESKTOP TASKBAR

You can also add a desktop app to the Desktop taskbar.

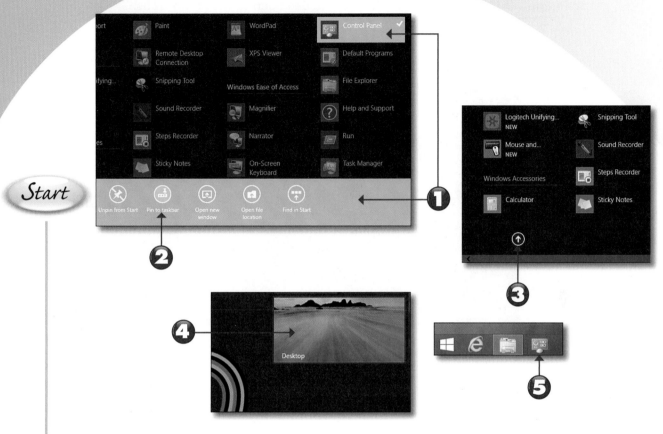

Start

1 Open the Apps bar and select the tile you want to pin to the Desktop taskbar.

2 Click **Pin to taskbar**.

3 Click the up arrow, or flick down to return to the Start screen.

4 Click the **Desktop** tile.

5 The app appears on the Desktop taskbar.

End

SWITCHING BETWEEN APPS

Windows 8 provides two ways to switch between apps: the new Switch List view hidden on the left edge of the Start screen, and the traditional Alt+Tab method of cycling through open apps. In this tutorial, you learn how to use each of these methods.

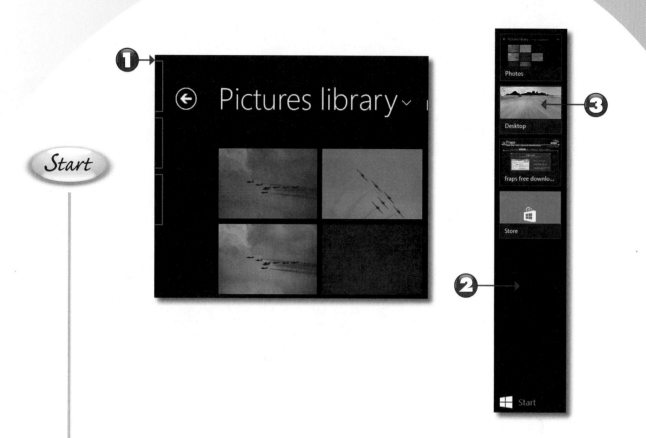

Start

1 After starting some apps, point to the upper-left corner of the screen until the right edge of program icons appear.

2 Slide the mouse pointer down the screen until all running programs are listed.

3 Click a program thumbnail.

Continued

NOTE

Desktop Equals App In Windows 8, the Windows desktop is considered an app. ∎

4 To scroll through a list of open apps, press **Alt+Tab**.

5 Repeat (hold down **Alt** and press **Tab**) until the program to which you want to switch is highlighted, and then release the keys.

6 The program you selected is now active.

End

TIP
Using Win+Tab You can also use Win+Tab in steps 4 and 5 to scroll through the list of running apps along the left edge of your display as shown in steps 2 through 3. To launch an app from Win+Tab, release the keys when the app you want to use is highlighted. ■

USING THE SNIPPING TOOL

If you want to turn what you see on your Windows desktop into a picture file, give Snipping Tool a try. Here's how to start it and put it to work.

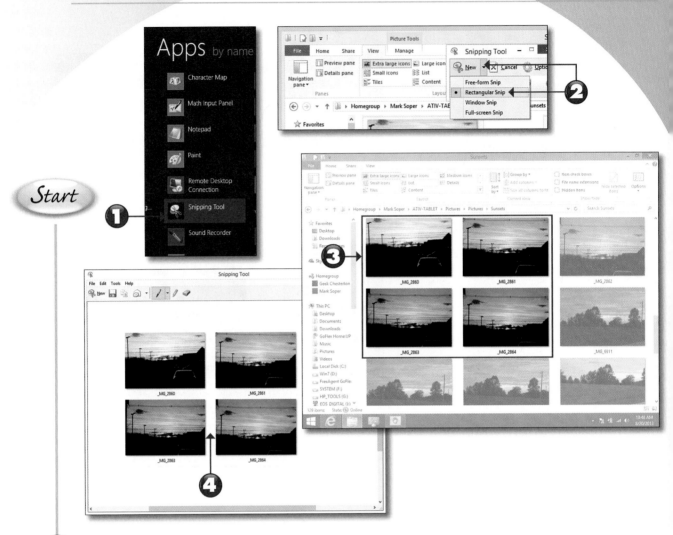

Start

1 From the Apps menu, select **Snipping Tool**.

2 Click **New** and select the type of snip you want.

3 Click and drag with your mouse, stylus, or finger until the information you want is highlighted.

4 Release the mouse button or remove your finger or stylus, and the snip is loaded into the Snipping Tool window.

Continued

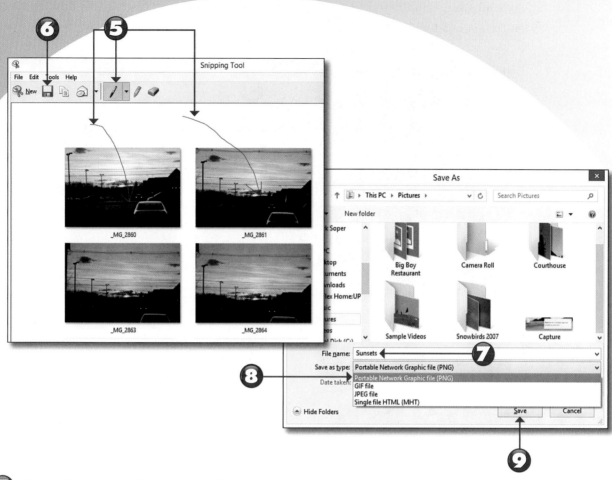

5 To mark up part of the snip, select the pen and draw on the snip.

6 Click **Save**.

7 Enter a new name for the picture file.

8 Select the type of file you want to save as. If you're not sure, go with JPEG.

9 Click **Save**.

Continued

NOTE

Ink Colors, Highlight, and Erase To change the ink color when drawing, open the Pen menu. To highlight part of the snip, use the Highlight tool. To erase ink or highlighting, use the Eraser tool. ■

USING STICKY NOTES

Sticky notes are valuable reminders on your desk, phone, and file cabinet, and the Windows version is just as useful for jogging your memory. Here's how it works.

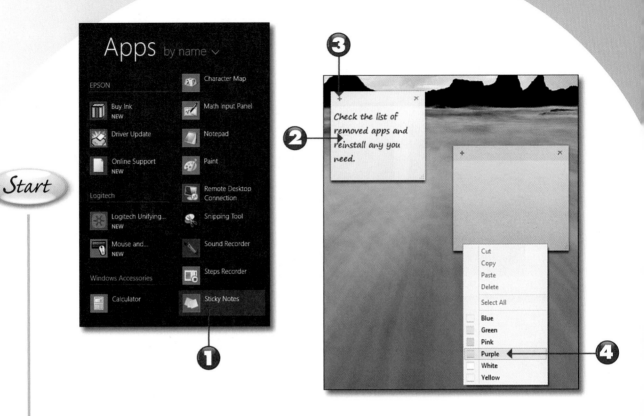

Start

1 From the Apps menu, select **Sticky Notes**.

2 Use your keyboard or on-screen keyboard to enter text for the note.

3 Click the plus sign to create a new note.

4 Right-click the note and select the color desired.

Continued

TIP

Viewing Your Notes When you close Sticky Notes, the notes vanish from the Windows desktop; however, the next time you run Sticky Notes, they are visible again. If you use Sticky Notes frequently, add it to the Taskbar. ∎

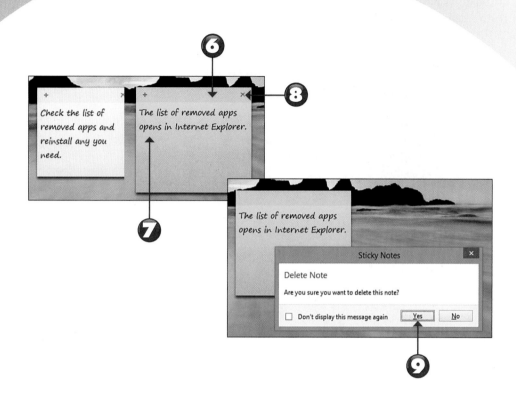

6 Click and drag the note to a new position.

7 Click the new note and enter the text you want.

8 Click the X to delete the note.

9 Click **Yes** to confirm.

End

NOTE

Making Your Notes More Exciting Click the lower-right corner of a note and drag it to resize the note and change its proportions. To add italic, bold, or underline to the note, highlight the text, and then press Ctrl+I (italic), Ctrl+B (bold), or Ctrl+U (underline). ■

USING CHARACTER MAP WITH WORDPAD

Windows includes the WordPad word processor so you can create or edit simple documents. If you need to add special characters to your WordPad documents or to other programs, you can use the Character Map utility included in Windows. Here's how to use them together.

Start

1 From the Apps menu, select **WordPad**.

2 Add text.

3 Open the Charms menu and click **Search**.

4 Type **character**.

5 Select **Character Map**.

Continued

TIP

Character Map via Start, Apps If you prefer, you can click the Start button in step 3, open the Apps menu, and start Character Map from the Apps menu.

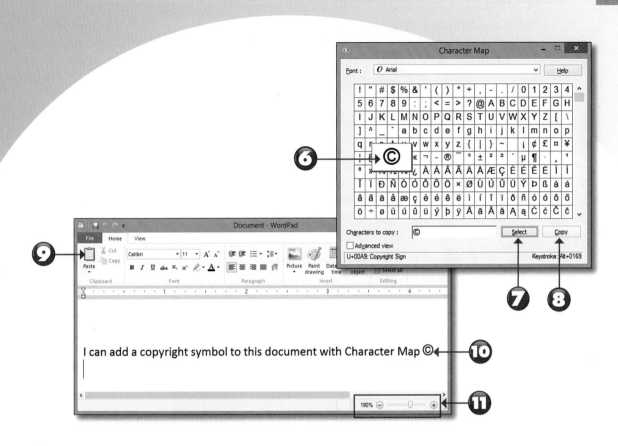

6 Click the Copyright character.

7 Click **Select**.

8 Click **Copy**.

9 Click **Paste.**

10 The character is added to the document.

11 Adjust the zoom control to see the character more easily.

End

It's always a good idea to preview your work before you print it. Windows 8 desktop applications typically include a Print Preview option that you can access from the Print menu or a Print dialog box. Here's how to preview your work in the WordPad application and start the print process.

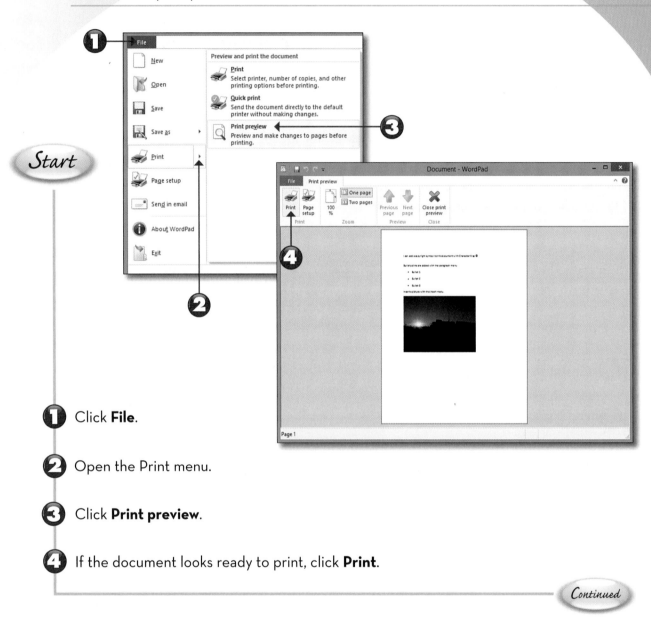

1 Click **File**.

2 Open the Print menu.

3 Click **Print preview**.

4 If the document looks ready to print, click **Print**.

Continued

TIP

Save, then Print Use the File, Save or Save As option to save a copy of your file before you print. ■

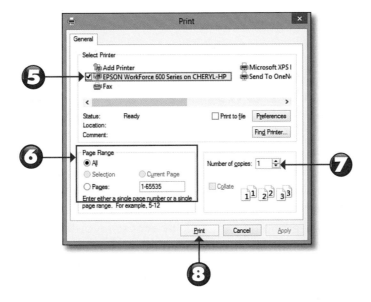

5 Select your printer.

6 Set a page range.

7 Set the number of copies.

8 Click **Print**.

End

NOTE

Adjusting Print Quality and Other Settings To change print quality, paper type, and other settings, click **Preferences**. ■

Chapter 17

MANAGING STORAGE WITH FILE EXPLORER

When it's time to work with your files in Windows 8, File Explorer (formerly called Windows Explorer) is the tool to use. In this chapter, you learn how to start File Explorer, copy and move files and folders, manage libraries, burn files to an optical disc, create a zip file archive, use Easy Access, select the best options for viewing and grouping files, quickly access favorite locations, and view file and folder properties.

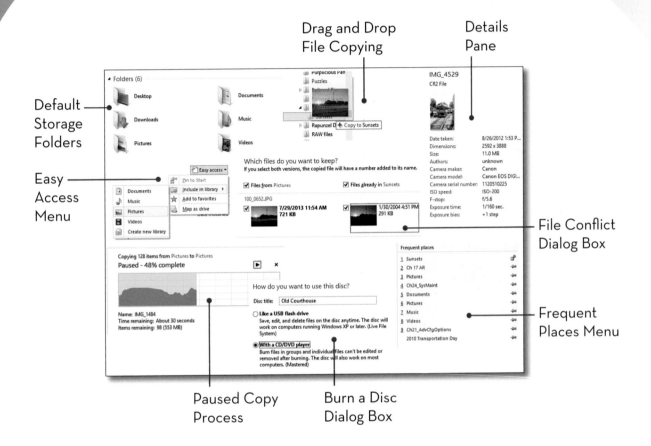

Drag and Drop
File Copying

Details
Pane

Default
Storage
Folders

Easy
Access
Menu

File Conflict
Dialog Box

Frequent
Places Menu

Paused Copy
Process

Burn a Disc
Dialog Box

STARTING FILE EXPLORER

File Explorer, a tool you can use to manage and organize your stored data, is just a couple of mouse clicks away from anywhere on your system. Here's how to access and start File Explorer from the Start screen.

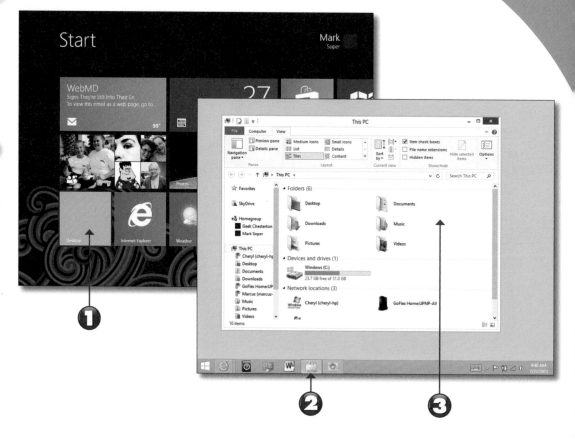

Start

1 Click the **Desktop** tile on the Start screen.

2 Click the **File Explorer** icon on the Desktop taskbar.

3 File Explorer displays the default folders used to store files on your computer.

End

NOTE

Computer, Meet This PC In Windows 8.1, File Explorer's default view is called This PC, instead of Computer as in Windows 8. ∎

INTRODUCTION TO FILE EXPLORER

File Explorer uses two panes in its default view. The left pane—called the Navigation pane—enables you to navigate to different locations, including the Windows desktop, default storage folders, Homegroup, and other computer and network locations. The right pane shows you details of the location selected in the left pane. Let's take a closer look at how File Explorer works.

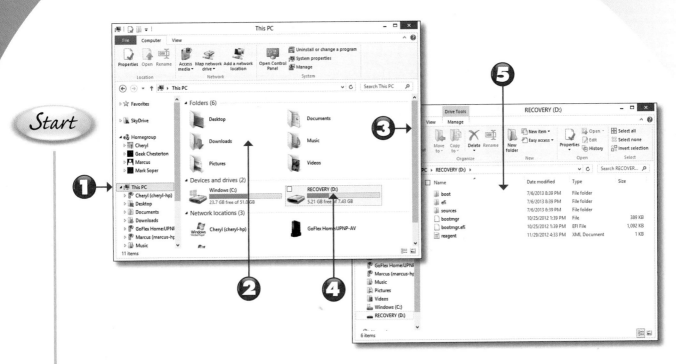

Start

1. The This PC node is expanded by default.

2. Contents of the selected node.

3. Scroll the right pane down to view all the contents of the selected node.

4. Double-click a drive letter to see its files and folders.

5. Contents of the selected drive.

End

NOTE

Nodes and Objects in File Explorer Each item listed in the Navigation pane is an object. Some objects contain other objects called *nodes*. Click the white pointer to expand it; click the black pointer to contract it. Click the back arrow on the top-left corner of the Navigation pane to return to the previous view. ■

USING THE HOME TAB

File Explorer uses a multi-tabbed ribbon menu that provides easier and faster access to new and improved features. Ribbon menus also change according to what tab you select. Here are some of the tasks you can perform using the Home tab.

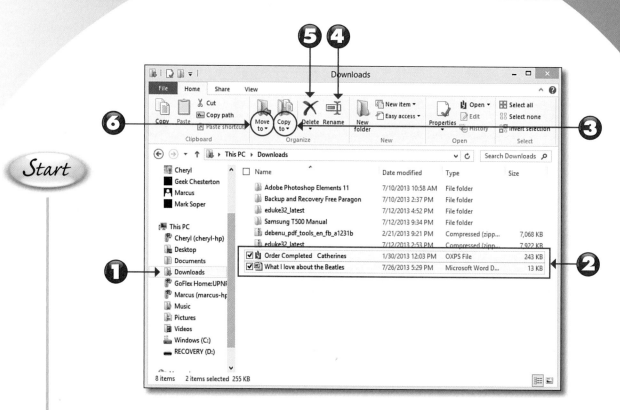

Start

1. Click a folder that contains files or other folders in the left pane.

2. Select one or more files or folders in the right pane.

3. Open to select a destination for copying selected items.

4. Click to rename selected items.

5. Click to delete selected items.

6. Open to select a destination for moving selected items.

Continued

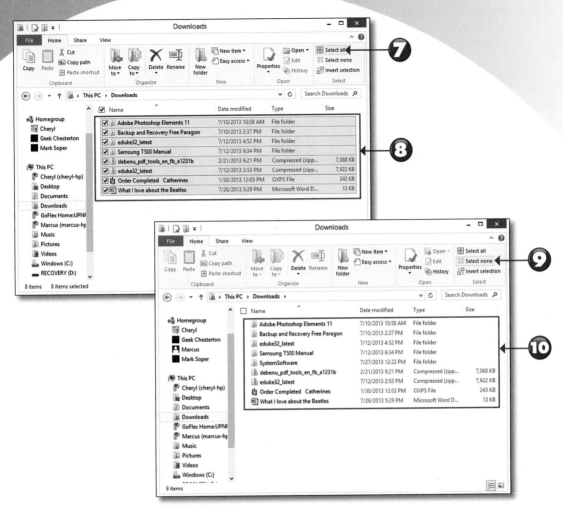

7 Click **Select All**.

8 This selects all files and folders in the window.

9 Click **Select None**.

10 Now there are no files or folders selected.

End

NOTE

Enabling Checkboxes To enable checkboxes, see "Selecting, Viewing, and Grouping Options" later in this chapter. ■

USING THE VIEW TAB

The File Explorer's View tab helps you select from a variety of settings so you can view drives, files, folders, and network locations in the most appropriate ways. Here are some examples of how to use the View tab.

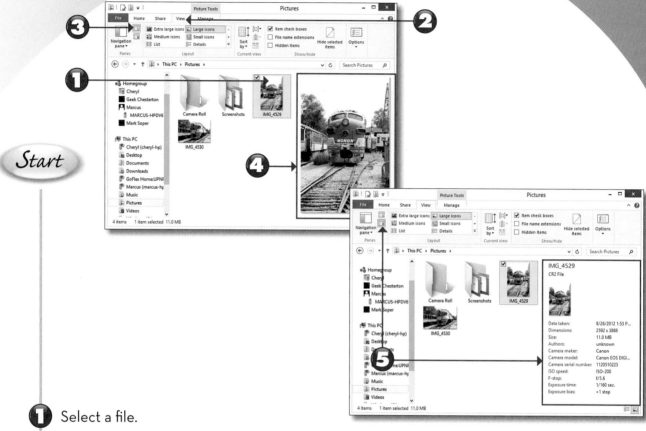

1 Select a file.

2 Click the **View** tab.

3 Click the **Preview pane** button.

4 Preview of selected file.

5 Click the **Details pane** button to see specific details about the selected file.

Continued

NOTE

Additional View Tab Options Use the Show/Hide section of the View tab to show or hide item check boxes (displayed in this example), show filename extensions, such as .docx or .jpg, and show hidden items. ■

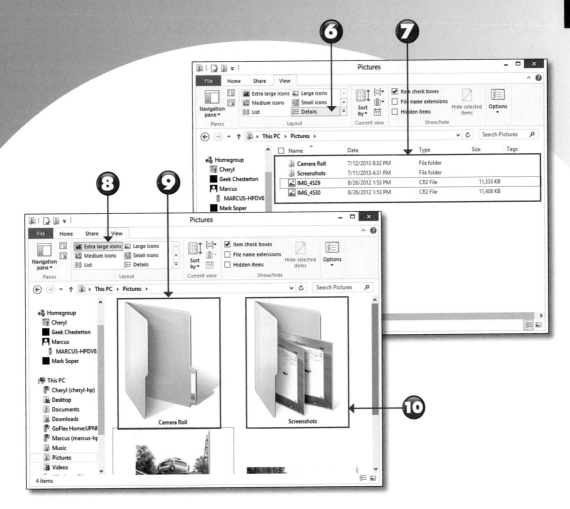

6 To see more data about files and folder in the main windows, select **Details** from the Layout menu.

7 You can now see extra details for files and folders.

8 Select **Extra Large Icons** from the Layout menu.

9 Empty folders appear empty in this view.

10 Folders containing files show a preview of their contents.

End

NOTE

Minimizing/Expanding the Ribbon To minimize the Ribbon menu to tab names only, click the up arrow next to the Help (question mark) button, near the upper-right corner of the File Explorer window. When the Ribbon menu is minimized, the arrow becomes a down arrow. Click it to expand the Ribbon. ■

COPYING AND MOVING FILES OR FOLDERS

If you need to have a file or folder in more than one place, use the Copy To command in File Explorer. The Move To command enables you to easily move files or folders to a different location. You can select from a listed destination or choose another location with either of these commands.

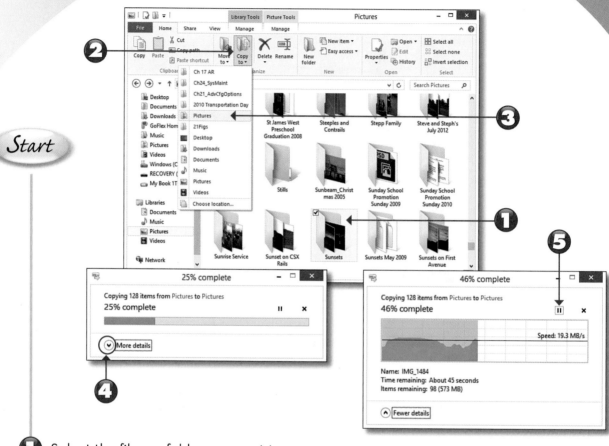

Start

1. Select the files or folder you want to copy.

2. Open the **Copy to** menu.

3. Click the destination.

4. To see more information about the process, click the down arrow next to **More details**.

5. To pause the process, click the **Pause** button. (Click the **Resume** button when you're ready to continue.)

Continued

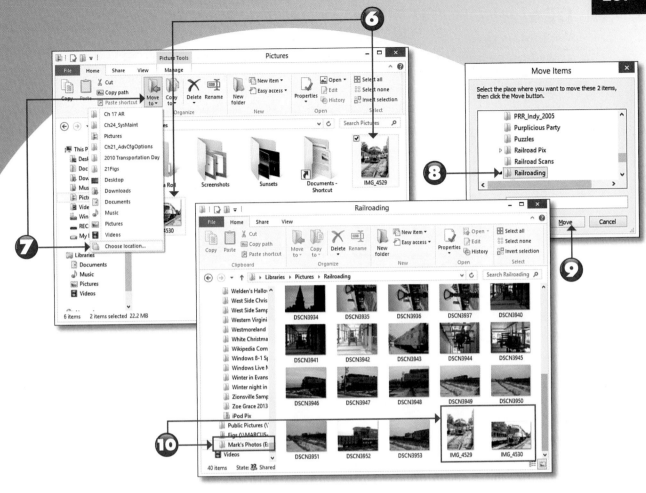

6 Select files or folders to move.

7 Open the **Move to** menu and select **Choose Location**.

8 Click a location.

9 Click **Move**.

10 Open the location you selected in step 8 to see the items you moved.

End

NOTE

Copy Speeds When you click the More Details button shown in step 4, you can see the average copy speed, number of items left to copy, and estimated time remaining. ◼

DEALING WITH FILENAME CONFLICTS

When you copy or move files with File Explorer, you might discover that some files being copied or moved have the same names as files already appearing in the destination location. Here's what to do.

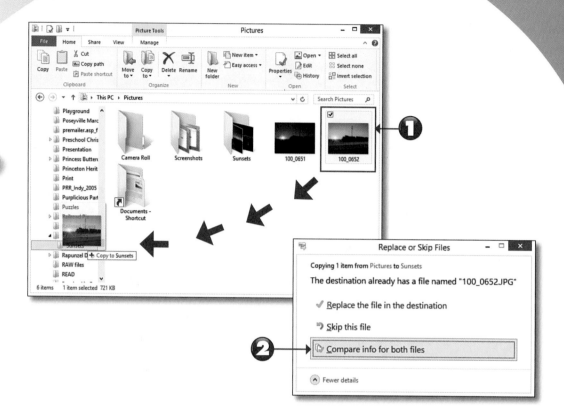

Start

1 Copy, move, or drag a file from one folder to another folder that contains a file with the same name.

2 Click **Compare info for both files**.

Continued

NOTE

Using Drag and Drop You can use drag and drop to easily copy or move files. To copy a selected file, hold down the Ctrl key while you drag the file using the primary mouse button. To use drag and drop to move a file, simply drag the file to the destination location and release the mouse button. This exercise uses drag and drop. ■

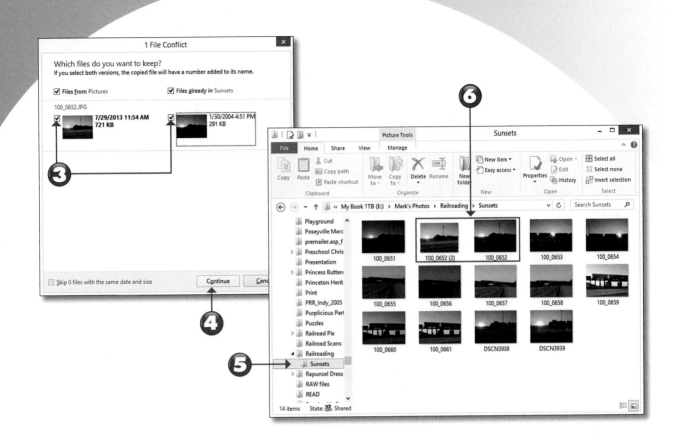

3 To keep both files, click both checkboxes.

4 Click **Continue**.

5 Open the destination folder.

6 The copied file with the name conflict is renamed to avoid replacing the original file.

End

NOTE

Dealing with Multiple Filename Conflicts If you copy or move more than one file or folder that has a name conflict, choose "Let me decide for each" in step 2. You are then prompted to choose what to do with each file. ■

BURNING DATA DISCS

You can use options on the Share tab in File Explorer to easily burn CDs or DVDs of your files. Here's how.

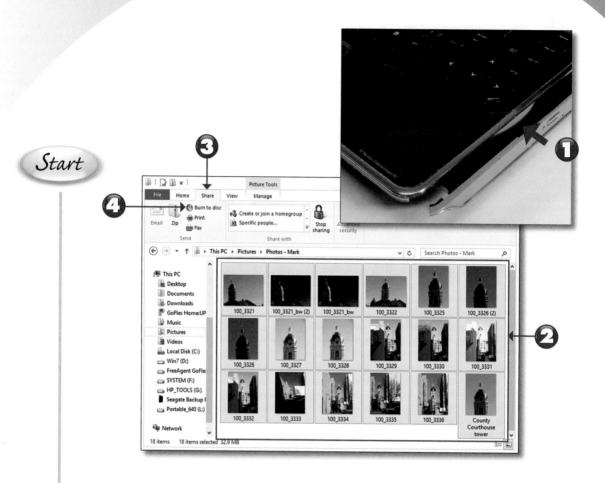

Start

1. Place a writeable disc in your optical drive and close the drive.

2. Select the files or folders you want to burn to an optical disc.

3. Click the **Share** tab.

4. Click **Burn to disc**.

Continued

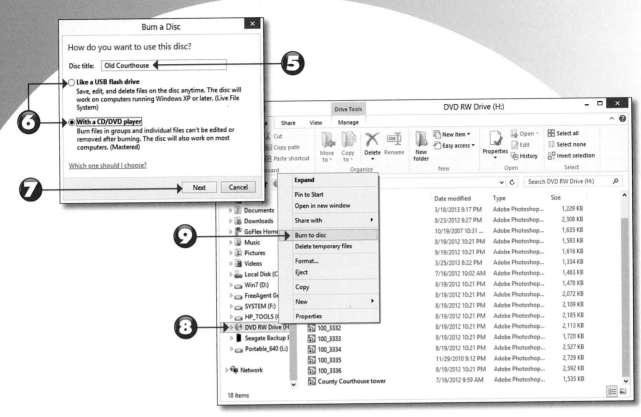

5 Enter a name for the disc.

6 Select the method to use.

7 Click **Next**.

8 Right-click or press and hold (touchscreen) the drive letter of your optical drive.

9 Select **Burn to disc**.

Continued

NOTE

Disk Formatting Options In step 6, choose the Like a USB flash drive option if you are using rewriteable (erasable) media such as a CD-RW, DVD-RW, or DVD+RW disc, and you are using the disc with Windows XP or later versions. Otherwise, choose the With a CD/DVD player option if you aren't sure what type of computer or device will be used with the media. ∎

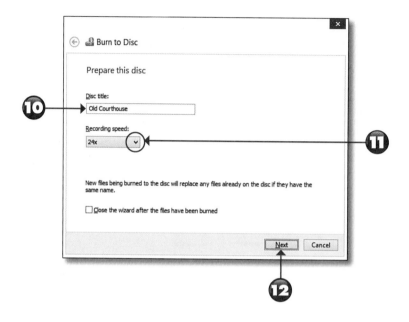

10 Confirm the disc name, or type a new name.

11 Confirm or change the recording speed.

12 Click **Next**.

Continued

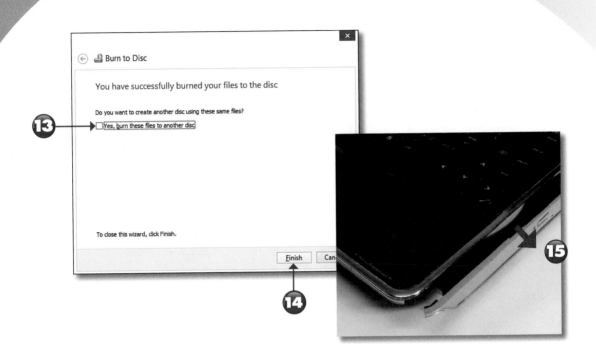

13 Click the empty checkbox if you want to burn another copy of the disc.

14 Click **Finish**.

15 Remove the disc from the drive.

End

TIP

Recording Speeds Choose a slower recording speed in step 11 if you have had problems using recorded media from your computer on another device, such as a CD player. ■

SELECTING, VIEWING, AND GROUPING OPTIONS

Windows 8 make selecting, viewing, and grouping files easier than in previous versions of Windows. This lesson uses some folders containing photos. However, the methods described here can also be used with music files, videos, or other types of documents.

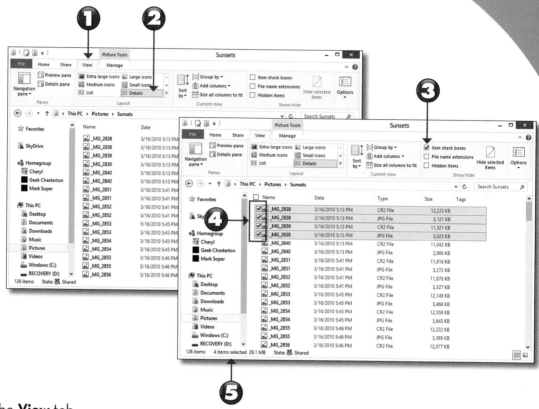

Start

1 Click the **View** tab.

2 Click **Details** to display filenames, date/time created, file types, file sizes, and tags.

3 Check the **Item check boxes** option box.

4 To select an item, hover the mouse over the item until the empty checkbox appears, and then click the checkbox.

5 You can see here the number of items selected and their total size.

Continued

TIP
Item Check Boxes and Your System Enable the Item check boxes option (step 3) to make it easier for you to select items to burn to disc, copy, move, delete, and so on. If you use a tablet device or touchscreen PC, this option might already be enabled. ∎

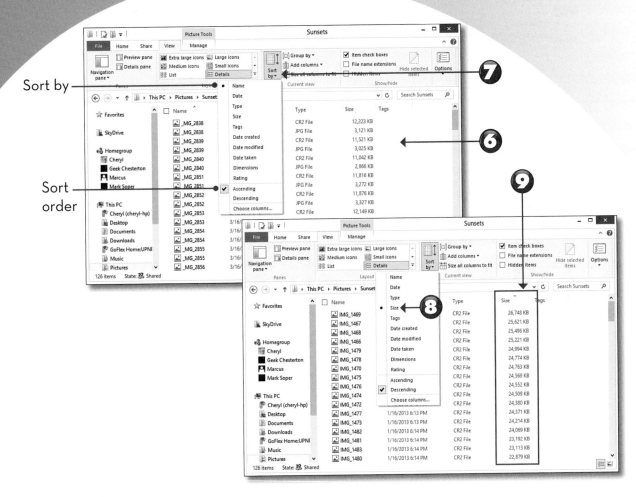

Sort by

Sort order

6 Click an empty area of the File Explorer window to deselect files.

7 Open **Sort by** to see the current sort option (dot) and direction (check mark).

8 Select **Size** as the **Sort by** setting.

9 Files are sorted smallest to largest.

Continued

TIP

Quick Toggling Between Views The icons in the lower-right corner of the File Explorer window enable instant switching to Details view (click left icon) or Large Icons view (click right icon). ■

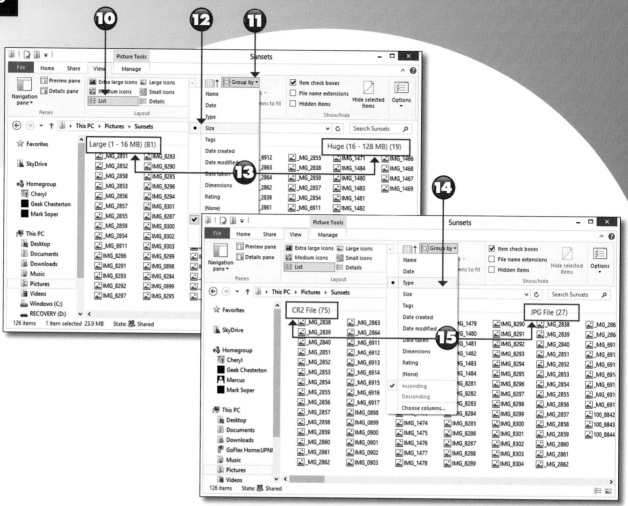

10 Select **List** as the view.

11 Open the **Group by** menu.

12 Select the **Size** grouping option.

13 Groups of files arranged by size.

14 Select the **Type** grouping option.

15 Groups of files arranged by type.

Continued

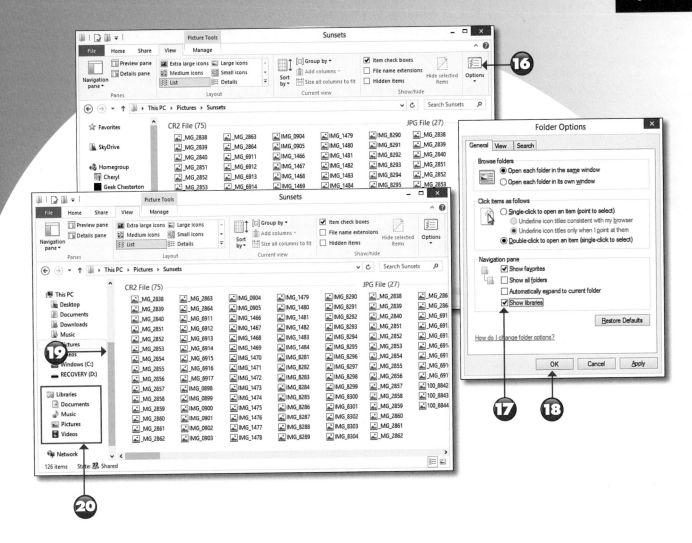

16 Click the **Options** icon.

17 Click the empty **Show libraries** checkbox. A library enables you to view multiple folders as a single logical folder.

18 Click **OK**.

19 Scroll down the Navigation pane.

20 Libraries.

End

CREATING COMPRESSED FILES WITH THE SHARE TAB

Compressed files, often called Zip files, are handy because you can store multiple files and folders into a single file that's usually smaller than the combined size of the original files. The resulting file is also easier to email. Windows 8 make this process easier than ever before by adding Zip file creation to the Share tab in File Explorer.

Start

1 Click the **Share** tab.

2 Select files or folders you want to include in a Zip file.

3 Click **Zip**.

4 Right-click (mouse), or press and hold (touchscreen) the Zip file icon.

5 Select **Rename**, and enter a new name for the Zip file.

End

NOTE

Easy File Selection with Grouped Files When files are grouped, you can select all the files in a group by clicking the group name, such as JPG File (as in step 2). ■

USING FREQUENT PLACES

The Frequent Places feature on the File tab makes it easy to return to locations you like to use: Open the tab and click a location to open it. You can even pin places to the Frequent places menu on the right side of the File tab.

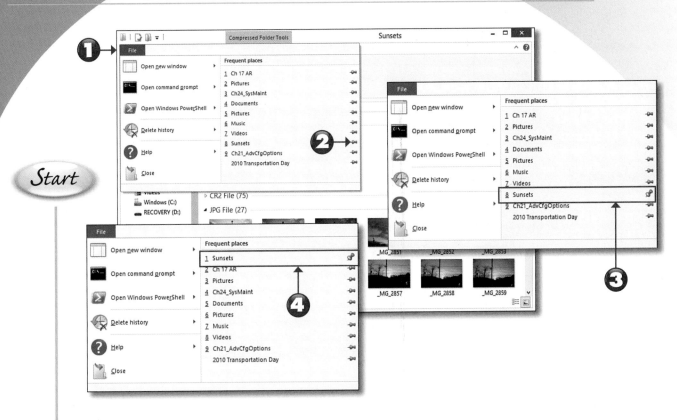

1 Click the **File** tab.

2 Click the pin icon for a location you want to keep on the list.

3 The pinned location stays on the list until unpinned.

4 The next time you open the File tab, pinned locations are at the top of the list.

End

NOTE

Unpinning a Location If a pinned location no longer needs to stay on the list, open the File tab and click the pin. Unpinned locations are removed from the list of Frequent Places when other locations are accessed more recently.

MANAGING DRIVES

The Manage Drives tab appears when you select a drive in File Explorer. In this exercise, you learn how to format (overwrite and remove all files from) a USB flash drive you want to empty and reuse, and discover other features of this tab.

① Click the drive's icon in File Explorer. Make sure any files on the drive aren't needed before you continue.

② Click the **Drive Tools** tab.

③ Click **Format**.

④ Change or add a volume label (optional).

⑤ Click **Start**.

Continued

NOTE

Drive Tools for Removable Media Use the Media section of the Drive Tools tab to open the AutoPlay menu, finish burning an optical disc, erase a rewriteable optical disc, or eject a disc. ■

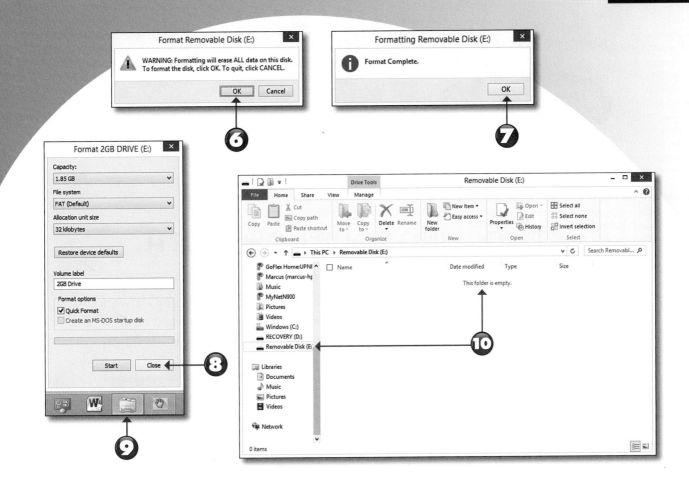

6 Click **OK** to continue.

7 Click **OK** when finished.

8 Click **Close**.

9 Open File Explorer.

10 Click or tab the drive's icon to see that it is now empty.

End

NOTE

Other Drive Tools Use Optimize (also known as Defragment) to put all the files on a drive next to each other to improve file access speed. Use Cleanup to remove unneeded files from a drive (typically needed only with the C: drive). ■

Chapter 18

NETWORKING YOUR HOME WITH HOMEGROUP

Windows 8 provides two interfaces for connecting to and managing network connections with the Internet and with other users on your home or small-business network. These interfaces are the Start screen and its PC settings screen for basic network settings using HomeGroup, and the desktop's Control Panel for fine-tuning HomeGroup networking. This chapter shows you how to work with the HomeGroup settings in each of these interfaces.

Joining a
HomeGroup

Setting
sharing for a
HomeGroup
network

Changing
sharing settings
for a folder

Connecting
to a secured
wireless
network

Playing media from
a shared folder

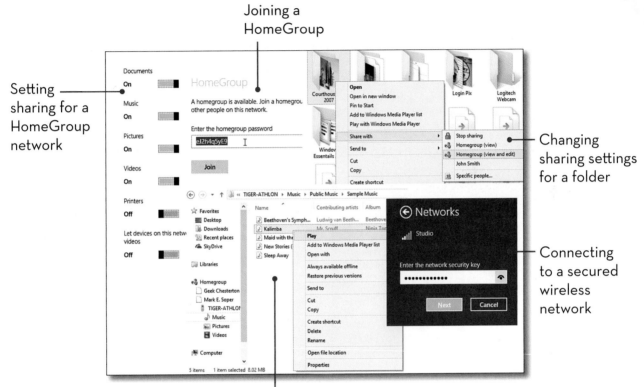

CONNECTING TO AN UNSECURED WIRELESS NETWORK

Your home and office networks should be secure networks (in other words, you should use a password with your home Wi-Fi network); however, wireless networks found in locations such as coffee shops, restaurants, and hotels are often unsecured. Here's how to connect to these networks.

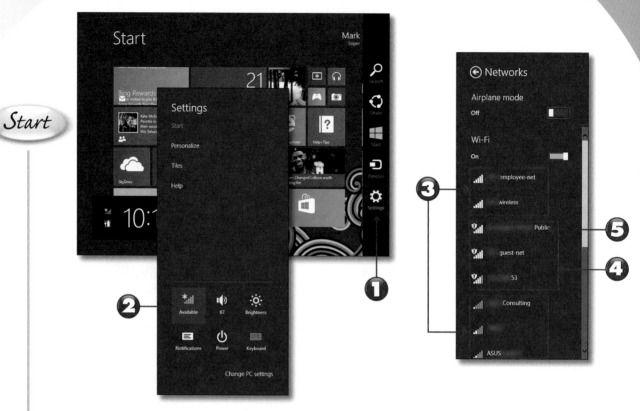

Start

1 Open the Charms menu and click **Settings**.

2 Click the wireless icon.

3 These are secured networks (the user must provide the encryption key).

4 These are unsecured networks.

5 Click the unsecured network's name (SSID) to connect to it.

Continued

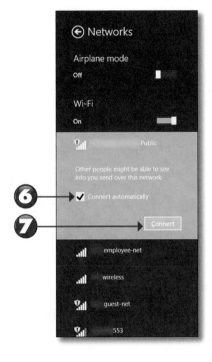

6 If you plan to connect to the network again, click the empty **Connect automatically** box.

7 Click **Connect**.

8 Your network connection is listed first and is marked Connected.

End

NOTE

The Windows Security Shield and Wireless Networks Unsecured networks—networks that do not use an encryption key—are marked with the Windows security shield to remind you that they are not secured by an encryption key. However, some of these networks, typically business networks, use a login for security rather than an encryption key. ■

NOTE

Starting the Connection Process from the Windows Desktop You can also start this process from the Windows desktop by clicking the wireless network icon in the notification area of the taskbar. ■

CONNECTING TO A SECURED PRIVATE NETWORK

A secured network uses a network security key, also known as an encryption key. The first time you connect to a secured network, you must enter the network security key. Windows 8 can remember your network security key and the rest of your connection details for you. Here's how this process works.

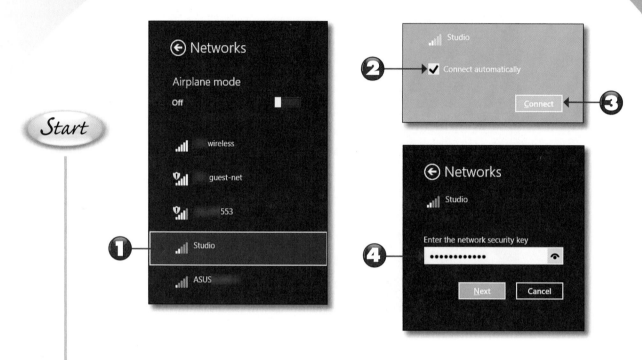

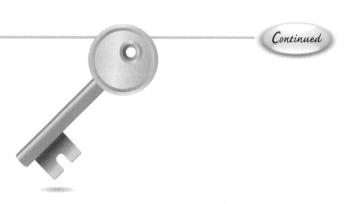

1 From the Networks screen (refer to the previous task), click a secure network.

2 To connect automatically from now on, click the empty checkbox.

3 Click **Connect**.

4 Enter the network security key.

Continued

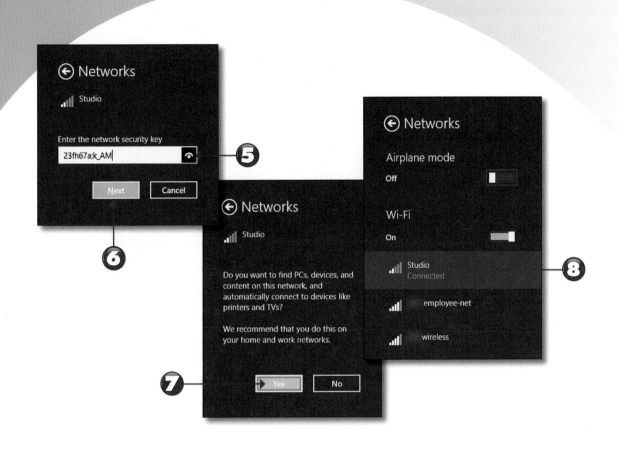

5 To see the hidden characters, click the eye icon.

6 Click **Next**.

7 Click **Yes** to turn on sharing and connect to devices.

8 Your network connection is listed first.

End

CONNECTING TO A HIDDEN NETWORK

Most wireless networks broadcast their names (SSIDs). However, some are set up so that you must know the name of the network if you want to connect to it. This tutorial shows you how to connect to a hidden wireless network.

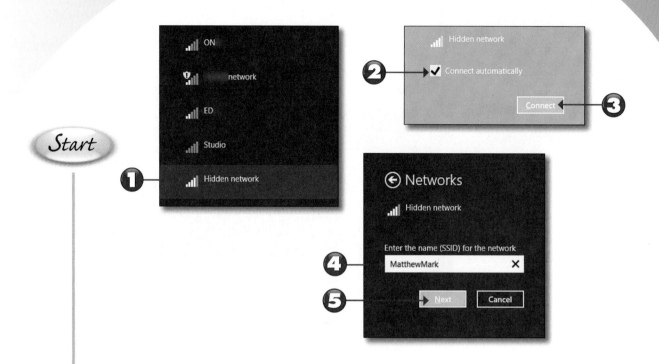

1 From the Networks screen (refer to "Connecting to an Unsecured Wireless Network"), click **Hidden network**.

2 Click the empty checkbox to connect automatically the next time.

3 Click **Connect**.

4 Type the name of the network (SSID).

5 Click **Next**.

NOTE

Finishing Your Connection To complete the process, for secured networks, refer to steps 4 through 8 in "Connecting to a Secured Private Network," p. 300, earlier in this chapter. ■

DISCONNECTING AND DISABLING WIRELESS ACCESS

When it's time to bid farewell to a wireless connection (also known as a Wi-Fi connection) or turn off wireless access altogether, Windows 8.1 makes it even easier than with Windows 8. Here's how.

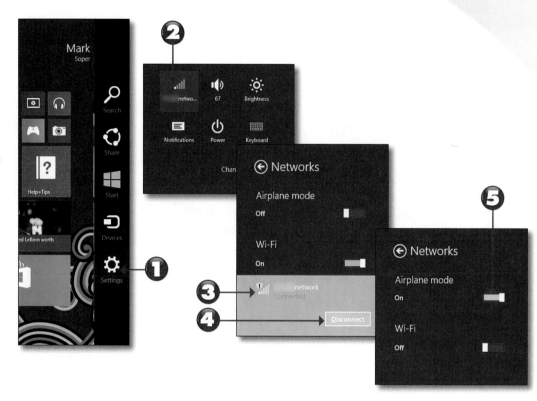

1. Open the Charms menu and click **Settings**.

2. Click the wireless icon.

3. Click the active connection.

4. Click **Disconnect**.

5. Turn on **Airplane Mode** to turn off all Wi-Fi connections.

CREATING A HOMEGROUP FROM THE START SCREEN

Windows 8 supports an easy-to-use, yet secure, type of home and small-business networking feature called a HomeGroup. HomeGroup networking enables home network users to share libraries and printers—you can specify which libraries to share and whether to share printers and devices on a particular system. All users of a HomeGroup use the same password but don't need to worry about specifying particular folders to share. You can create a new HomeGroup from the Start screen.

Start

1 Open the Charms menu.

2 Select **Settings**.

3 Click **Change PC settings**.

4 Click **Network**.

Continued

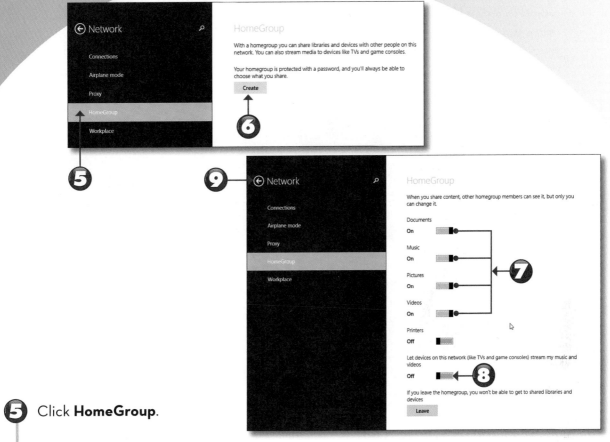

5 Click **HomeGroup**.

6 Click **Create**.

7 Move sliders to the right to share content in libraries and printers.

8 Move the Media devices slider to the right to enable access to streaming media for playback.

9 Click the back arrow when you are finished.

End

NOTE

Your HomeGroup, Your Choice In steps 7 and 8, you can select any or all of the items listed to share. Sharing Documents, Music, Pictures, and Videos with HomeGroup members provides them with read-only access to all the items in each folder. To learn more about folders, see Chapter 17, "Managing Storage with File Explorer." ■

VIEWING THE PASSWORD FOR YOUR HOMEGROUP

A HomeGroup needs at least two computers to share data and devices. You can add any Windows 8 computer—or a Windows 7 computer with its network location set as Home—to your HomeGroup. They'll need the HomeGroup password, which you can display directly from the HomeGroup menu in PC settings.

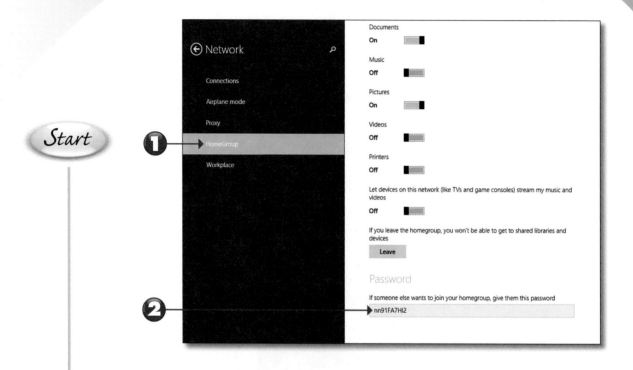

1 From the Network screen, click **HomeGroup**.

2 Scroll down to **Password**. Use the password on other computers you want to add to the HomeGroup.

NOTE

How to Print the HomeGroup Password If you want to print the HomeGroup password and instructions for joining a HomeGroup, see "Setting Up a HomeGroup from Network and Internet." ∎

JOINING A HOMEGROUP FROM THE START SCREEN

Microsoft introduced HomeGroups in Windows 7, so if you have one or more Windows 7 or Windows 8 computers in your home or small office, you might already have a HomeGroup. Here's how to add your Windows 8 computer to an existing HomeGroup from the PC settings screen.

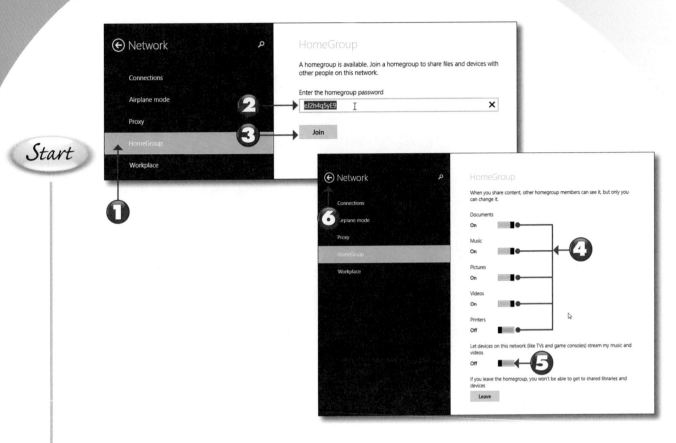

Start

1 From the Network screen, click **HomeGroup**.

2 Enter the HomeGroup password.

3 Click **Join**.

4 Move sliders to the right to share content in folders and printers.

5 Move the Media devices slider to the right to enable access to streaming media for playback.

6 Click the back arrow when you are finished.

End

OPENING THE NETWORK AND INTERNET WINDOW IN CONTROL PANEL

If you want more control over HomeGroup and streaming media settings, use the Network and Internet window in Control Panel. Here's how to open it from the Start screen.

Start

1 Open the Apps screen.

2 Click **Control Panel**.

Continued

TIP

Instant Search from the Start Screen You can also type control panel from the Start screen to quickly locate Control Panel in step 1. ■

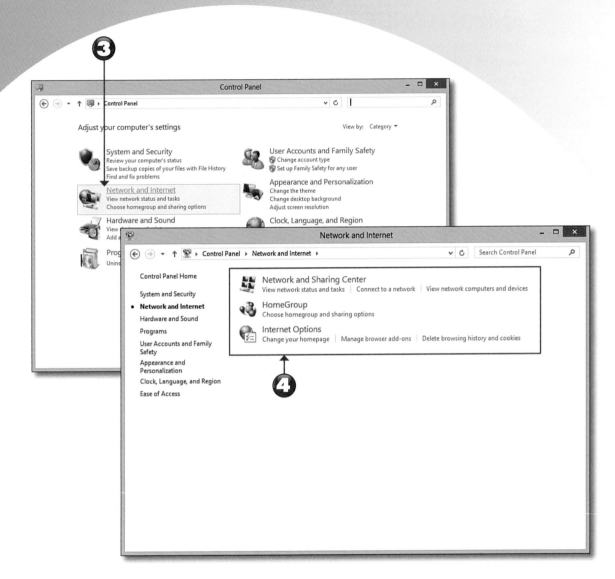

③ Click **Network and Internet**.

④ This page gives you access to the settings available in Network and Internet.

End

> **NOTE**
>
> **How to Use the Network and Internet Window** Use the Network and Sharing Center to set up and view connections. Use HomeGroup to set up or connect to a HomeGroup, an easy-to-manage, secure network of Windows 7 and/or Windows 8 computers. Use Internet Options to configure the Internet Explorer browser. ■

SETTING UP A HOMEGROUP FROM NETWORK AND INTERNET

If you're more comfortable setting up and managing a HomeGroup from the Windows Control Panel, Windows 8 provides the same HomeGroup options that Windows 7 provides. The HomeGroup setting in Control Panel's Network and Internet window also provides more options than the Windows 8 Start screen. Here's how to set up a HomeGroup from the Windows desktop.

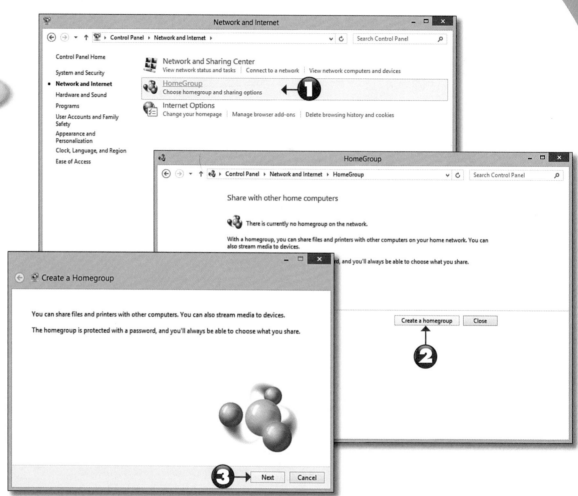

1 From the Network and Internet window, click **HomeGroup**.

2 Click **Create a homegroup**.

3 Click **Next**.

Continued

 4 Select the items you want to share.

5 Click **Next**.

6 Write down the HomeGroup password.

7 Click to print the password and instructions for other computers.

8 Click **Finish**.

End

NOTE

HomeGroups Are Lonely with Just One Member Before a HomeGroup can be used to share information and printers, other users must join it, or you must join an existing HomeGroup. ■

JOINING A HOMEGROUP FROM NETWORK AND INTERNET

If your network already has a HomeGroup, you should connect to it rather than create a new one. If you created the HomeGroup, other users on your network must connect to it. This tutorial covers the steps for connecting a Windows 8 computer to a HomeGroup, but the steps are similar for Windows 7 computers.

 From the Network and Internet window, click **HomeGroup**.

2 Click **Join now**.

3 Click **Next**.

Continued

NOTE

Rules for Joining a HomeGroup A computer running Windows 7 can join a HomeGroup only if its network location is set as Home. To change the network location, use the Network and Sharing Center. A computer running Windows 8 can join a HomeGroup only if you select the Yes, Turn on Sharing and Connect to Devices option when you connect to the network. ■

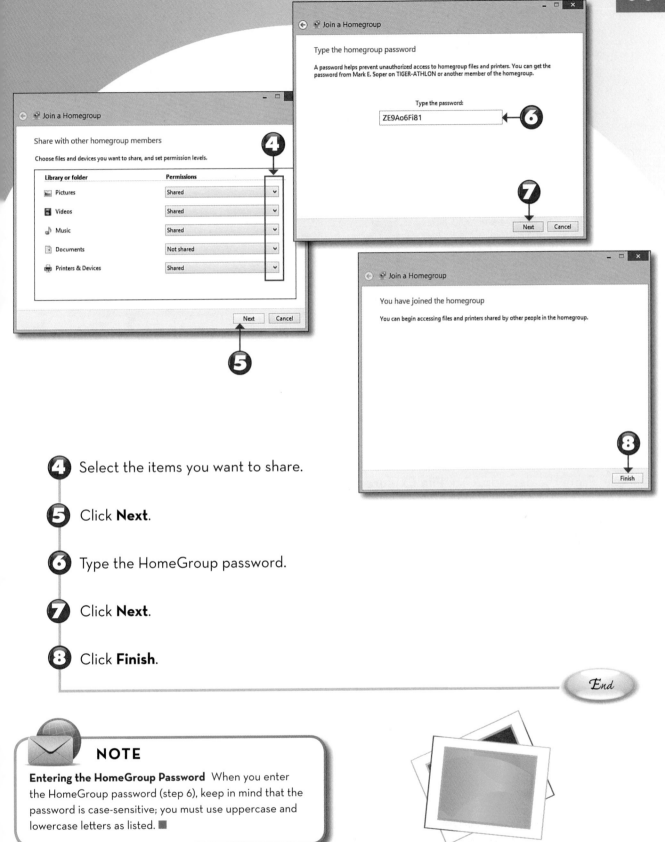

4 Select the items you want to share.

5 Click **Next**.

6 Type the HomeGroup password.

7 Click **Next**.

8 Click **Finish**.

End

NOTE

Entering the HomeGroup Password When you enter the HomeGroup password (step 6), keep in mind that the password is case-sensitive; you must use uppercase and lowercase letters as listed. ■

OPENING HOMEGROUP FILES

As soon as two or more computers with shared folders are part of your HomeGroup, you can access folders and files on the HomeGroup as easily as you access your own files from the Windows desktop. Here's how to open and enjoy those files from the Windows desktop. You can also open these files with the appropriate app on the Start screen.

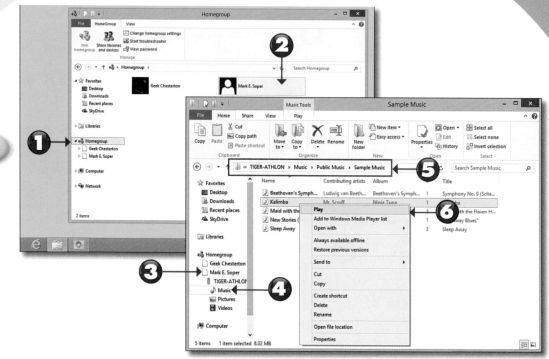

Start

① From the desktop, click **File Explorer**.

② Click **Homegroup**.

③ Click a user's name.

④ Click a category.

⑤ Navigate to the folder that includes the file you want to use.

⑥ Right-click an item and select what you want to do with it.

End

TIP

Double-Clicking to Open an Item You can also double-click an item to open it in its native application. ■

CUSTOMIZED SHARING FOR FOLDERS YOU CHOOSE

The normal setting for a HomeGroup permits read-only access to files in shared libraries. However, if you need to share files that might need to be changed by other HomeGroup members, you must specify this on a folder-by-folder basis. Here's how it works.

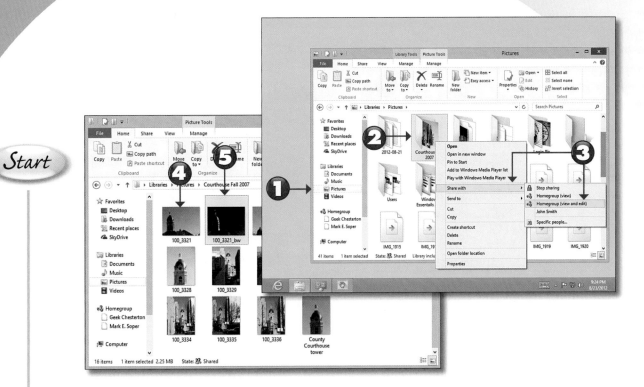

1 Open File Explorer.

2 Locate a folder or library you want other users to be able to edit.

3 Right-click the folder or library and point to **Share with** and select **Homegroup (view and edit)**.

4 The original photo.

5 The version of the photo edited by another user on the HomeGroup.

NOTE

Sharing with Specific Users on the Network If you want to share with a specific user on the network, you can select the name and click Add in step 4. ■

VIEWING A FOLDER'S SHARING SETTINGS

If you customize sharing for individual folders, it might sometimes be difficult to remember exactly which folders are shared in a particular way. Use the folder's Properties dialog box to see how a folder is shared.

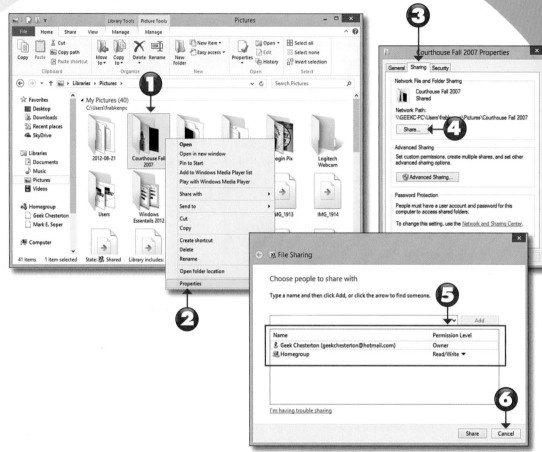

Right-click a folder in File Explorer.

Click **Properties**.

Click the **Sharing** tab.

Click **Share**.

Note the sharing settings.

Click **Cancel**.

LEAVING A HOMEGROUP FROM THE NETWORK SCREEN

A HomeGroup is an easy way to share files and devices, but if you need to leave a HomeGroup, you can do so from either the Network screen or from the HomeGroup window in Control Panel. This lesson covers leaving a HomeGroup from the Network screen.

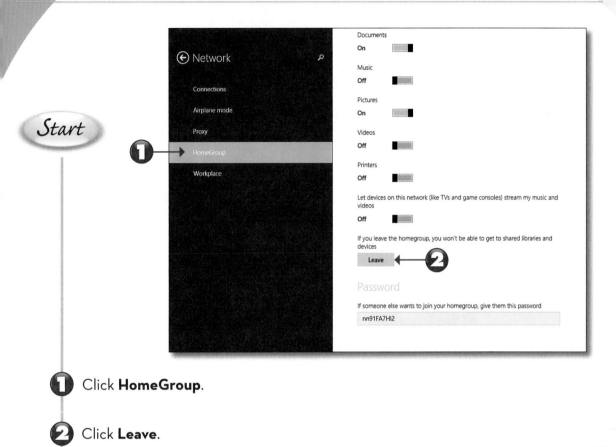

Start

1 Click **HomeGroup**.

2 Click **Leave**.

End

NOTE

Persistent Passwords If you decide to rejoin the HomeGroup later, Windows 8 remembers the password and supplies it for you. However, if the HomeGroup password has been changed, you will need to enter the new password. ■

Chapter 19

WORKING WITH PHOTOS AND MUSIC FROM YOUR DESKTOP

You can access photos and music from your desktop with two Windows desktop apps: Windows Photo Viewer and Windows Media Player. Here's how to use them to help you enjoy your media.

Starting media sync
with a portable
media player

Importing photos
from a digital camera

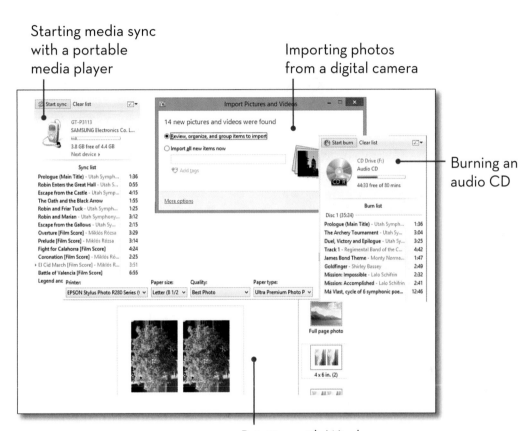

Burning an
audio CD

Printing with Windows
Photo Viewer

ADDING PICTURES TO YOUR PICTURES LIBRARY

If you upgraded to Windows 8, your Pictures library includes the contents of the Pictures or My Pictures folders from your previous version of Windows. However, if you have a preinstalled version of Windows 8 on a new computer, your Pictures library doesn't include any of your photos. Here's how to copy photos from another location, such as an external hard disk or optical disc, into your Pictures library.

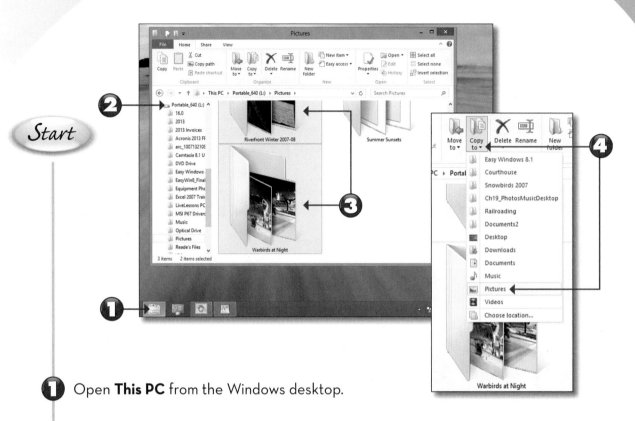

Warbirds at Night

1 Open **This PC** from the Windows desktop.

2 Open a location that contains pictures.

3 Select one or more folders that contain pictures.

4 Open the **Copy To** menu and select **Pictures**.

Continued

TIP

Folders or Photos? If you have folders that contain pictures, I recommend selecting the folders for copying (which will also select the pictures they contain) rather than opening the folders and selecting individual pictures. If you follow these instructions but select individual pictures, they'll all be copied into the pictures folder and you'll be faced with the task of sorting through them. ∎

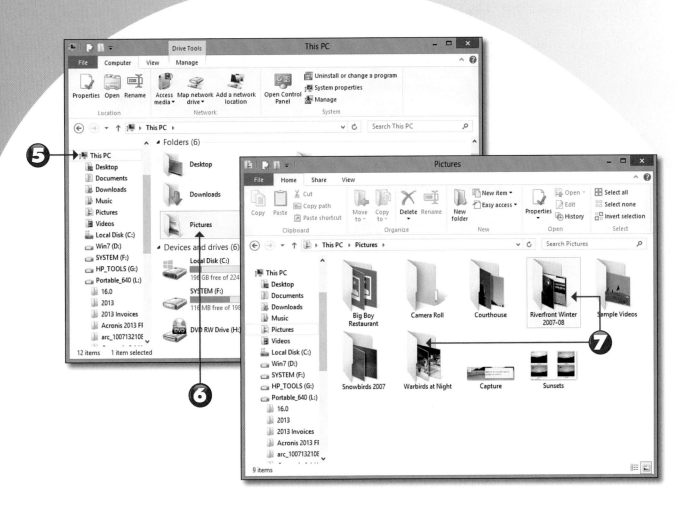

5 Click **This PC**.

6 Open the **Pictures** folder.

7 Any folders you copied here now appear.

End

IMPORTING PICTURES

When you take photos with your digital camera, the next logical stop for them is your Pictures library. Here's how to import your photos from your camera.

Start

1 Connect the USB cable for your digital camera to your camera and to a USB port on your computer.

2 Turn on the camera.

3 Press the **Playback** key if the camera is not recognized.

4 Right-click the camera icon in This PC.

5 Select **Import pictures and videos**.

6 Click **Next**.

Continued

TIP

Keeping Your Camera On During File Transfer To prevent your camera from shutting off during picture transfer, tap the camera's shutter button lightly or increase its auto shutoff time.

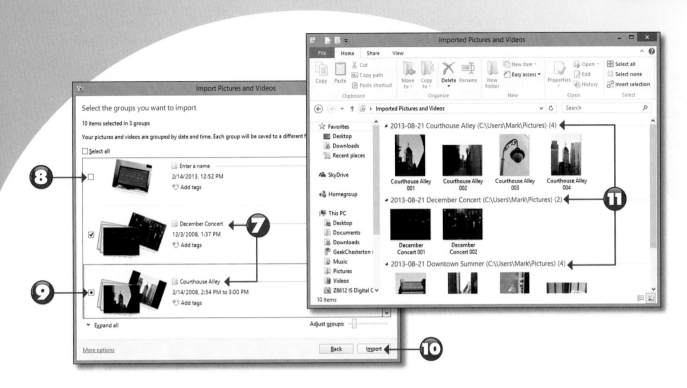

7 Enter a name for each group of photos.

8 Clear the check boxes from groups you don't want to import.

9 Not all photos were selected; click **View all...items** to select some photos only.

10 Click **Import**.

11 Your photos are placed into new subfolders of the Pictures folder.

End

NOTE

Changing Folder and Filename Settings
If you prefer to keep your pictures' original filenames or want to change settings for folder names, see "Selecting Import Options," p. 324, this chapter. ■

TIP

RAW Photos Displayed as Icons Windows displays preview icons for JPEG photos, but RAW photos, which are proprietary to different camera models, are displayed as icons. To enable you to see RAW previews, install Microsoft Digital Camera Codec Pack from Windows Update, or contact your digital camera vendor for a RAW image codec made for Windows 8. ■

SELECTING IMPORT OPTIONS

The standard import options in This PC change the name of your pictures and create a folder that includes the import date and the group name. If you prefer other import options, you can change these settings.

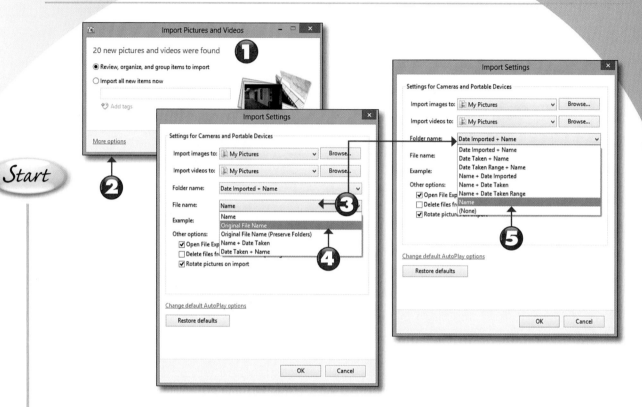

 Start

1 Start the import process as listed in steps 1–6 of the previous lesson.

2 Click **More options**.

3 The default settings for file (picture) name and folder name.

4 Select to keep the original filename.

5 Select to use group name only for folder name.

Continued

NOTE

Photo Organizers Help Find Photos by Date If you use a photo-organizing program such as Adobe Lightroom or Photo Gallery, you can find photos by date or date range, so you don't need to include the date as part of the folder name. Photo Gallery is available free from Microsoft as part of Windows Essentials 2012. ■

6 New folder and filename settings.

7 Open to choose a new default folder for video imports (such as Videos).

8 Click to restore the defaults.

9 Click **OK** to return to the Imported Pictures and Videos window.

10 Imported photos and folder using the new import settings.

End

NOTE

Why Use the Original Filename for Photos? If you need to use photos for evidence in a civil or criminal case, the filenames should not be changed. Another benefit of using the original filenames for photos is to make it easier to determine which camera you used—different camera brands use different numbering schemes for their photos. ■

USING WINDOWS PHOTO VIEWER

Do you want to see your photos in an adjustable-size window? Or, maybe you'd like to make a copy of a photo before you edit it. You can use Windows Photo Viewer for these and other tasks. Here's how to start and use this application.

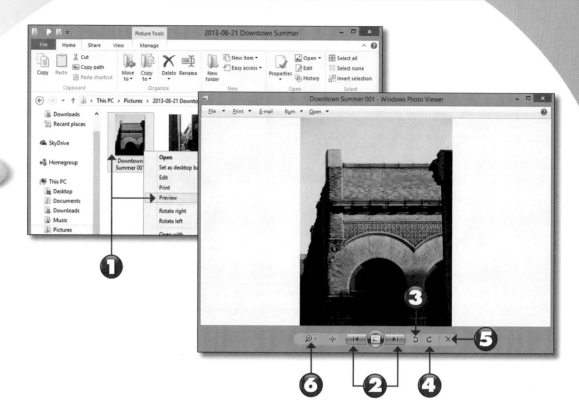

Start

1 Right-click a photo and select **Preview**.

2 Move to the previous or next photo.

3 Rotate the photo to the left.

4 Rotate the photo to the right.

5 Delete the current photo.

6 Click to open zoom control.

Continued

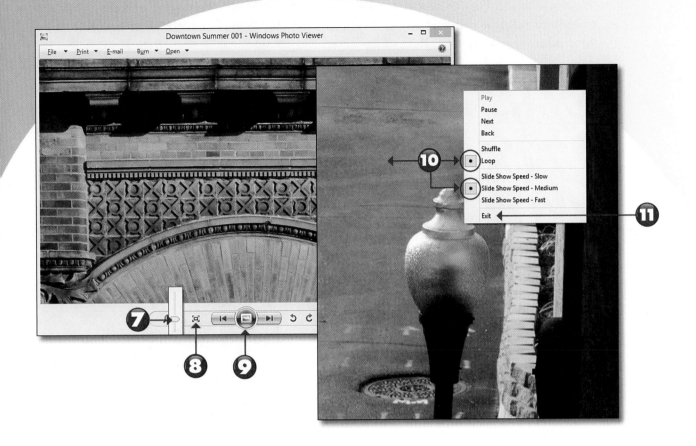

7 Click and drag up to see closer details; click inside the image to drag the view window around; click and drag down to see more of the image.

8 Toggle between Actual size and Fit to window.

9 Click **Play slide show**.

10 Right-click the image in the slide show to view or change the slide show settings; dots indicate current settings. Click to change settings.

11 Click **Exit** to end the slide show.

End

NOTE

File and Open Menus Help Edit Photos Safely Use the File menu to make a copy of a photo before you edit it. To open the photo in another program, such as the Start menu's Photos app or others, use the Open menu. ◼

PRINTING PHOTOS WITH WINDOWS PHOTO VIEWER

Windows Photo Viewer makes it easy to print photos in different sizes and place multiple photos on a single sheet of paper. You also can select the best settings for printing your photos.

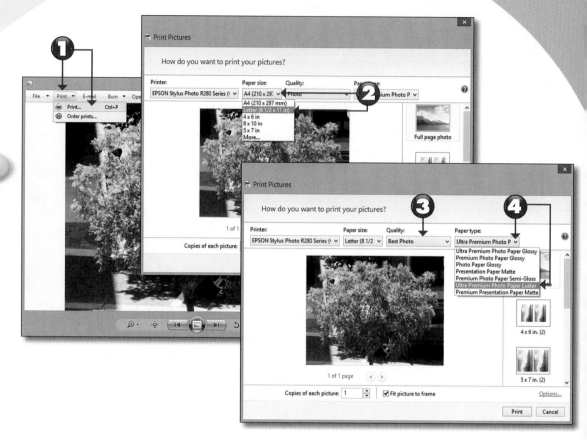

Start

① Open the Print menu and select **Print**.

② Select the correct paper size.

③ Choose the desired print quality.

④ Select the paper type.

Continued

NOTE

Solving Limited Photo Printing Options If you are using a printer driver included with Windows 8, you might not be able to adjust settings for print quality or paper type. Sometimes you can download and install an updated Windows 8 printer driver from your printer vendor that gives you access to these settings. ■

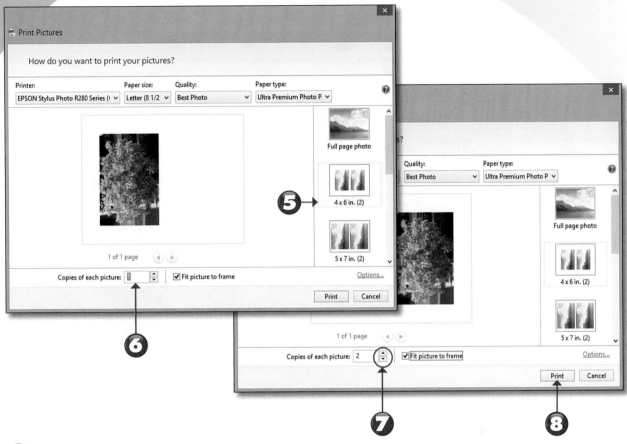

5 Click the desired print size.

6 The normal setting prints one copy per sheet, even if you select a smaller print size.

7 Adjust the number of copies to fill the sheet.

8 Click **Print**.

End

TIP

Printing with Plain Paper Some vendor-supplied printer drivers might not include Plain Paper as an option in Windows Photo Viewer's Print utility. Select the original driver provided with Windows 8 or open your photos in a different program, such as Paint, and use its Print menu to choose your printer and its print options. ■

STARTING WINDOWS MEDIA PLAYER

Windows Media Player enables you to play and create digital music tracks from CDs, watch video clips, and share media with other users. In this lesson, you discover how to launch Windows Media Player and add it to the Windows taskbar.

Start

From the Start menu, click the **Apps** button or flick upward (touchscreen).

Click **Windows Media Player**.

Continued

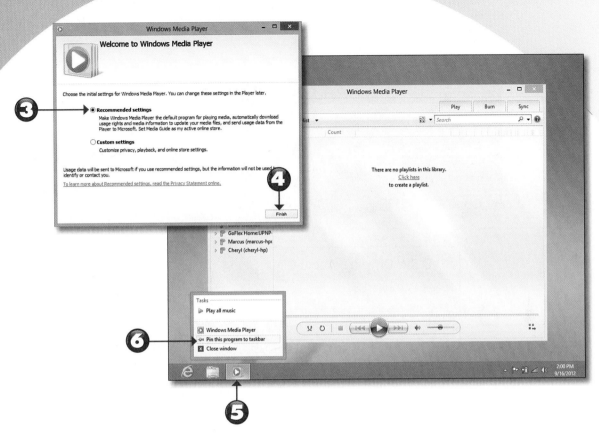

3 Click **Recommended Settings**.

4 Click **Finish**.

5 Right-click the Windows Media Player icon on the taskbar.

6 Select **Pin this program to taskbar**.

End

PLAYING AN AUDIO CD

You can use Windows Media Player to play audio CDs. And, playing audio CDs puts you just a couple of clicks away from ripping them to digital music tracks.

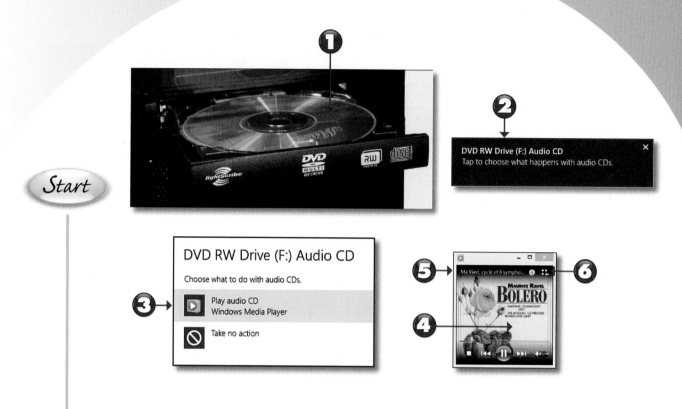

DVD RW Drive (F:) Audio CD
Tap to choose what happens with audio CDs.

DVD RW Drive (F:) Audio CD

Choose what to do with audio CDs.

▶ Play audio CD
Windows Media Player

⊘ Take no action

Start

① Insert an audio CD into your computer's optical drive.

② Click the AutoPlay notification.

③ Click **Play audio CD - Windows Media Player**.

④ The current album.

⑤ The current track playing.

⑥ Point to the playback window and click the **Switch to Library** button.

Continued

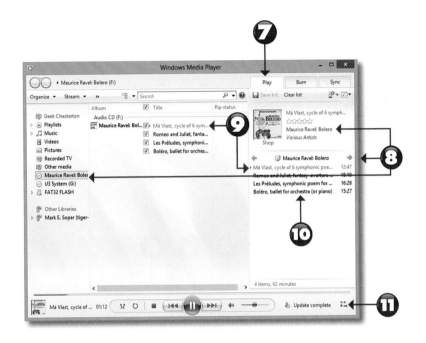

7 Click the **Play** tab.

8 The current album.

9 The current track.

10 The current playlist.

11 Click to switch back to **Now Playing** mode.

End

USING PLAYBACK CONTROLS IN WINDOWS MEDIA PLAYER

Windows Media Player makes it easy to play your media in any order you choose or pause it when it's time to grab a phone call. Here's an explanation of these and other playback controls in Windows Media Player.

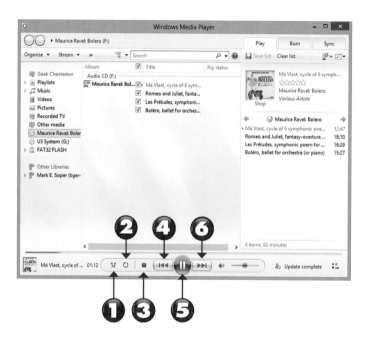

1 Shuffle playback.

2 Repeat current playlist.

3 Stop playback or recording.

4 Go to previous track.

5 Pause playback.

6 Go to next track.

Continued

7 Click and drag to desired position in current track (Seek).

8 Click to pause/resume playback.

9 Click to mute volume; click again to restore volume.

10 Drag to adjust playback volume.

End

NOTE

Controls in Now Playing Mode The Now Playing view also includes stop, previous/next track, pause/play, and volume controls. ■

RIPPING (COPYING) AN AUDIO CD

Tired of shuffling CDs in and out of a boom box? If you haven't yet discovered how easy it is to convert your CDs into audio tracks, let Windows Media Player do the work for you. In this example, you learn how to rip a CD that has already been inserted into your computer's optical drive.

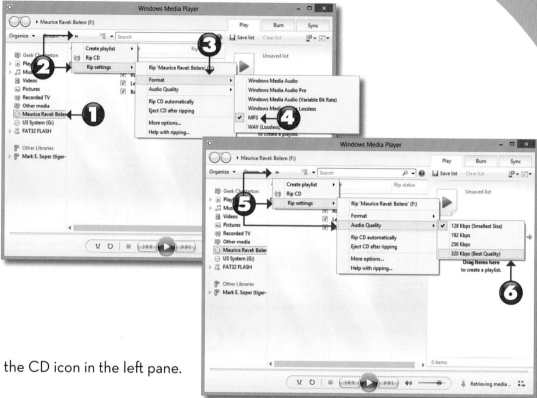

Start

1 Click the CD icon in the left pane.

2 Expand the menu (if necessary) and point to **Rip settings**.

3 Point to **Format**.

4 Click **MP3**.

5 Select **Rip settings** again, and then point to **Audio Quality**.

6 Click **320Kbps (Best Quality)**.

Continued

NOTE

MP3 Versus WMA MP3 files can be played by all digital media players. Windows Media Audio formats work well with Windows-based players but don't work with Apple iPods, iPhones, or iPads. ∎

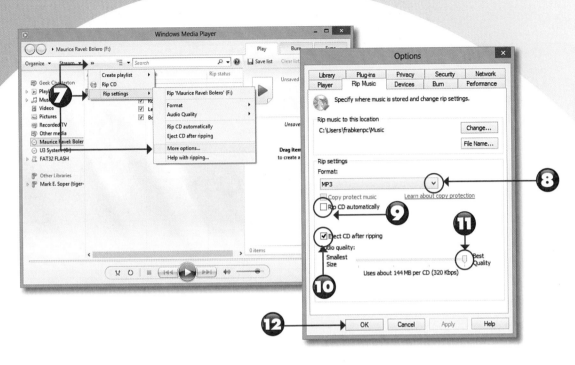

7 Select **Rip settings**, and then click **More options**.

8 Click to select a different file format.

9 Click the empty checkbox if you want to rip CDs automatically when you insert them.

10 Click the empty checkbox to eject a CD after ripping it.

11 Drag to adjust quality/size settings for ripping.

12 Click **OK**.

Continued

NOTE

Full-Screen View and WMP Menus If you run Windows Media
Player in full-screen view and all menu items are visible, you will not
see the >> symbol. This symbol is displayed if some menu items are
hidden due to space limitations. ∎

13 Expand the menu and click **Rip CD**.

14 A ripped track.

15 A track being ripped.

16 Expand the menu and click to stop rip.

17 Tracks waiting to be ripped.

Continued

NOTE

Toggling the Playlist Pane On and Off The Playlist pane shown in this section can be toggled off and on. To learn how, see the section "Setting Up Playlists," later in this chapter. ■

18 All tracks ripped.

19 Expand the **Music** category.

20 Click **Album**.

21 The album is listed in the Music library.

End

TIP

Ripping Another CD Windows Media Player sometimes has difficulty figuring out whether you're finished with a CD. To get ready to rip another CD, right-click the CD in Windows Media Player and select Eject. After the disc is ejected, remove it and close the drive. If the track list is still on-screen, open File Manager, open Computer, and double-click the optical drive icon. When it changes from the disc icon to the drive icon, Windows knows the drive is empty. Return to Windows Media Player, and the track list should be empty. You can now insert another disc and rip it. ■

SELECTING AND PLAYING ALBUMS AND INDIVIDUAL TRACKS

Downloaded music, music ripped from CDs, and audio you record yourself are all digital music tracks, as far as Windows Media Player is concerned. You can view and play albums or individual tracks in a variety of ways.

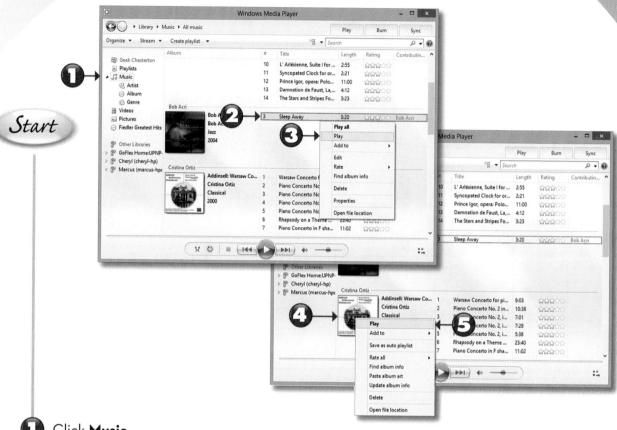

Start

1 Click **Music**.

2 Right-click a track.

3 Select **Play** to play the current track only.

4 Right-click an album.

5 Select **Play** to play all tracks in the album.

Continued

6 Click **Artist**.

7 Click an artist.

8 The number of tracks (songs) by artist.

9 The total time and current rating.

Continued

TIP

How to Rate Albums and Songs To change the rating for an album, right-click it, select Rate All (Songs), and select the rating desired (1–5 stars or Unrated). Windows Media Player also assigns ratings based on how often you play a song; all songs (and hence all albums) start out with a three-star rating. To rate a song, open the Album view and highlight the stars in the Rating column. ■

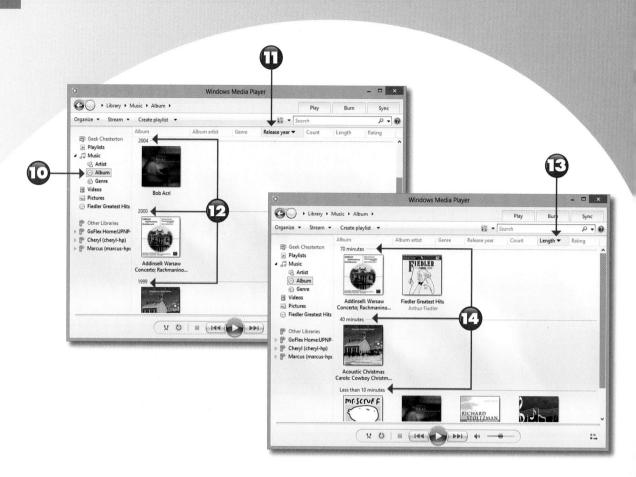

10 Click **Album**.

11 Click **Release year**.

12 The albums listed from most recent to oldest.

13 Click **Length**.

14 The albums listed from longest to shortest playing time.

Continued

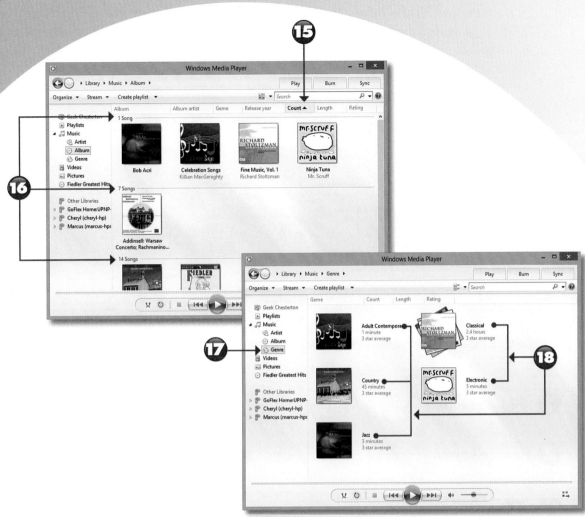

15 Click **Count**.

16 The albums are grouped by number of songs (tracks).

17 Click **Genre**.

18 The songs are stacked by genre.

End

SETTING UP PLAYLISTS

With Windows Media Player, you can create a mix of tracks just for playback on your PC, sync music with a digital media player, or burn a CD of your personal "greatest hits." First, you need to set up a playlist. Here's how to make one.

Start

1 Click **Organize**.

2 Point to **Layout**.

3 Select **Show list**.

4 Click **Music**.

5 Right-click a track and point to **Add to**.

6 Select **Play list**.

Continued

TIP

Selecting by Artist, Album, or Genre Selecting Music in step 4 enables you to scroll through all the albums in your collection; however, if you prefer to select by other categories, choose Artist, Album, or Genre in step 4 after clicking Music (if necessary). ■

NOTE

Hiding/Displaying the Playlist Pane If the Playlist pane is already visible on the right side of the Windows Media Player window, skip steps 1–3. To hide the Playlist pane, uncheck Show List in step 3. ■

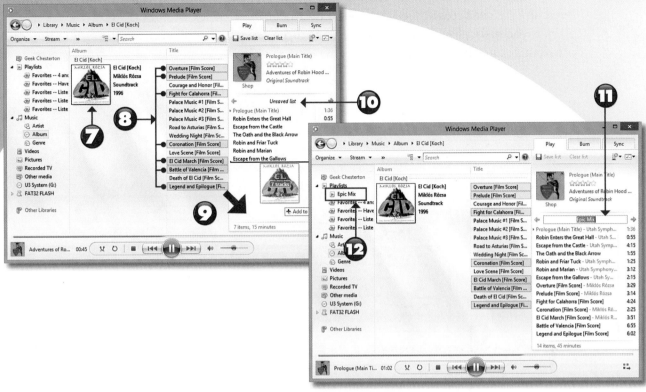

7 Select another album.

8 Click the first track, then hold down the **Ctrl** key and click additional tracks.

9 Drag them into the list window.

10 Click **Unsaved list**.

11 Enter a name for the list.

12 The new playlist is now available.

End

TIP

Editing a Playlist To edit a playlist, click it. Then, click a song and drag it to a new position, or right-click the song in the playlist and select Remove from List, Move Up, or Move Down. ■

SYNCING FILES TO A MEDIA PLAYER

You can sync files from a list you create on the spot in Windows Media Player or from a playlist you have already created. In this tutorial, we use the playlist we created in the previous tutorial.

Start

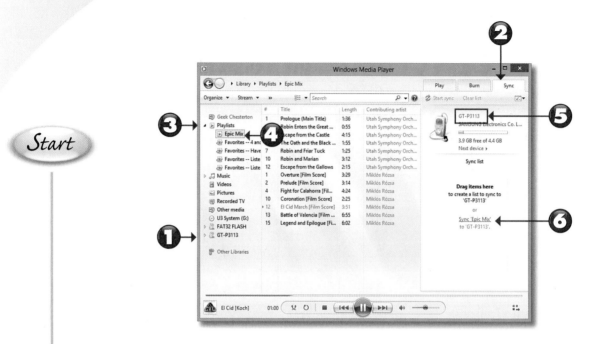

1 Connect a media player to your computer.

2 Click the **Sync** tab.

3 Click **Playlists** if the list is not expanded.

4 Click a playlist.

5 Verify that the correct device is listed on the Sync tab.

6 Click to start the sync process.

Continued

7 The available space on the device.

8 Click **Start sync**.

9 After the sync process is over, click to see sync results.

10 The sync results.

End

TIP

What Else Is On the Media Player? Click the Music, Videos, or Pictures categories listed under the media player in the left pane to see other media content. ■

BURNING (CREATING) A MUSIC CD

In Windows Media Player, you can select music and burn it to a CD that will play in most CD players. You can use a playlist you have already created or use drag and drop to create a new list specifically for the CD. We use the second method in this tutorial.

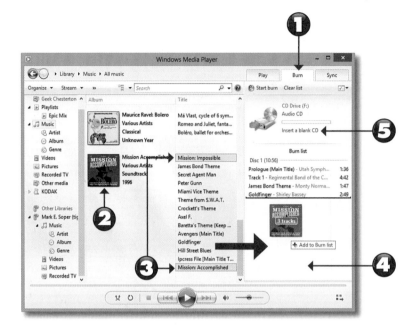

Start

1 Click the **Burn** tab.

2 Select an album.

3 Select music tracks. Use the Ctrl key to select more than one track from an album or other category.

4 Drag the tracks to the Burn list window.

5 Insert a blank CD.

Continued

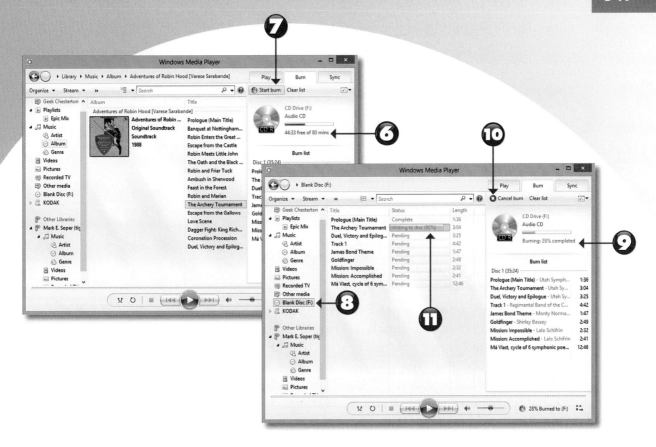

6 The space available on the CD.

7 Click **Start burn**.

8 Click the **Blank Disc** icon.

9 The burn process indicator.

10 Click here if you choose to cancel the burn.

11 The track being burned.

End

NOTE

Finishing Up Your Disc At the end of the burn process, the CD is ejected and you can label the disc. ■

Chapter 20

WEB BROWSING FROM YOUR DESKTOP

Windows 8.1 includes Internet Explorer 11 (IE11), the latest version of Microsoft's web browser. When you launch IE11 from the Start screen, you are using a touch-optimized version of the browser that has limited support for plug-ins. If you use IE11 from the Windows desktop, however, you have a full-featured web browser that fully supports Adobe Flash, a wider variety of plug-ins, favorites, and other familiar Internet Explorer features. This chapter shows you how to use IE11's most important features when you run it from the Windows desktop.

Bing Mapping
Web Accelerator

InPrivate
Browsing

Browsing
History

Favorites
Center

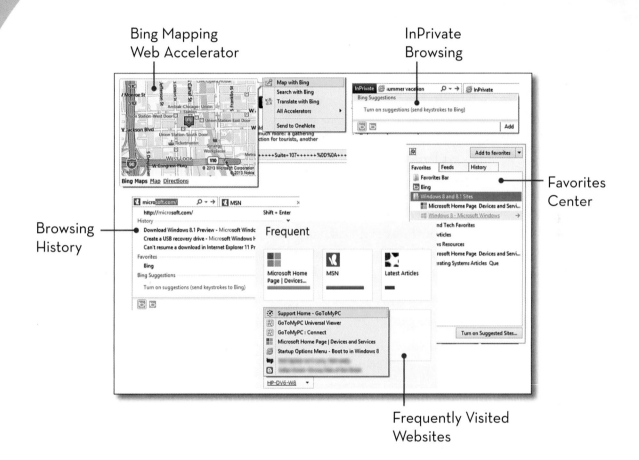

Frequently Visited
Websites

STARTING IE11 FROM THE DESKTOP

To access the desktop version of IE11, you need—surprise—to open the Desktop first. Here's how to do it.

Start

End

1. Click the Desktop tile on the Start screen.

2. Click the IE icon on the Windows taskbar.

3. Use the IE11 address bar to enter web addresses to visit.

4. Click the **new tab** button to create a blank tab.

5. The IE11 Home, Favorites, and Tools icons let you control how you use IE.

NOTE

Browsing the Web from the Start Screen Refer to Chapter 5, "Browsing the Web from the Modern UI," for details on how to browse the web by launching Internet Explorer from the Start screen. ■

ENTERING A WEBSITE ADDRESS (URL)

Internet Explorer 11 displays more than just the address (URL) when you enter a URL you've previously visited. This feature makes it easier to go back to an address you've previously visited, even if you have visited several pages in the same domain.

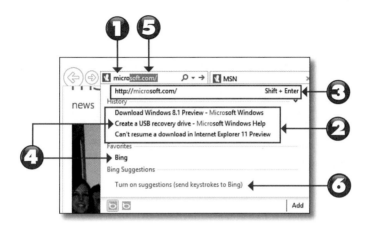

Start

1 Begin typing the name of a website. You do not need to add the "www."

2 If you have already visited a web page with the text in either the website name (URL) or the web page title, these appear in the History list.

3 To choose the first match, press **Shift+Enter**.

4 Select a website from the list.

5 To go to the exact match for what you typed, press **Enter**.

6 Click to turn on suggestions from Bing search.

End

TIP

Keyboard Navigation In step 4, you can also use the down arrow to highlight the page you want to load, and then press Enter. ■

WORKING WITH TABS

Internet Explorer 11 includes tabbed browsing. In this tutorial, you learn how to open and work with new tabs in IE11.

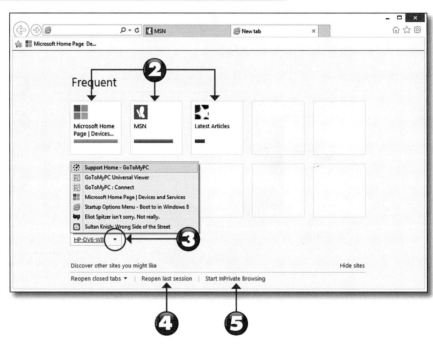

1 Click to open a new tab.

2 Click to reopen a website you visit frequently.

3 Open to select from other recent websites.

4 Click to reopen your last browsing session's tabs.

5 Click to open an InPrivate Browsing window.

End

NOTE

InPrivate Browsing For information about opening a window in IE11 for InPrivate Browsing, see "Using InPrivate Browsing from the Desktop," later in this chapter. ■

SETTING YOUR HOME PAGE

You can change your Internet Explorer 11 home page whenever you want, and you also can use a tab group as a home page. Here's how to do it.

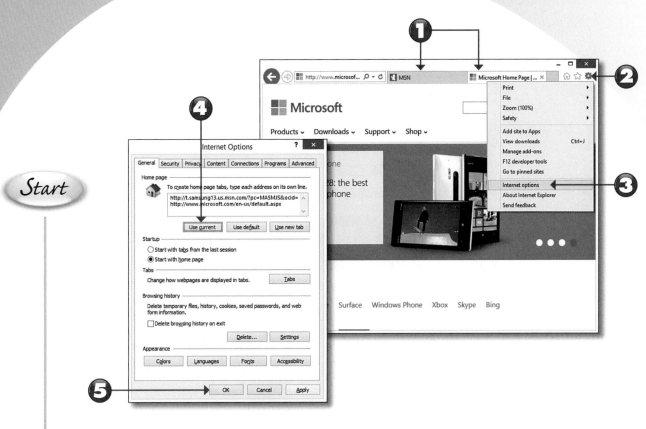

Start

1 Open the page(s) you want to use as your home page.

2 Open the **Tools** menu.

3 Click **Internet options**.

4 Click **Use current**.

5 Click **OK**.

End

NOTE

Selecting a Single Tab when Multiple Tabs Are Open If you have opened multiple tabs in IE11 but want to use only one tab for your home page, the easiest way to do it is to close the other tabs before you open Internet Options in step 3. ■

OPENING A LINK

Because Internet Explorer 11 supports tabbed browsing, you can open a link to another website in three ways—as a replacement for the current page, as a new tab in the same window, or in a new window. When you click on a link, the link could open in the same window or in a new window. To control how the link opens, use the method shown in this tutorial.

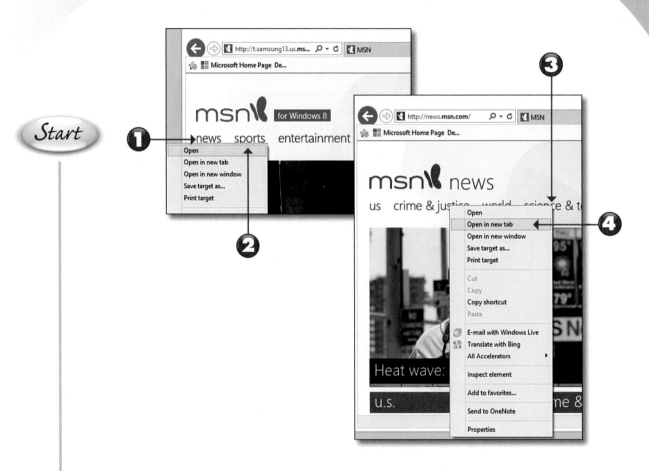

Start

1 Right-click (mouse/touchpad), or press and hold a link (touchscreen).

2 To open the link in the current tab, select **Open**.

3 Right-click a link.

4 Select **Open in new tab**.

Continued

5 To view the contents of the new tab, click it.

6 Right-click a link on the new tab.

7 Select **Open in new window**.

8 A new window opens to display the link.

End

USING PAGE ZOOM

Page Zoom enables you to increase or decrease the size of text and graphics on a web page. By increasing the size, you make pages easier to read, and by reducing the size, you enable page viewing without horizontal scrolling. By enabling the status bar, you can make Page Zoom easier to use.

Start

1 Right-click the browser window's top border.

2 Select **Status bar**.

3 Click the page zoom control and select **200%**.

End

NOTE

When to Zoom The 200% view shown in step 3 makes the text and pictures on a web page easier to see, but you must scroll left to right as well as up and down to see the entire page. Use zoom settings smaller than 100% if you want to see more of the page without scrolling. These settings do not affect how the page prints. ◼

NOTE

Enabling More Bars in IE11 You can also enable the Menu bar (displays File, View, Tools, and other menus), Favorites bar (quick access to favorite websites), and Command bar (quick access to printing and other features) in step 2. ◼

PREVIEWING AND PRINTING A WEB PAGE

Internet Explorer 11 enables you to preview and print web pages intelligently. Whether you want to save paper or make full-size page printouts, IE11 does the job the way you want it.

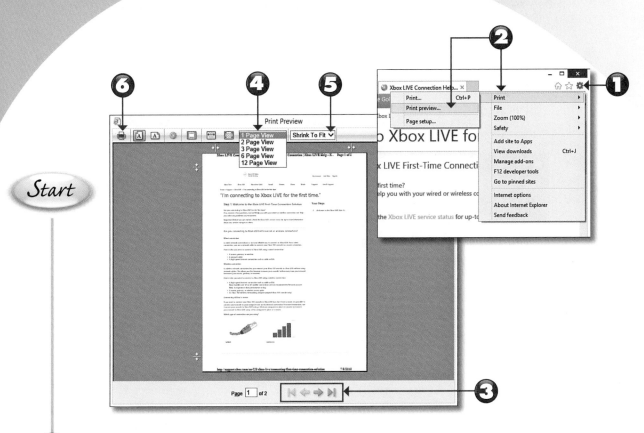

Start

1. Click **Tools**.

2. Point to **Print**, and select **Print preview**.

3. Click to move through pages.

4. Select viewing options.

5. Select print size options.

6. Open the Print dialog box.

End

OPENING THE FAVORITES CENTER

The Favorites Center remembers your favorite websites so you can go to them with just a couple of mouse clicks whenever you want. Here's how to open it.

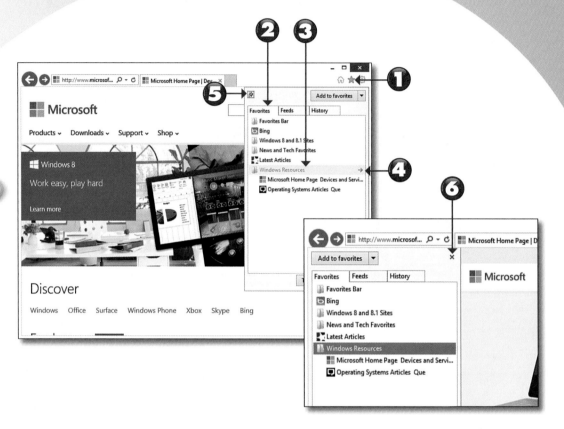

Start

1 Click the **Favorites** button to view favorite websites or categories.

2 Click the **Favorites** tab to make it active.

3 Click a folder to view the website links it contains.

4 Click the right-arrow icon to open all the links as a tab group.

5 Click to pin the Favorites Center to the left of the browser window and keep it open at all times.

6 Click **Close** to close the Favorites Center.

End

ADDING FAVORITES TO THE FAVORITES BAR

Internet Explorer 11 makes it even easier to get to your favorite websites with the Favorites Bar. The Favorites Bar sits just below the address bar, providing one-click access to the sites you use most often. Here's how to add sites to the Favorites Bar.

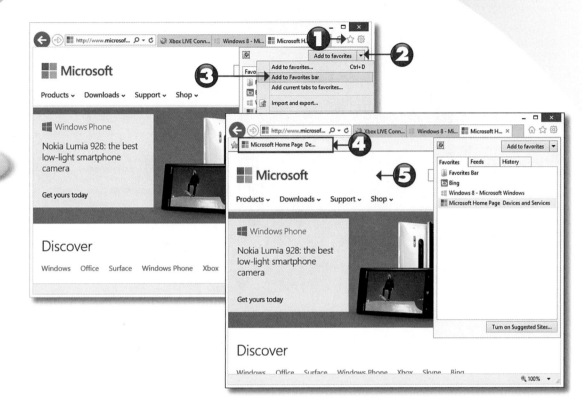

Start

1 With the website you want to add to the Favorites Bar in view, click the **Favorites** button.

2 Open the **Add to favorites** menu.

3 Click the **Add to Favorites bar** menu option.

4 The website is added to the Favorites Bar.

5 To close the Favorites Center, press **Esc**, or click any part of the web page that does not have a link.

End

NOTE

Avoiding an Overcrowded Favorites Bar Use the Favorites Bar only for websites you want to visit frequently, because it can get very crowded in a hurry. See the next section to learn how to add favorites to the Favorites Center. ■

ADDING FAVORITES TO THE FAVORITES CENTER

If you want to revisit some websites—but don't need one-click access to them in the Favorites Bar—add them to the Favorites Center.

Start

1 With the site you want to add on-screen, click the **Favorites** button.

2 Click **Add to favorites**.

3 To add the link to a new folder, click **New Folder**. (Or skip to step 8 if you want to add to the Favorites folder.)

4 Enter a folder name.

5 Click **Create**.

Continued

TIP

Saving the Current Tab as a Favorite If the website is the only tab in use, you can also save it by clicking Favorites, Add to Favorites and specifying where to save the favorite. For more details, see "Saving a Tab Group as a Favorite," later in this chapter. ■

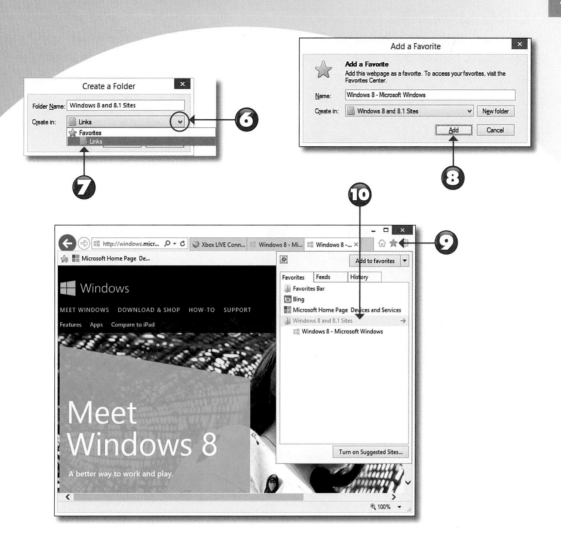

6 To add the link to an existing folder, click the **Create in** arrow.

7 Select the folder.

8 Click **Add**.

9 To see the new favorite, click **Favorites**.

10 Click the folder to expand the category.

End

ORGANIZING FAVORITES

Internet Explorer 11 enables you to organize your favorites even after you create them. You can create new folders, delete favorites you no longer use, and move favorites as desired. In this tutorial, you learn how to move a favorite from one folder to another.

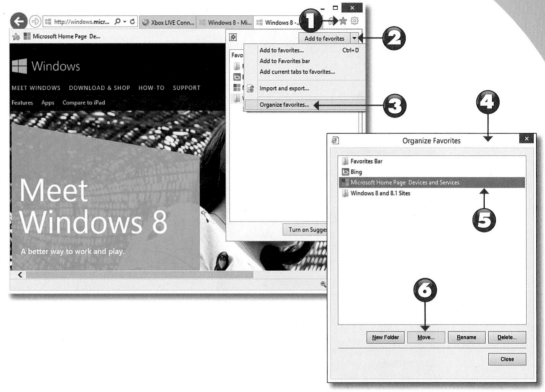

Start

1 Click **Favorites**.

2 Open the **Add to favorites** menu.

3 Click **Organize favorites**.

4 The root Favorites folder opens. To organize a different folder, click it.

5 Select the favorite to move.

6 Click **Move**.

Continued

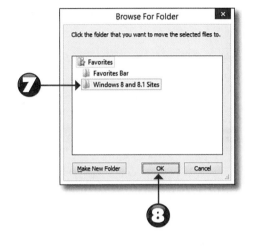

7 Select the folder where you want to move the favorite.

8 Click **OK**.

9 Click **Close**.

End

NOTE

Favorites, Feeds, and History You can also use the Favorites Center to subscribe to RSS feeds (Feeds tab) and to view websites visited by date (History tab). ■

SAVING A TAB GROUP AS A FAVORITE

If you have several websites you rely on throughout the day, such as a web-based email client, news, and sports sites, you can save time by opening them in separate tabs and then saving the tab group as a favorite. In this tutorial, you learn how to set up three tabs and save them as a tab group.

Start

1 Open the first website you want in your tab group.

2 Click **New Tab**.

3 Open the second website.

4 Click **New Tab**.

5 Open the third website.

Continued

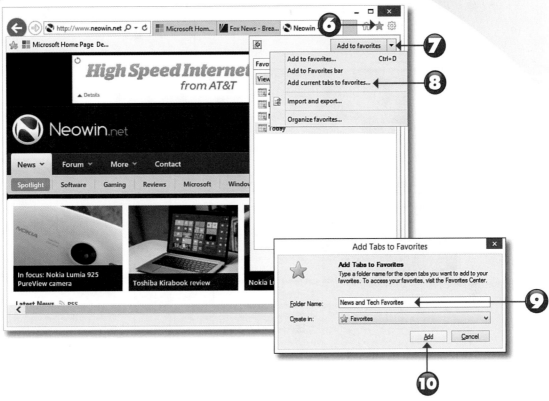

6 Click **Favorites**.

7 Open the **Add to favorites** menu.

8 Click **Add current tabs to favorites**.

9 Enter a name for the folder used to store the tab group.

10 Click **Add**.

End

TIP

Storing Your Tab Group in a Subfolder If you want to store your tab group in a different folder, open the Create In menu and select the folder you prefer. ■

OPENING A FAVORITE WEBSITE OR TAB GROUP

The Favorites Center enables you to open either individual favorites or tab groups whenever you want.

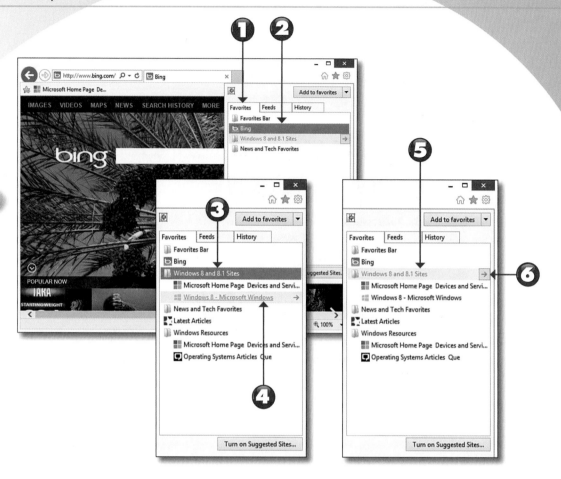

Start

1. Click the **Favorites** tab.

2. Click the favorite.

3. Click the category containing the favorite you want to open.

4. Click the favorite.

5. Hover the mouse over a folder.

6. Click the right arrow next to a folder to open its contents as a tab group.

End

USING ACCELERATORS

The Accelerators feature in Internet Explorer 11 makes it easier than ever to research names, places, or other information in any web page. Here's how to use the accelerators built in to IE11.

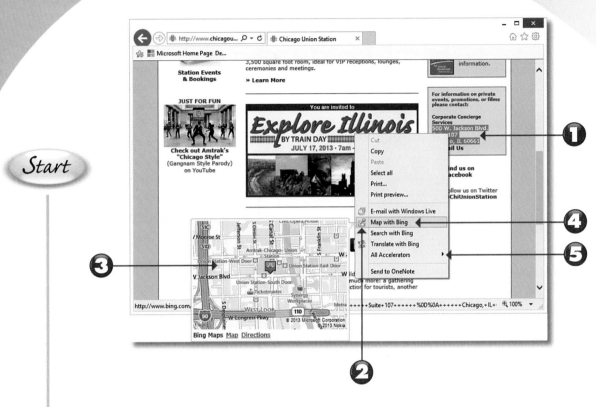

1 Highlight text in a web page and right-click it.

2 Hover the mouse over an accelerator.

3 Some accelerators display results in a popup window when you point to them.

4 To open the results of the accelerator in a new page, click the accelerator link.

5 Point to **All Accelerators** to see more accelerators.

TIP

In Search of More Accelerators To get more accelerators, open the All Accelerators menu and click Find More Accelerators. ■

USING INPRIVATE BROWSING FROM THE DESKTOP

Worried about leaving traces of where you've been online on a public computer, such as in a library or Internet cafe? The InPrivate Browsing feature in Internet Explorer 11 covers your tracks. When InPrivate Browsing is enabled, your browsing history, temporary Internet files, form data, cookies, usernames, and passwords are not retained. What happens in the InPrivate Browser window is forgotten as soon as you close it. As you learn in this section, you can use InPrivate Browsing from the desktop as well as from the Start screen.

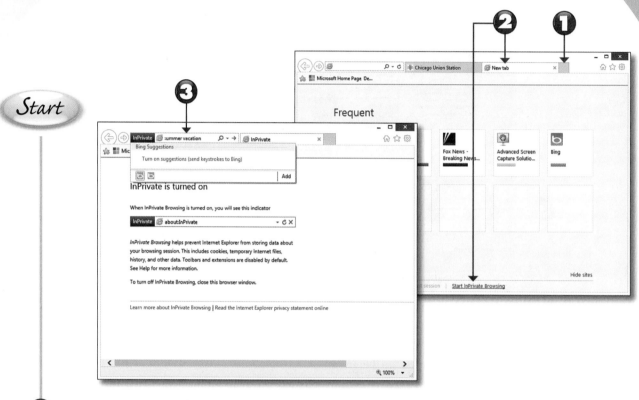

1 Click a blank tab.

2 When the tab opens, click **Start InPrivate Browsing**.

3 A new InPrivate window opens. Enter the URL or search terms.

Continued

NOTE

Blocking Access to InPrivate Browsing To block access to InPrivate browsing for other accounts, enable parental controls for those accounts. Refer to Chapter 22, "User Accounts and System Security," for details on how to enable parental controls. ■

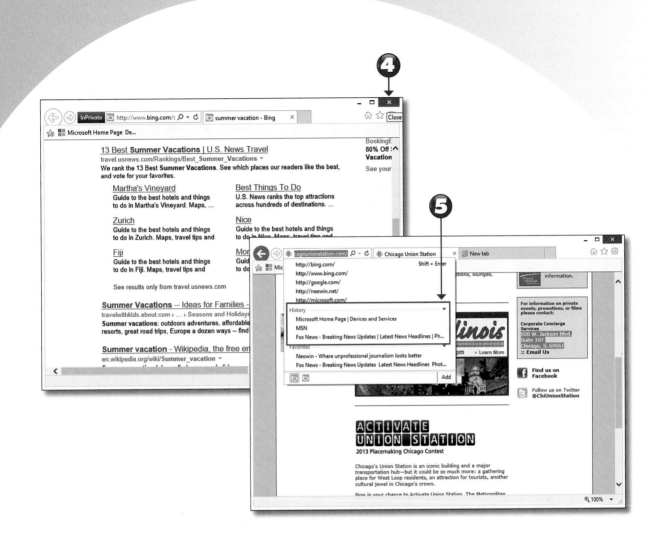

4 When you're finished browsing, close the InPrivate window.

5 Your browser history does not list any sites you visited while using InPrivate browsing.

End

MANAGING POPUPS

By default, Internet Explorer 11 blocks popups. However, if you need to use a site that relies on popups, you can disable the popup blocker temporarily, turn it off for the site, or disable popup blocking entirely. The Popuptest.com website provides a convenient way to try these methods.

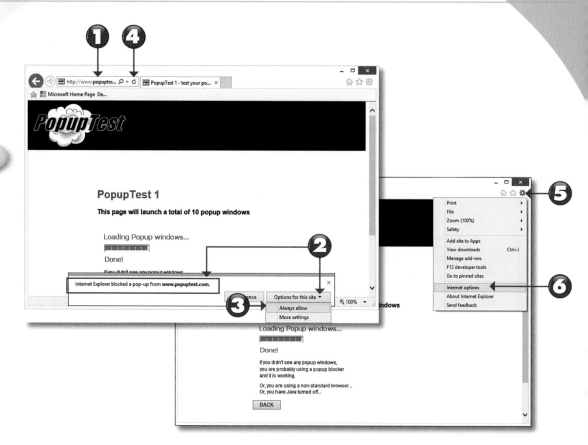

Start

1 Open a website that uses popups.

2 IE11 blocks the popup. Open the **Options for this site** menu to set options.

3 Click to always allow popups from the current site.

4 Click **Refresh** to see popups if the page doesn't display them automatically.

5 To manually add an allowed site, click the **Tools** button.

6 Click **Internet Options**.

Continued

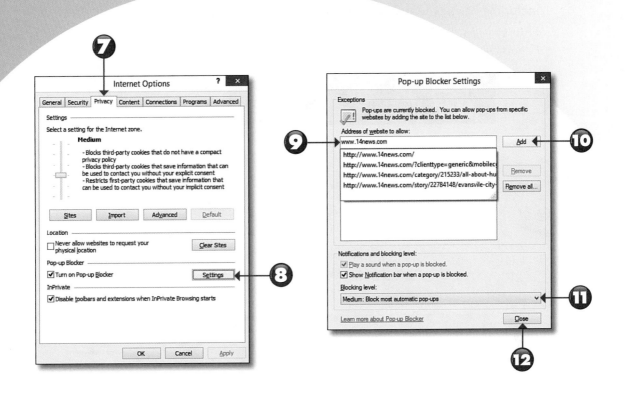

7 Click the **Privacy** tab.

8 Click **Settings**.

9 Enter a URL to allow.

10 Click **Add**.

11 Adjust the blocking level.

12 Click **Close**.

End

NOTE

Removing Allowed Sites To remove a site from the Allowed sites list, select it and then click Remove. To remove all listed sites, click Remove all. ■

SETTING INTERNET PRIVACY FEATURES

The Internet Options settings are used to configure many features of Internet Explorer 11, including privacy features. Here's how to help protect your privacy.

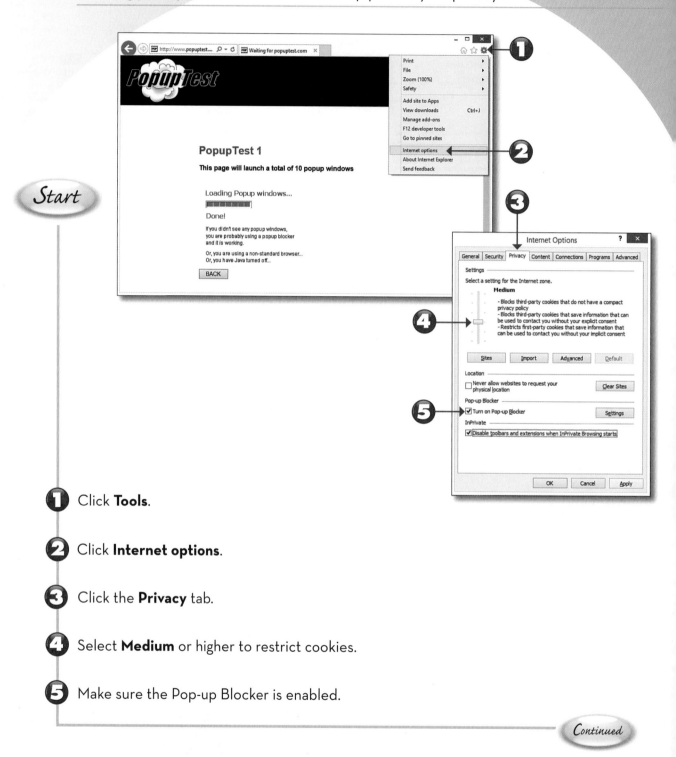

Start

1 Click **Tools**.

2 Click **Internet options**.

3 Click the **Privacy** tab.

4 Select **Medium** or higher to restrict cookies.

5 Make sure the Pop-up Blocker is enabled.

Continued

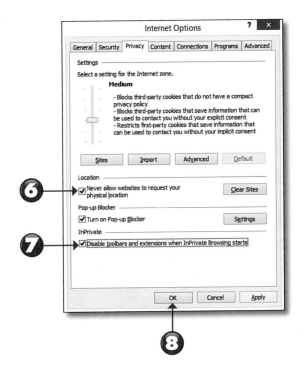

6 Click the **Never allow websites to request your physical location** box to enable this option.

7 Make sure the **Disable toolbars...** box is checked.

8 Click **OK** to save your changes and close the dialog box. (Click **Cancel** if you don't want to save your changes.)

End

NOTE

Privacy Tradeoffs If you select the Never allow websites... option (step 6), websites that use your physical location to provide localized searches or information might not work correctly. ∎

DELETING SELECTED ITEMS FROM YOUR HISTORY LIST

Internet Explorer 11 enables you to delete specified listings from your website history. Here's how to delete these sites.

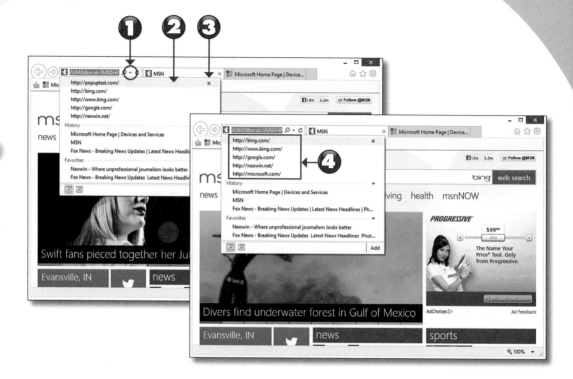

 Start

1 Open the **History** menu in the address bar.

2 Point to the entry you want to remove.

3 Click the **X** beside the entry.

4 The entry is removed.

End

TIP

Removing History Items from the Favorites Center You also can remove an entry from the History tab in the Favorites Center. Select the date, right-click the entry, click Delete, and click Yes to confirm the deletion. ∎

DELETING ALL ITEMS FROM YOUR HISTORY LIST

In addition to deleting selected items from your History list, Internet Explorer 11 also enables you to clear all items from your History list. You also can delete other files created during web surfing.

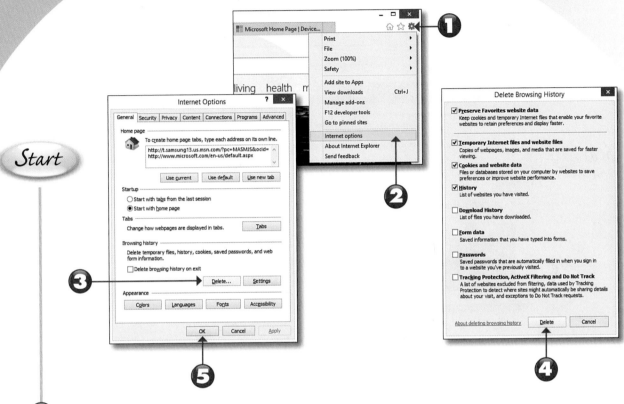

 Click **Tools**.

 Click **Internet options**.

3 From the **General** tab, click **Delete**.

4 Click **Delete** to delete History, Cookies, and Temporary Internet files. (Make sure their check boxes are enabled.)

5 Click **OK**.

End

NOTE

You're In Charge of What Is Removed In step 4, you can check and uncheck the options you want to delete from your browsing history. ■

NOTE

No History, If That's What You Prefer The Internet Options General tab (step 3) also has a checkbox you can select that will delete your browsing history each time you exit the browser. ■

SAVING A WEB PAGE

Internet Explorer 11 can save web pages as a single MHTML (also known as a web archive) file for easy retrieval or emailing to other users. You can also save pages in other formats. Here's how to build a library of web pages.

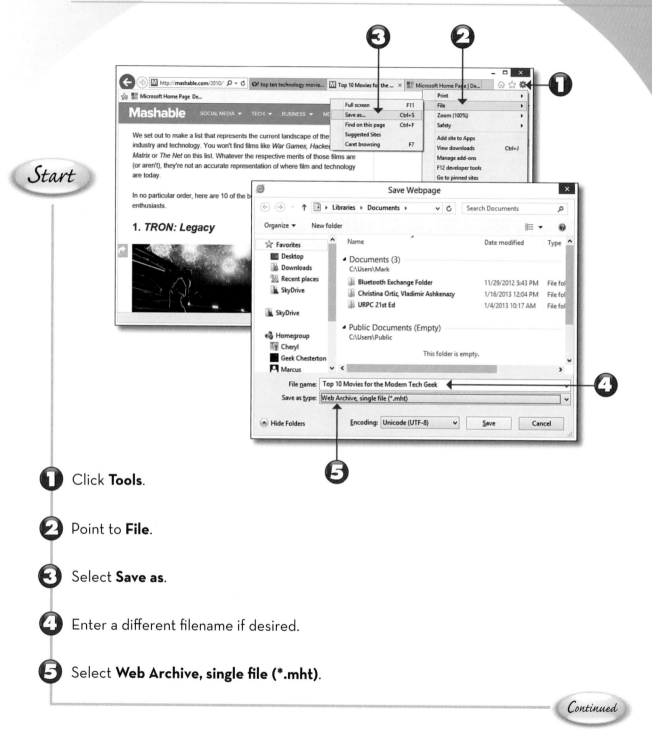

Start

1 Click **Tools**.

2 Point to **File**.

3 Select **Save as**.

4 Enter a different filename if desired.

5 Select **Web Archive, single file (*.mht)**.

Continued

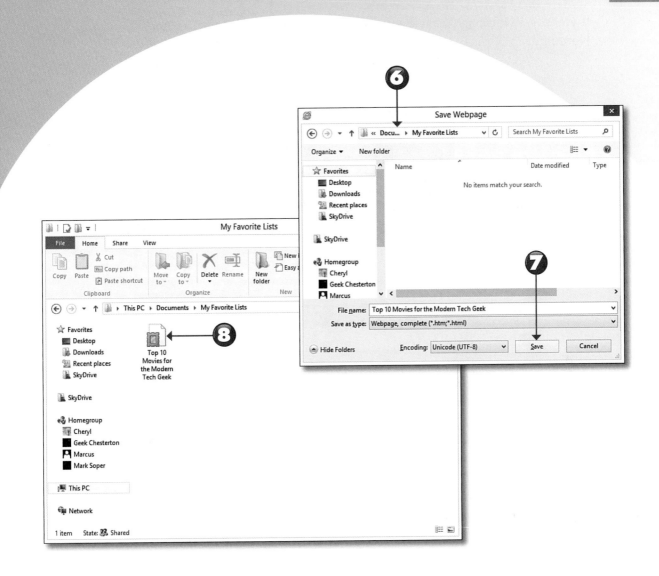

6 Select where to save the file.

7 Click **Save**.

8 The saved web page as it appears in File Explorer.

End

NOTE

Lots of File Types to Choose From Other file format options include Webpage, complete (saves images and other components to a folder below the target folder); Web Page, HTML only (*.htm, *.html; saves HTML code only); and Text File (.txt; plain text only). ■

EMAILING A WEB PAGE OR LINK

If you see a web page or link you'd like to share with someone, it's easy to email it with IE11. Here's how.

Start

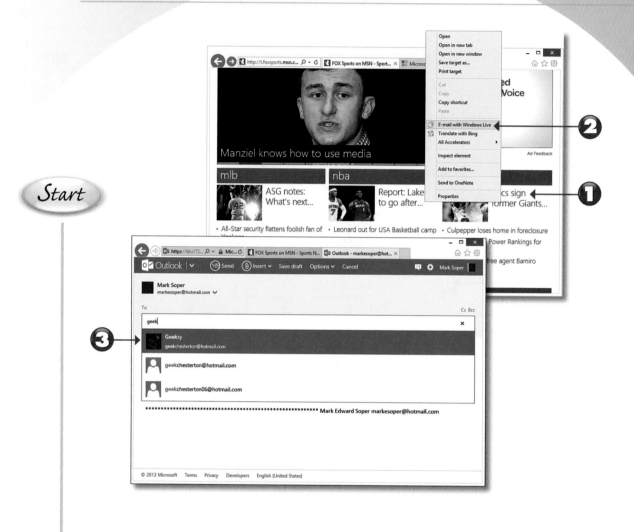

1 Right-click a link you want to email.

2 Click **Email** (with the email account you want to use).

3 Enter or select a recipient.

Continued

NOTE

Windows 8 and Your Email The exact wording you see in step 2 depends on the type of email account (or accounts) you have configured with Windows 8. ■

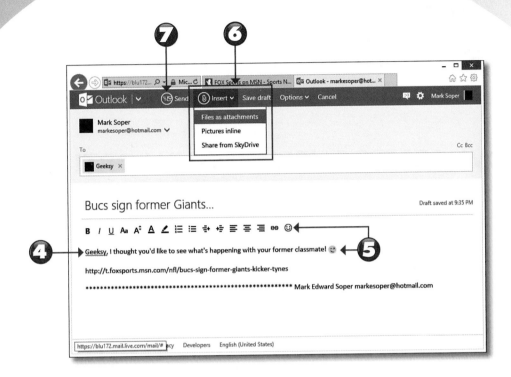

381

4 Enter additional text.

5 Add emoticons as desired.

6 Add any attachments desired.

7 Click **Send**.

End

NOTE

Your Screens Might Vary This example shows Outlook.com, which is the default email service I use. If you use Gmail or other email services and programs, your screen will look different than in this example. ■

Chapter 21

ADVANCED CONFIGURATION OPTIONS

Windows 8's standard configuration provides settings that many users like. However, you might want to change some of these settings. In this chapter, you learn how to connect and use an additional display, customize your desktop background and borders, manage your hardware, and use Task Manager.

Extending the Windows
Desktop to an
Additional Display

Creating a Custom
Window Border/
Taskbar Color

Searching for
Task Manager

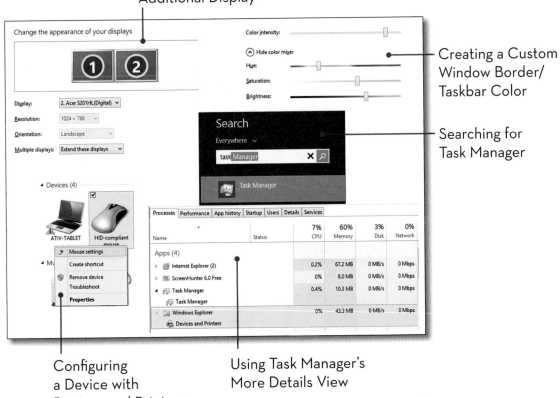

Configuring
a Device with
Devices and Printers

Using Task Manager's
More Details View

CONFIGURING WINDOWS UPDATE

Windows Update is normally set to automatically download and install updates to Microsoft Windows 8 and to other Microsoft apps, such as Office. However, you can change the default settings if you need to install updates on your own schedule. Here's how to tweak Windows Update settings from the Control Panel.

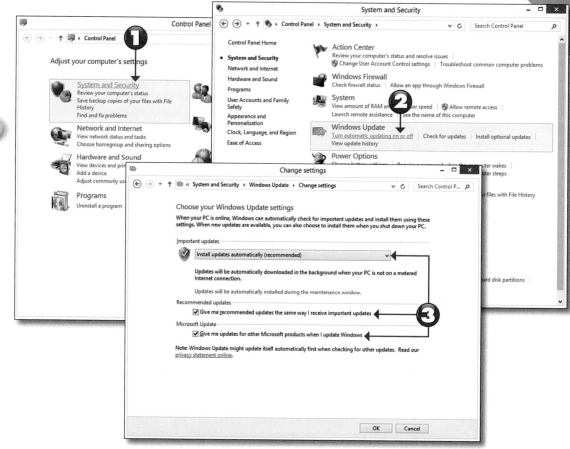

Start

1 Click **System and Security**.

2 Click **Turn automatic updating on or off**.

3 Note the default Windows Update settings.

Continued

NOTE

When Changing from Automatic Updates Makes Sense If you connect remotely with your computer or your computer runs backups on a regular basis, keep in mind that some Windows updates will cause the computer to reboot. This can prevent remote connections or backups from running. In those situations, it makes sense to specify when updates will be installed. ■

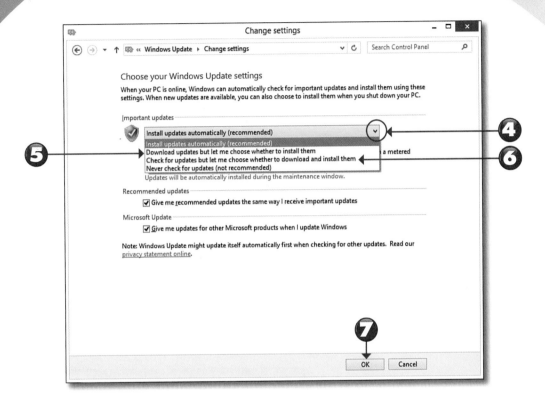

4 Click to change the automatic update setting.

5 Choose this option if you want to specify when your system is updated.

6 Choose this option if you want to specify whether to download updates.

7 Click **OK** to accept and use your settings.

End

CAUTION

The No Updates Option Is Not Recommended The dialog box shown in steps 4-7 also includes an option to Never Check for Updates. This option is intended primarily for corporate computers whose updates are managed centrally. At home or in a small office, let Windows figure out when to download your updates. ■

ADDING AND USING AN ADDITIONAL DISPLAY

You can add an additional display by using a laptop's video port or a second video port on a desktop computer that already has a display connected to it. You can use the additional display to duplicate the first display, but for normal use, you might prefer to set it up as an extended desktop. With an extended desktop, you can run different programs on each display. Once you've connected the cable from your monitor to an unused video port, here's how to make it happen on a typical laptop computer.

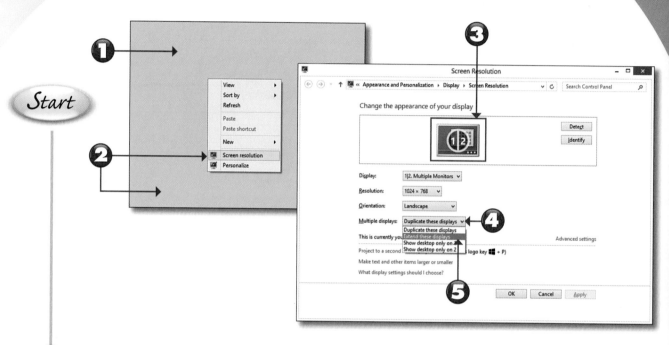

Start

1. Open the Windows desktop.

2. Right-click the desktop and select **Screen resolution** (make sure the monitor is on).

3. When the second display is detected; it is configured to duplicate what's on the first display.

4. Open the **Multiple displays** menu.

5. Click **Extend these displays**.

Continued

NOTE

Laptops Versus Desktops in Display Setup This example shows how to add a second display to a laptop. On a desktop, the second display icon might be displayed with a black frame (indicating it is inactive) as soon as you turn it on. To make it active, follow steps 4 and 5. ■

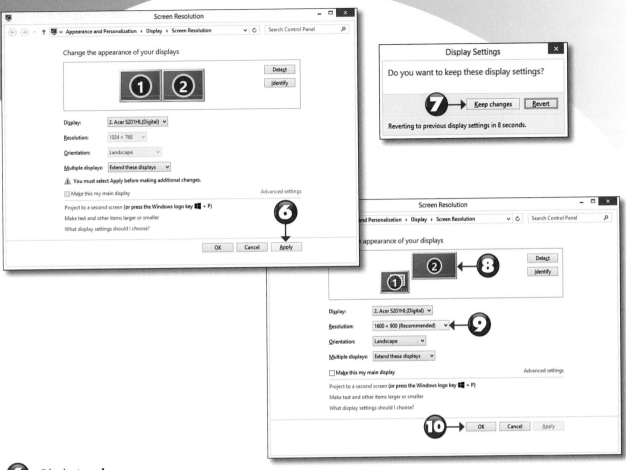

6 Click **Apply**.

7 Click **Keep changes**.

8 Drag the #2 display icon as needed to match your actual display orientation.

9 Verify whether your display is set to its recommended resolution.

10 Click **OK** to close.

End

NOTE

Using the Extended Desktop Drag a program to the second display, and when you close that program, Windows remembers which display was last used for the program. When you open the program again, Windows uses the additional display to run the program. ▪

PERSONALIZING YOUR DESKTOP BACKGROUND

Windows 8 normally uses a photo background for the Windows desktop. If you want to change to a different background, a plain background, or select multiple pictures for your desktop background, this tutorial shows you how.

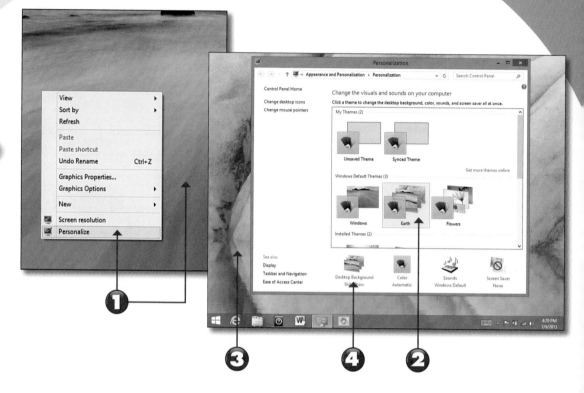

Start

① Right-click the desktop and select **Personalize**.

② Choose a theme.

③ You'll see a preview of the theme appear in the background.

④ Click **Desktop Background** to select images or background colors.

Continued

NOTE

Desktop Background = Wallpaper If you're a longtime user of Windows, you might remember that desktop backgrounds were once called *wallpaper*. ■

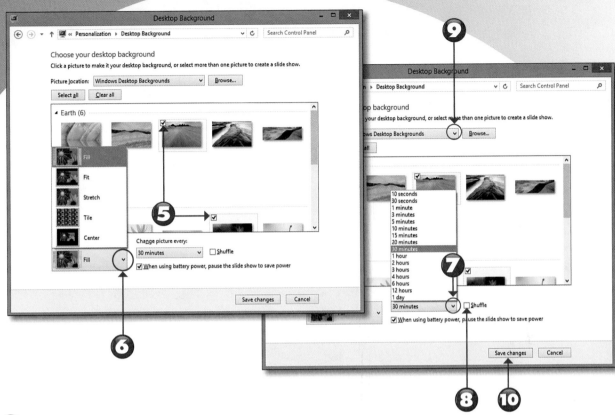

5 Click empty checkboxes to select images.

6 Open to select the picture position.

7 Open to select how often to change the picture.

8 Click to shuffle pictures.

9 Open to select other backgrounds.

10 Click **Save changes**.

End

TIP

Need More Background Choices? If you are not satisfied with the standard desktop backgrounds, use the Browse button to locate a picture folder as a background source. You also can select a solid color for the desktop. ■

SELECTING A STANDARD WINDOW COLOR

The Personalization window also includes options for selecting your preferred window and taskbar color. Here's how to choose your favorite.

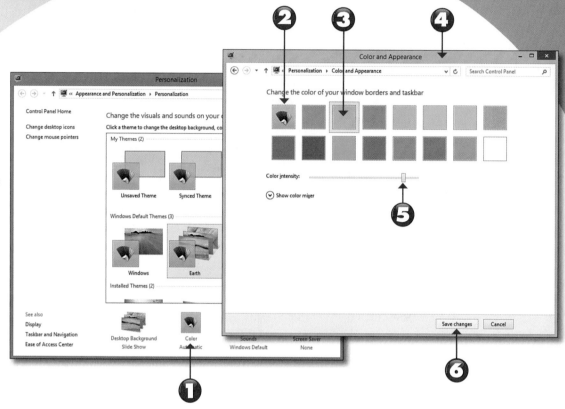

Start

1 Click **Color**.

2 Automatic is the default selection.

3 Click a different color.

4 You can see a preview of the selected color on the window's title bar.

5 Adjust the slider to lessen (left) or increase (right) color intensity.

6 Click **Save changes**.

End

CREATING A CUSTOMIZED WINDOW COLOR

The Color and Appearance window also includes a color mixer. Here's how to create and select a custom window and taskbar color.

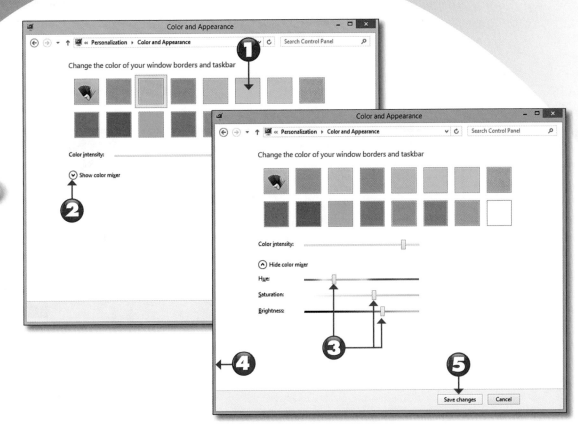

Start

1. From the Color and Appearance window (see previous task), select a standard color.

2. Click **Show color mixer**.

3. Adjust the **Hue**, **Saturation**, and **Brightness** sliders.

4. The window (and title bar) color changes in real time as you adjust sliders.

5. Click **Save changes**.

End

TIP

Starting Over with Another Color To abandon your changes, click Cancel in step 5. To use a different color, click any color desired and continue from step 1. ■

SELECTING A SCREEN SAVER

The Windows 8 screen saver function helps to protect the privacy of your display when you're away from your computer. This feature also helps to prevent an image being permanently burned into your screen—still a concern if you use a plasma HDTV with your computer. This tutorial shows you how to select and customize your favorite screen saver from the Personalization window.

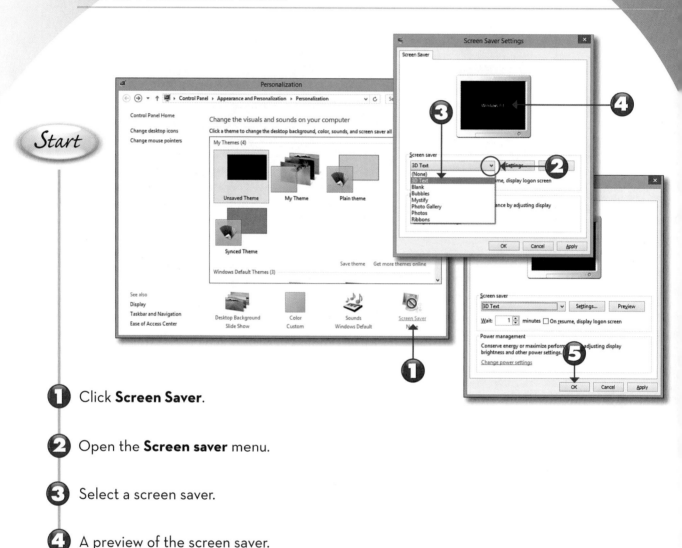

1. Click **Screen Saver**.

2. Open the **Screen saver** menu.

3. Select a screen saver.

4. A preview of the screen saver.

5. Click **OK**.

TIP

Keeping Your System Secure with Screen Saver You can also select an option to display your logon screen after the screen saver works. Enable this option in the Screen Saver Settings dialog box if you use your computer where someone might want to snoop around its contents. ■

SAVING A DESKTOP THEME

A desktop theme is the combination of desktop background, window color, sound effects, and screen saver. After you have made changes to any or all of these settings, you can save your selections as a new theme from the Personalization window. Here's how.

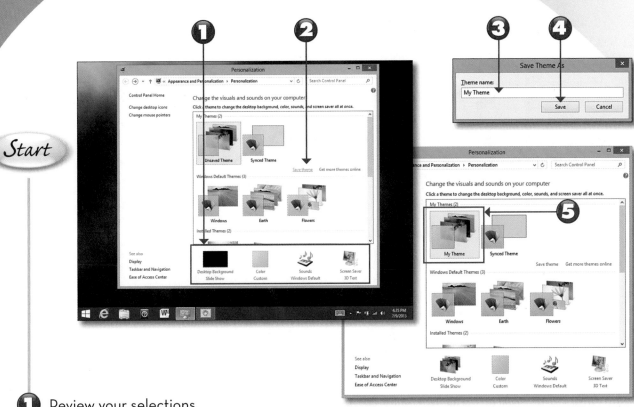

1 Review your selections.

2 Click **Save theme**.

3 Type a name for the theme.

4 Click **Save**.

5 Your new theme, as it appears in the Personalization window.

NOTE

Choosing Sound Effects for Your Theme You can select different sound effects for Windows events by clicking the Sounds option shown in step 1 and selecting different sounds for listed actions. The sound scheme you select is also saved as part of your theme. If you download a theme, custom sound effects might be included as part of the theme. ■

MANAGING DEVICES AND PRINTERS FROM THE WINDOWS DESKTOP

If you need to diagnose device problems, update software for a device, or manage devices and printers, use Control Panel's Devices and Printers window. In this example, we use the Devices and Printers window to adjust mouse settings.

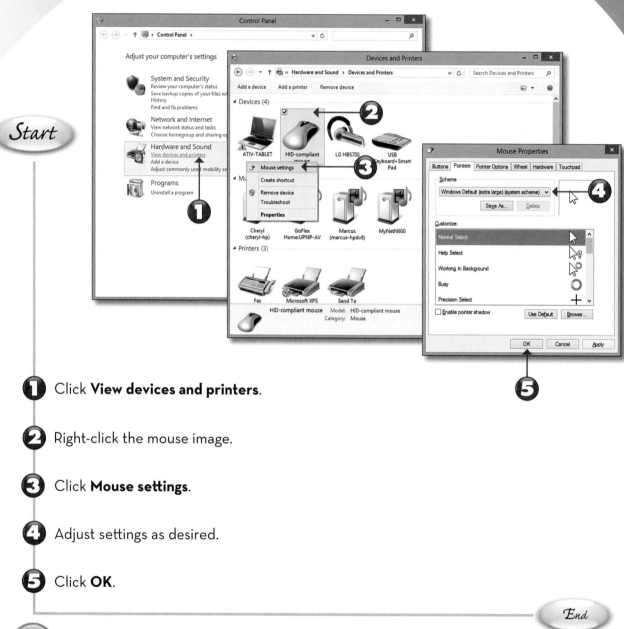

1. Click **View devices and printers**.

2. Right-click the mouse image.

3. Click **Mouse settings**.

4. Adjust settings as desired.

5. Click **OK**.

NOTE

Menu Options Vary with the Device You Select The options next to Add a Device and Add a Printer above the Devices section of the window change according to the item you select. For example, if you select the optical drive, you can also eject the media or adjust AutoPlay settings. ■

SEEING WHAT PROGRAMS ARE RUNNING WITH TASK MANAGER

You can have many programs running at the same time with Windows 8.1, even if you see only one program window visible. To find out what programs and apps are running at a given moment, you can open the Windows Task Manager from the Windows desktop. Here's how.

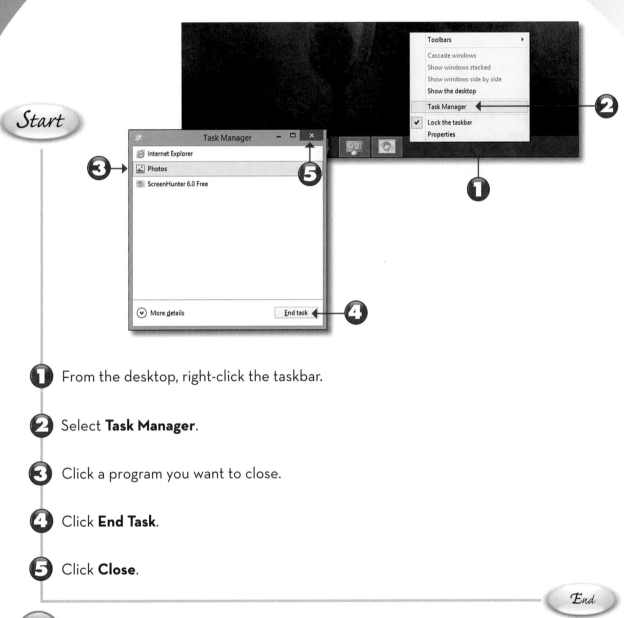

1 From the desktop, right-click the taskbar.

2 Select **Task Manager**.

3 Click a program you want to close.

4 Click **End Task**.

5 Click **Close**.

NOTE

Starting Task Manager the Old-Fashioned Way If you are using a non-touchscreen computer, you might prefer to press the Ctrl+Alt+Delete keys at the same time as step 1 and select Task Manager from the menu that appears in step 2. ■

Chapter 22

USER ACCOUNTS AND SYSTEM SECURITY

Windows 8 provides new ways to log in to your system, keep it secure, and monitor what younger members of the family are doing. Like its predecessors, Windows 8 is designed to support multiple users, and with features such as Administrator, Standard, and Windows 8.1's new Child accounts and Family Safety, you can provide users of different ages and capabilities just the right level of access to Windows 8 features and the Internet.

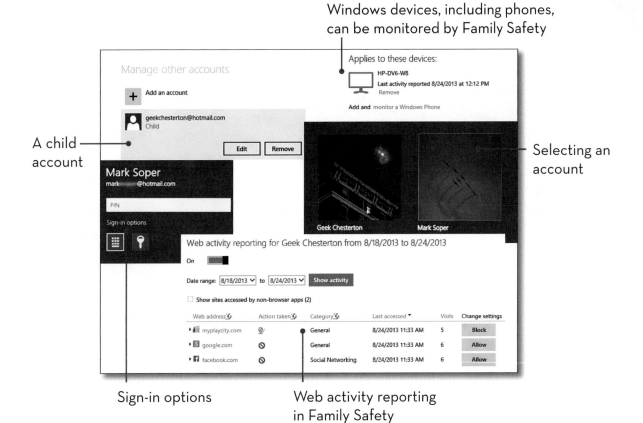

Windows devices, including phones, can be monitored by Family Safety

A child account

Selecting an account

Sign-in options

Web activity reporting in Family Safety

SETTING UP WINDOWS 8 FOR MULTIPLE USERS

A Windows 8 computer always has at least one user account; however, if you share your computer with other users at home or work, each user should have his or her own account. By using this feature, Windows 8 can provide customized settings for each user. As this lesson shows, this task is performed from the Windows 8 Start screen.

Start

1 Open the Charms menu.

2 Click **Settings**.

3 Click **Change PC settings**.

4 Click **Accounts**.

Continued

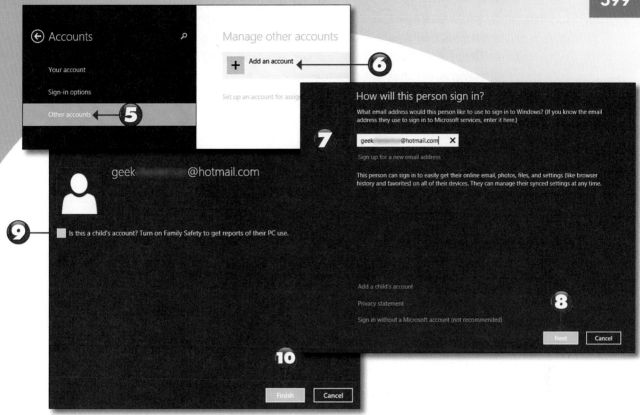

5 Click **Other accounts**.

6 Click **Add an account**.

7 Enter the user's email address.

8 Click **Next**.

9 Click this box if you want this account to be monitored and controlled by Family Safety.

10 Click **Finish**.

End

NOTE

Family Safe and a Child's Accounts In Windows 8.1, the Family Safety feature is designed to monitor and manage a child's accounts. If you didn't click the checkbox in step 9, you can turn a standard account into a child's account by editing account settings. ∎

CHANGING AN ACCOUNT TYPE

When you create an additional user account in Windows 8, it's a standard account. However, if you want another user's account to be set as administrator of the computer or as a child's account, you can change that user's account type. Here's how.

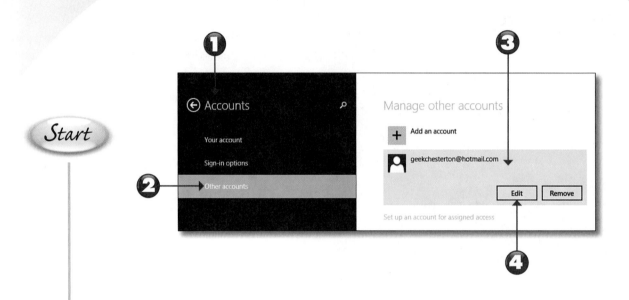

Start

1 Open the Accounts menu (refer to the previous task).

2 Click **Other accounts**.

3 Select the account to change.

4 Select **Edit**.

Continued

NOTE

Using Assigned Access Use the **Set up an account for assigned access** link shown in steps 3 and 4 if you want an account to be limited to a single task, such as running a presentation. ■

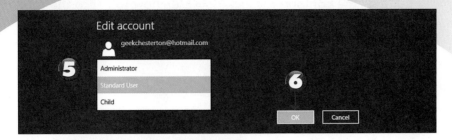

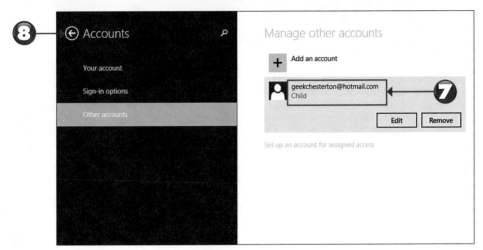

5 Select the account type desired.

6 Click **OK**.

7 The new account type is now listed.

8 Click the back arrow key to return to PC settings.

End

NOTE

Standard, Administrator, and Child Accounts A standard account can use the computer for most tasks but needs administrator permission (specifically, an admin password) to complete tasks that could change the computer. An administrator account can perform all tasks. A child account is similar to a standard account but can also be monitored by Windows' Family Safety features. ■

NOTE

Why You Might Need Two Administrators When would you want to create more than one administrator account for a computer? There might be times when the original administrator is not available while the computer is in use, and when systemwide changes need to be made—such as new programs or hardware installations. Be sure that the user you select is trustworthy and not likely to mess around with the computer just for fun. ■

SELECTING AN ACCOUNT TO LOG IN TO

After you add one or more additional users, Windows 8 offers you a choice of accounts at startup or whenever the computer is locked. Here's how to get to the account selection screen.

Start

11:44
Saturday, August 24

①

Geek Chesterton
geek   @hotmail.com **②**
Password

③

① Press any key (such as the spacebar) or tap the screen (if you have a touchscreen).

② If the account you want is displayed, log in as usual.

③ If the account is not displayed, click the left arrow.

Continued

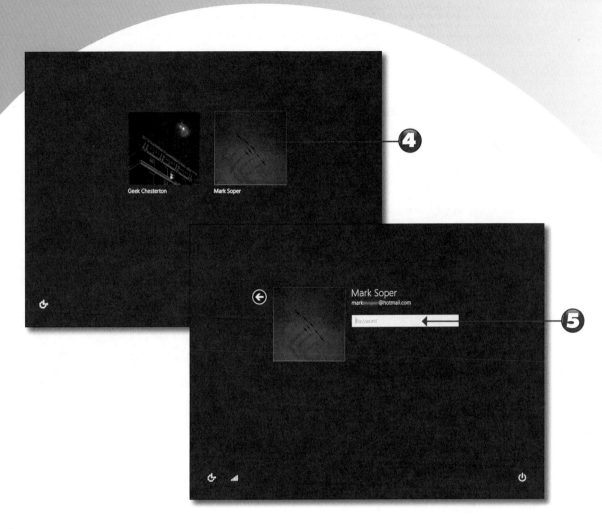

4 Click the account you want to log in to.

5 Log in to the selected account.

End

SETTING UP PIN NUMBER ACCESS

Windows 8 enables users with Microsoft accounts to set up a PIN number as an alternative to a regular password. You must set a regular password before you can set up PIN number access. Using a PIN number for login can be easier for tablet users or users with limited typing ability. Here's how to do it.

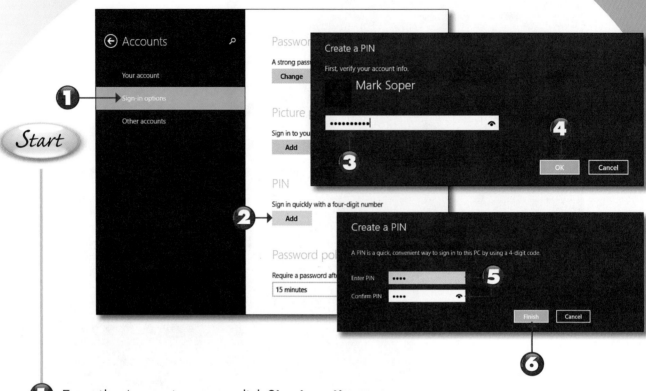

Start

1 From the Accounts screen, click **Sign-in options**.

2 Click **Add** in the PIN section of the dialog box.

3 Enter your password.

4 Click **OK**.

5 Enter and reenter a four-digit PIN.

6 Click **Finish**.

Continued

7 The Sign-in options dialog now provides the options to change or remove the account's PIN.

8 Type your PIN in the login screen.

9 Click to display sign-in options.

10 Click to use a password for login.

End

CONFIGURING PARENTAL CONTROLS WITH FAMILY SAFETY

Windows 8 enables you to keep a watchful eye on how children use a computer through its Parental Controls (Family Safety) feature. Here's how to configure this feature from the Control Panel. To access Control Panel, see steps 1 and 2 of "Opening the Network and Internet Window in Control Panel," p. 308, Chapter 18.

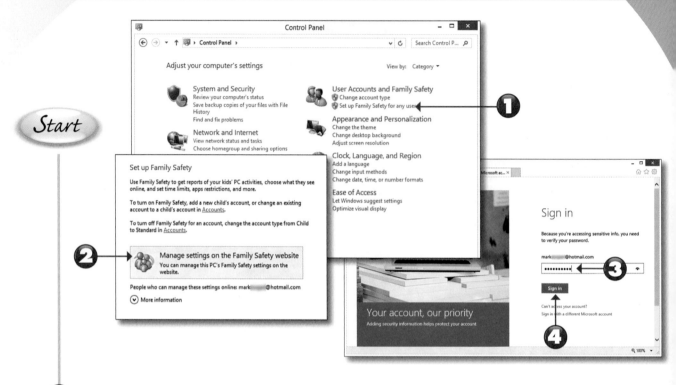

1 Click **Set up Family Safety for any user**.

2 Click **Manage settings on the Family Safety website**.

3 Enter your password.

4 Click **Sign in**.

Continued

NOTE

Family Safety Settings Vary By Account Each child account on a PC can be set up with different Family Safety settings. ■

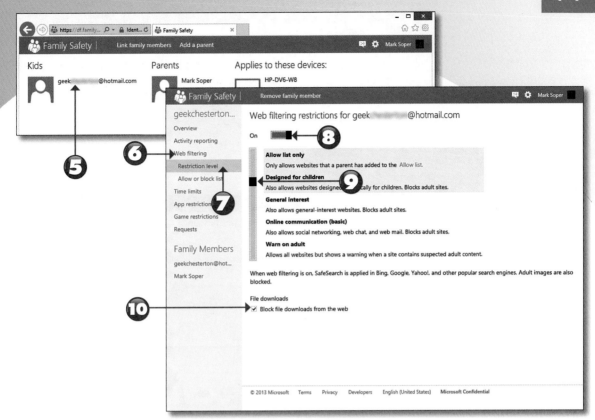

5 Click a child's account.

6 Click **Web filtering**.

7 Click **Restriction level**.

8 Turn on web filtering.

9 Drag to set the web filtering level.

10 Click the empty checkbox to block file downloads.

Continued

NOTE

Dealing with Blocked Websites, Games, or Apps When a child account attempts to access a blocked website, game, or app, a dialog box appears. The parent can provide their account password to bypass the block, but if the parent isn't home, the child can send a request via email. With a website block, the child is also directed to kid-friendly websites. ■

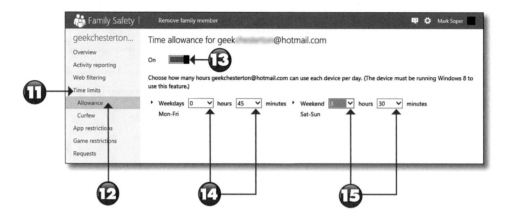

11 Click **Time limits**.

12 Click **Allowance**.

13 Turn on time allowance.

14 Select hours and minutes per weekday.

15 Select hours and minutes per weekend day.

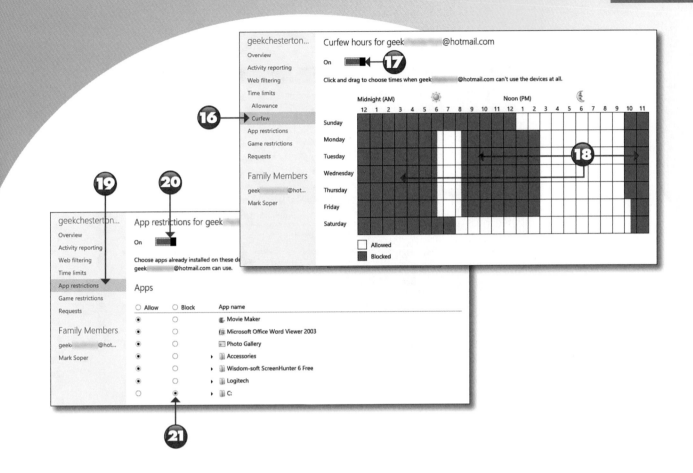

16 Click **Curfew**.

17 Turn on this setting.

18 Click and drag across the calendar to specify blocked time periods (shown in blue).

19 Click **App restrictions**.

20 Turn on this setting.

21 Click **Block** to block an app.

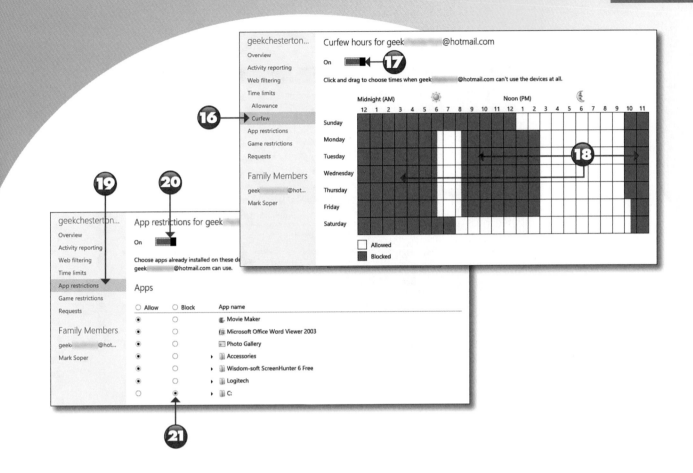

Continued

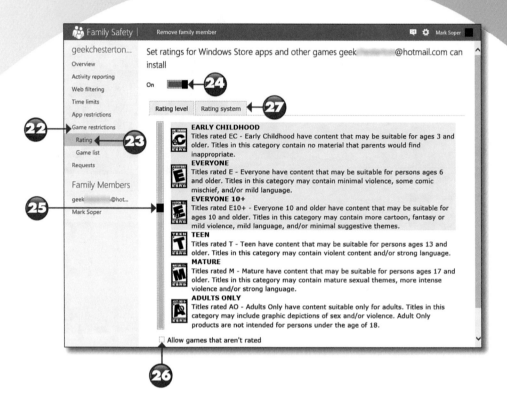

22 Click **Game restrictions**.

23 Click **Rating**.

24 Turn on this setting.

25 Drag the rating level to highlight the highest game rating allowed.

26 Click the empty checkbox to permit the child to play games without a rating.

27 Click to select a different rating system.

Continued

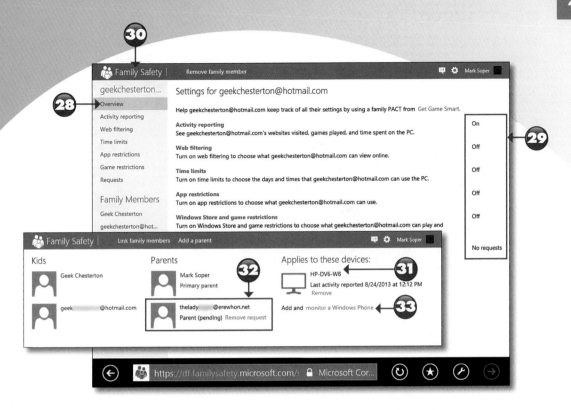

28 Click **Overview**.

29 Current settings.

30 Click to return to the main Family Safety window.

31 The current device.

32 Pending request for a parent.

33 Click to add a Windows phone.

End

NOTE

Adding a Parent Step 30 shows a request made to an additional parent to manage Family Safety. To add a parent, click the link, enter the parent's email address, and click Send request. As soon as the parent accepts the request, that parent will receive notifications from Family Safety. ■

NOTE

Closing Family Safety When finished, close the browser window. ■

REVIEWING FAMILY SAFETY LOGS

When you enable Family Safety monitoring for an account, you can view activity reports from PC Settings' Accounts dialog or through Control Panel. In this tutorial, we cover using the PC Settings method.

Start

① From the Settings charm, select PC Settings and click **Accounts**.

② Click **Other accounts**.

③ Click **Manage Family Safety settings online**.

④ Click a user monitored by Family Safety.

Continued

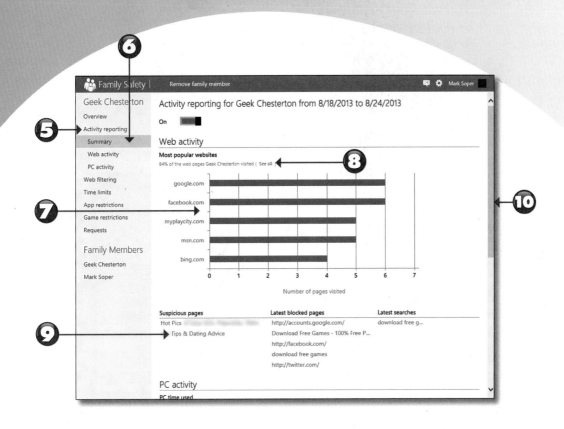

5 Click **Activity reporting**.

6 Click **Summary**.

7 The summary screen shows you an overview of the activities.

8 Click to see all web pages visited.

9 Click an item to see details.

10 Scroll down to see more categories.

Continued

NOTE

Changing Date Ranges If no activity is displayed, change
the date range on the Web activity or PC activity tabs. ■

11 Click **Web activity**.

12 Adjust the time periods to choose a date range to view.

13 Click to show activity.

14 Current settings for listed websites; click to change.

Continued

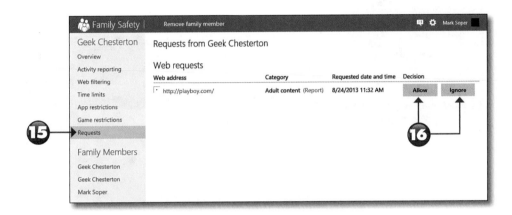

 Click **Requests**.

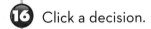 Click a decision.

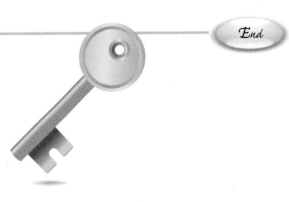

End

SETTING UP AND USING A PICTURE PASSWORD

Windows 8 not only gives you a choice of account types and the option to type in your password or a PIN number, but if you have a touchscreen computer, tablet, or multitouch-enabled touchpad, you can also create a picture password. This tutorial starts in the Accounts screen.

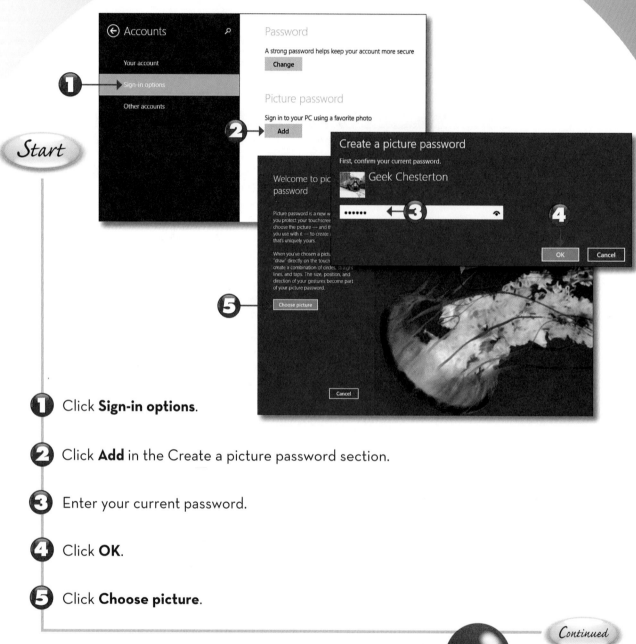

1 Click **Sign-in options**.

2 Click **Add** in the Create a picture password section.

3 Enter your current password.

4 Click **OK**.

5 Click **Choose picture**.

Continued

TIP

Passwords First, Then Picture Passwords You cannot create a picture password for an account until a regular password has been created. ■

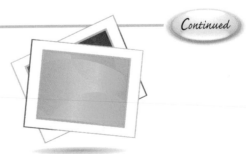

6 Click a folder.

7 Select a photo.

8 Click **Open**.

9 Click the photo and drag it into the desired position.

10 Click **Use this picture**.

Continued

11 Draw three gestures (taps, circles, or straight lines) on your touch surface.

12 Confirm your gestures.

Continued

NOTE

Your Picture, Your Choice In this example, we used one of each of the allowable gestures (tap, circle, and straight line). You can use any combination of these gestures that you want, but they must be performed in the same order and on the same areas of the picture. ▪

13 Click **Finish**.

14 On the next login screen, log in using the picture password gestures.

15 Click **Switch to password** if you prefer not to use the picture password.

End

TIP

Changing or Removing Your Picture Password Return to the Accounts section of the PC Settings screen if you want to change or remove your picture password. ■

Chapter 23

PROTECTING YOUR SYSTEM

Today's computers and storage devices don't cost much to buy or replace, but the information you store on them—from documents to photos, video, and music—is priceless. In this chapter, you learn about a variety of easy-to-use features in Windows 8 that are designed to help you protect your computer's contents.

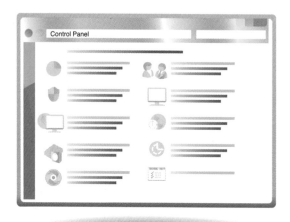

File history after
being turned on

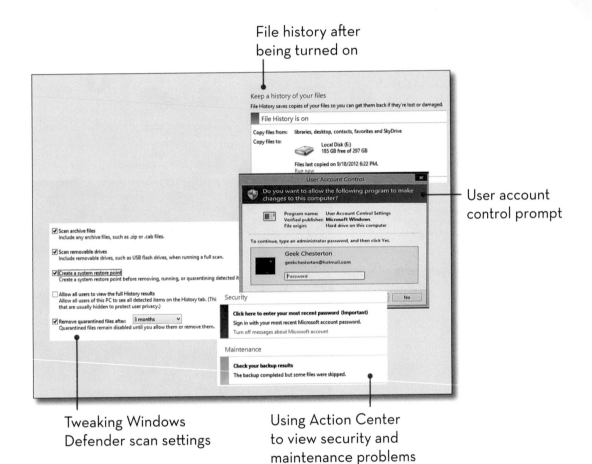

User account
control prompt

Tweaking Windows
Defender scan settings

Using Action Center
to view security and
maintenance problems

LOOKING AT USER ACCOUNT CONTROL

The User Account Control (UAC) feature helps protect your system from unwanted changes. Program installations and Windows tasks marked with a shield might prompt an administrator to approve the operation. They also will prompt a standard user to get permission from an administrator to perform that task. Here's how User Account Control works and what the prompts look like.

Start

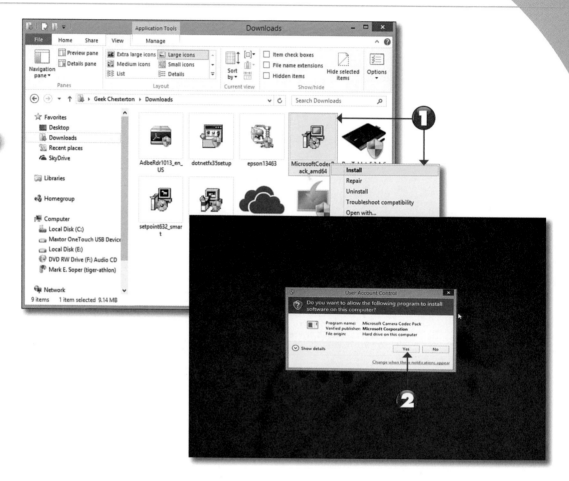

1 If you are logged in as administrator, right-click a downloaded program file and select Install.

2 The UAC dialog box appears. Click **Yes** to continue.

Continued

NOTE

Changing UAC Settings The normal (default) UAC settings are suitable for most systems; however, UAC settings can be modified in Control Panel. Click the Change User Account Control Settings link under Action Center in Control Panel's System and Security window (see step 3). ■

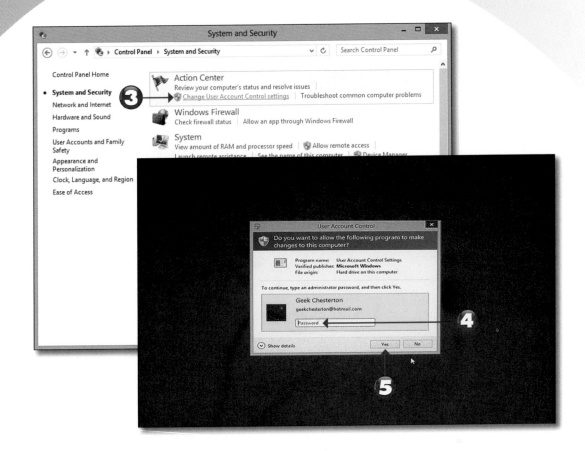

3 If you are logged in as a standard user, click a task marked with a shield.

4 Enter the administrator password.

5 Click **Yes** to continue.

End

NOTE

Two Administrators, No Waiting If your system has two or more administrators, you will see each administrator listed in the UAC dialog box shown in steps 4 and 5. You need only one administrator password to continue. ■

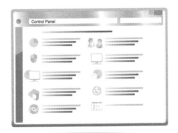

CONFIGURING WINDOWS UPDATE

Windows Update is normally set to automatically download and install updates to Microsoft Windows 8 and to other Microsoft apps such as Office. However, you can change the default settings if you need to install updates on your own schedule. Here's how to tweak Windows Update settings from the Control Panel.

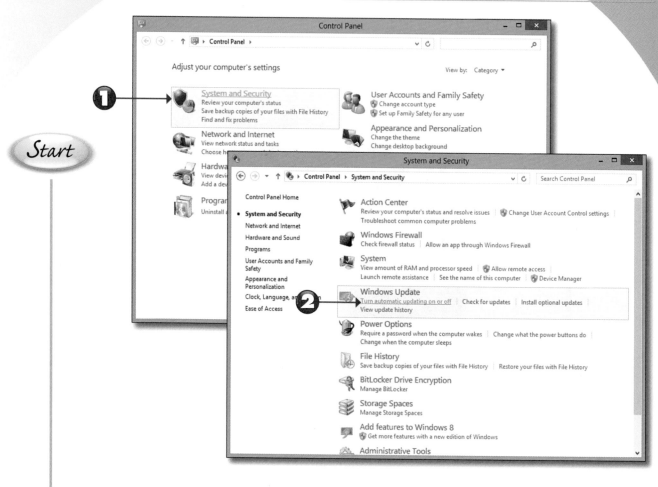

1 Click **System and Security**.

2 Click **Turn automatic updating on or off**.

NOTE

When Changing from Automatic Updates Makes Sense If you connect remotely with your computer or your computer runs backups on a regular basis, keep in mind that some Windows updates will cause the computer to reboot. This can prevent these operations from taking place. In those situations, it makes sense to control when updates will be installed. ■

Continued

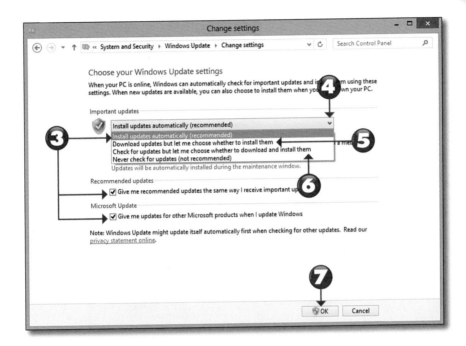

3 Notice the default Windows Update settings.

4 Click to change the automatic update setting.

5 Choose this option if you want to specify when your system is updated.

6 Choose this option if you want to specify whether to download updates.

7 Click **OK** to accept and use your settings.

End

CAUTION

The No Updates Option Is Not Recommended The dialog box shown in steps 3–7 also includes an option to Never Check for Updates. This option is intended primarily for corporate computers whose updates are managed centrally. At home or in a small office, let Windows figure out when to download your updates. ■

PROTECTING YOUR FILES WITH FILE HISTORY

Previous versions of Windows included a variety of backup programs, but many users never back up their files. Windows 8's new File History feature makes backing up files in your libraries, favorites, and contacts easy to set up and make automatic. Now, there's no reason to worry about losing your files. Here's how it works.

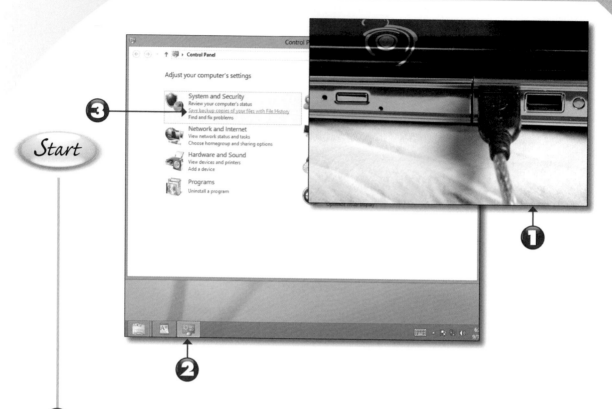

Start

3

2

1 Connect an external hard disk to your computer.

2 Open Control Panel.

3 Click **Save backup copies of your files with File History**.

Continued

TIP
Tweaking File History To adjust how often to save files, how much disk space (offline cache) to use, or how long to keep files in File History, click the Advanced Settings link shown in the left pane of the File History window. ■

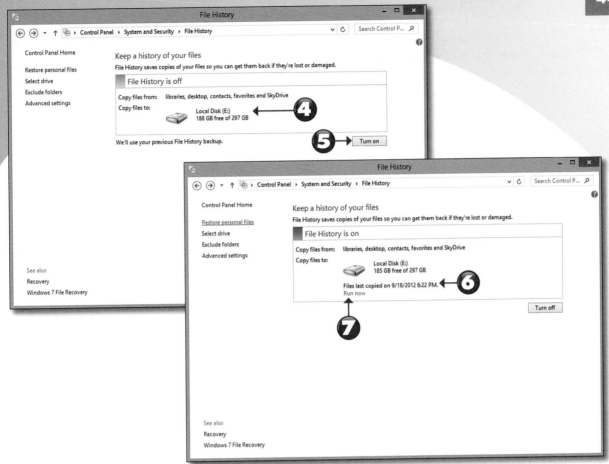

4 The drive recommended by File History.

5 Click **Turn on**.

6 File History backs up your files.

7 Click **Run now** to run File History again immediately.

End

TIP

Choosing Your Preferred Drive If you have more than one external hard disk, the drive selected by File History might not be the one you want to use. Use the Select Drive link in the left pane of the File History window to choose a particular drive before turning on File History. ■

NOTE

Recommending This Drive to Your HomeGroup If your computer is connected to a HomeGroup, you will see a prompt asking whether you want to recommend this drive to other members of the HomeGroup. Click Yes if you want other HomeGroup members to use the drive for File History; otherwise, click No. Clicking the No option is recommended if you expect to use most of the drive's capacity for the computer to which it is connected. ■

RECOVERING FILES WITH FILE HISTORY

File History creates backups of your files so if a file is erased or damaged, you can get it back. If you haven't yet enabled File History in Windows 8, refer to "Protecting Your Files with File History," earlier in this chapter. Here's how to retrieve a lost file or folder.

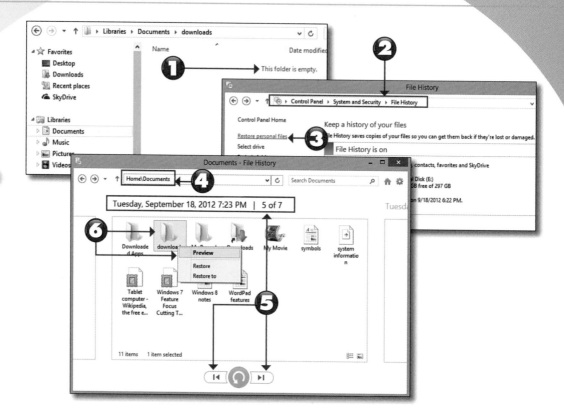

Start

1. The contents of a folder called downloads, in the Documents folder, have been accidentally deleted.

2. Open **File History** from the Control Panel.

3. Click **Restore personal files**.

4. Navigate to the folder's original location.

5. Select a version to restore.

6. Right-click the folder and select **Preview**.

Continued

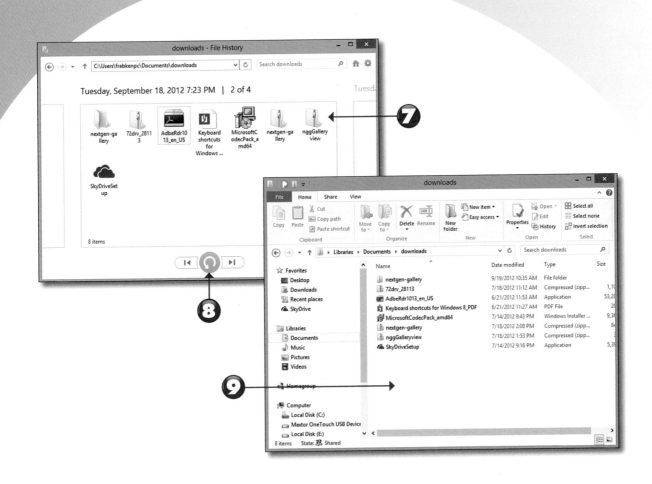

7 The folder opens. Review its contents to make sure it contains what you want to restore.

8 Click the green **Restore** button.

9 File Explorer opens. The folder and its contents are returned to their original location.

End

NOTE

Restore Options To restore the folder or file to a different location, select the Restore to option in step 6, and then specify the location. ■

TIP

Restoring Selected Files To restore only selected files, click the first file you want to restore, and then use Ctrl+Click to select additional files. Click the Restore button—only the files you selected will be restored. ■

CHECKING SECURITY SETTINGS WITH WINDOWS ACTION CENTER

Windows Action Center keeps an alert eye on security and maintenance issues that might happen and gives you specific instructions on how to fix them. Here's how to use Windows Action Center to keep your system safe.

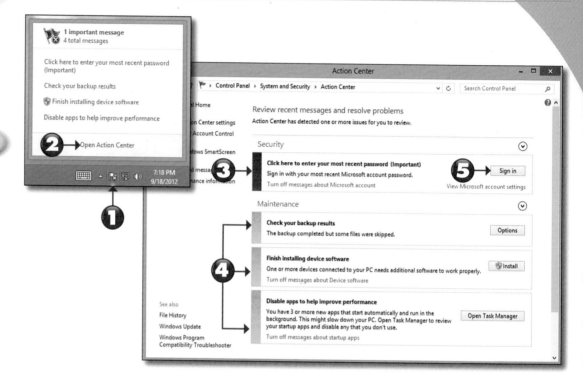

Start

1. Click the **Windows Action Center** icon in the notification area of the taskbar.

2. Click **Open Action Center** for more information.

3. Important issues are marked with a red banner.

4. Other problems are marked with a yellow banner.

5. Click the action button to solve the problem listed.

Continued

NOTE

Running Action Center from Control Panel You don't need to wait for a warning to run Action Center. It's available from the System and Security section of the Control Panel. ∎

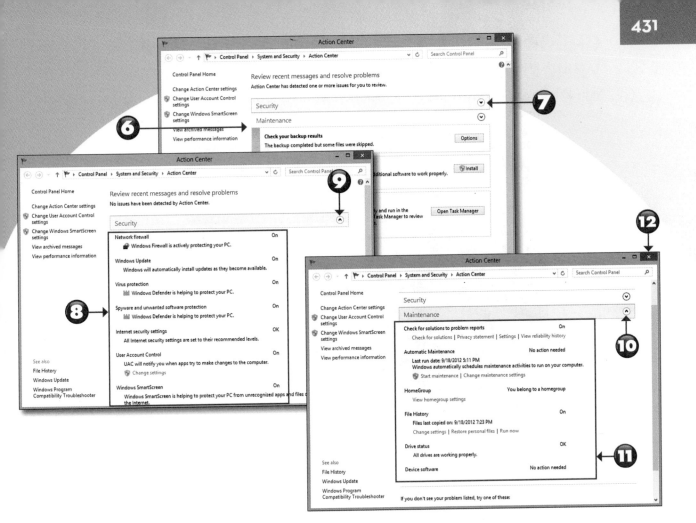

6 After you resolve the problem, the problem is removed from the list.

7 Click to see other security items monitored by Action Center.

8 The status of monitored security items.

9 Click to collapse the Security category.

10 Click to expand the Maintenance category.

11 The status of Maintenance items.

12 Click **Close**.

End

CHECKING FOR VIRUSES AND SPYWARE WITH WINDOWS DEFENDER

The Windows Defender program included with Windows 8 provides protection against spyware, viruses, and malware. Here's how to open Windows Defender and run a scan.

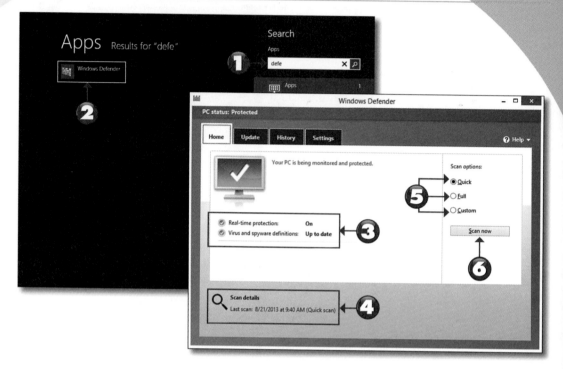

Start

1 From the Start screen, type **defe** and Windows Search opens automatically.

2 Click **Windows Defender**.

3 The current status.

4 The last scan details.

5 Choose a scan type.

6 Click **Scan now** to start a scan.

End

NOTE

Updating Windows Defender If Windows Defender displays a message that its definitions are out of date, use the Update tab to install updates. ∎

SETTING WINDOWS DEFENDER OPTIONS

Windows Defender's normal (default) options provide suitable protection for most users, but if you want to check additional locations for malware or make other changes to Windows Defender settings, this lesson shows you how.

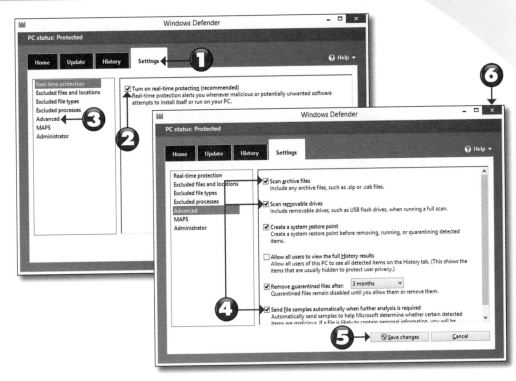

Start

1 From Windows Defender, click the **Settings** tab.

2 Make sure the Real-Time Protection box is checked.

3 Click **Advanced**.

4 If these boxes are empty, click them to enable these settings.

5 Click **Save changes**.

6 Click **Close**.

End

NOTE

Turning on Real-time Protection If Windows Defender's real-time protection is disabled, use the Settings tab to turn it on unless you use another antivirus or antimalware program. ∎

Chapter 24

SYSTEM MAINTENANCE AND PERFORMANCE

Windows includes a wide variety of features that help your system to run at peak performance. Some of these programs were first introduced in Windows 8, while others are familiar from Windows 7 and earlier versions, such as System Restore and Disk Cleanup. In this chapter, you learn how to keep your computer system running at peak performance.

Hardware details from
Windows System Information

Windows 8.1
warns about
a drive with
problems

Creating
a task

Preparing to
run System
Restore

Preparing to run
Windows Memory
Diagnostics

Refreshing your PC

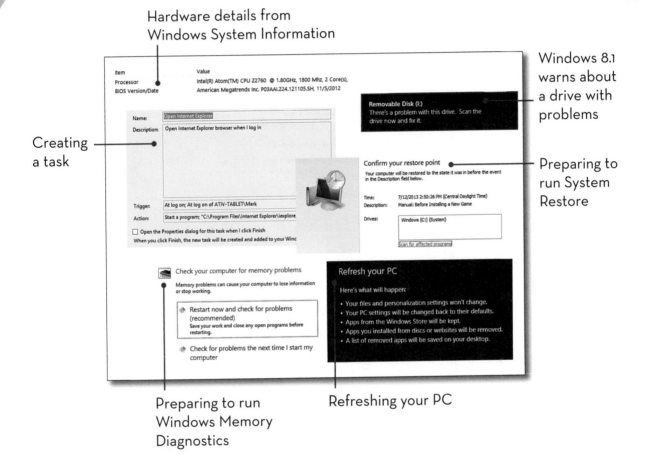

SELECTING A POWER SCHEME

You can select a power scheme in Windows that will stretch battery life as far as possible or keep your system running at top speed all the time. Here's how to select the power scheme you want from the Windows desktop.

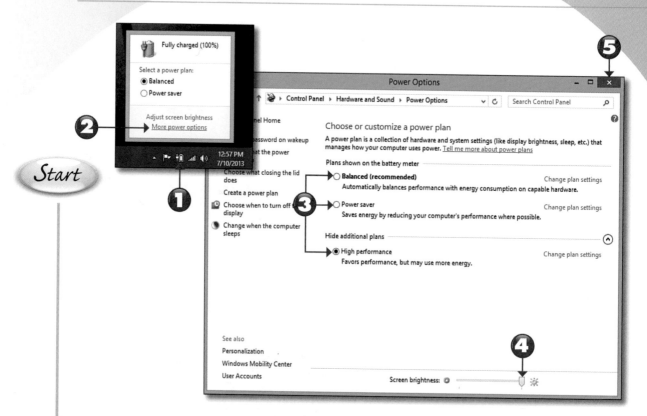

Start

① If you have a laptop or tablet computer, click the **power** (battery meter) icon in the notification area of the Windows desktop.

② The most common power options are shown. To see additional options, click **More power options**.

③ Choose a plan setting from those listed.

④ To adjust screen brightness, use the slider.

⑤ Close the dialog when finished.

End

NOTE

Paths to Power Options Power Options is also available from the System and Security section of Control Panel. Use this method to adjust power options for a desktop computer. ∎

VIEWING DISK INFORMATION

How much space is left on your drive? What drive letter does your external hard disk use? Use the This PC view in File Explorer for answers to these and other questions about the drives built in to and connected to your computer.

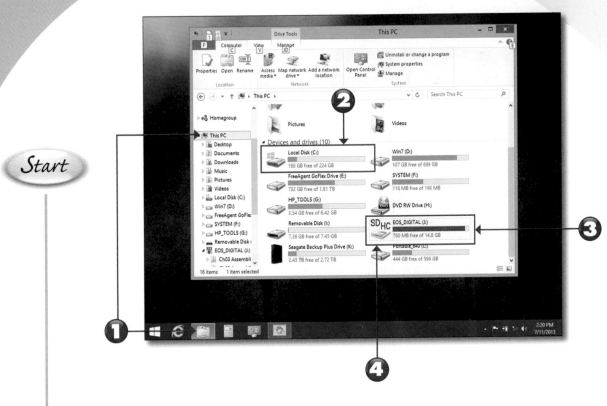

Start

1 Open File Explorer and click **This PC**.

2 The blue bar indicates how much used space the disk has.

3 The red bar indicates the drive has 10% or less free space.

4 Double-click a drive to see what folders it contains.

End

NOTE

Using the View Tab If you do not see red and blue bars for drive capacity, open the View tab and select Tiles from the Layout menu. ∎

NOTE

Drive Tools Click a drive to display the Drive Tools tab. Click this tab to access options for setting up BitLocker disk encryption (Windows 8.1 Pro only), Optimize, Cleanup, Format, AutoPlay, Eject, Erase, Finish Burning, and Erase this disc. Some options are available only with optical media. ∎

CHECKING DRIVES FOR ERRORS

Windows watches the drives connected to your system for errors. If an error is detected, you will see a message. Here's what to do next.

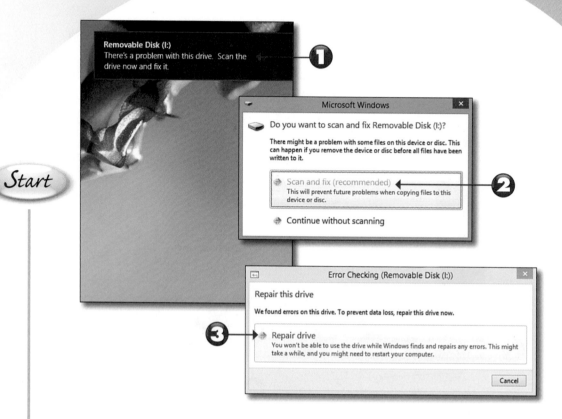

Removable Disk (I:)
There's a problem with this drive. Scan the drive now and fix it.

1

Microsoft Windows ☒

Do you want to scan and fix Removable Disk (I:)?

There might be a problem with some files on this device or disc. This can happen if you remove the device or disc before all files have been written to it.

> ● Scan and fix (recommended)
>   This will prevent future problems when copying files to this device or disc.

2

● Continue without scanning

Error Checking (Removable Disk (I:)) ☒

Repair this drive

We found errors on this drive. To prevent data loss, repair this drive now.

3

> ● Repair drive
>   You won't be able to use the drive while Windows finds and repairs any errors. This might take a while, and you might need to restart your computer.

Cancel

Start

① This just-inserted flash drive has a problem—click the notification.

② Click **Scan and fix**.

③ Click **Repair drive**.

Continued

4 View the results. On drives with minor errors, you might see a message like this one.

5 If the drive has significant problems, click **Show Details**.

6 Click **Close**.

End

NOTE

Miss the Notification? No Problem! The notification window shown in step 1 stays on-screen for just a few seconds. If it disappears before you can click it, right-click or press and hold a drive until its context menu opens. Select Properties, and then click the Tools tab. Error-checking is available from the Tools tab. ■

USING WINDOWS TROUBLESHOOTERS

Windows includes a number of troubleshooters you can run from Control Panel to help solve problems with your system. Here's how to use a troubleshooter to fix an audio playback problem. In this example, the speakers were muted.

Start

1 Click **Find and fix problems** in Control Panel.

2 Click **Troubleshoot audio playback**.

3 Click **Next**.

Continued

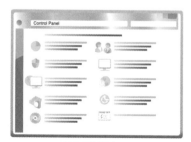

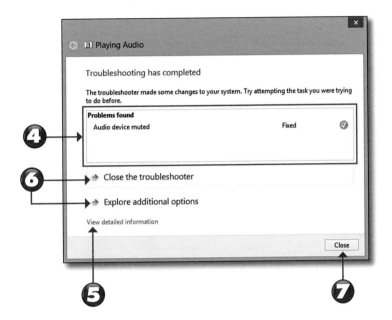

4 Review the results.

5 Click to see more detailed information.

6 Choose an option to complete the task.

7 Click **Close** to close the window.

End

NOTE

Making Changes Yourself If you need to turn on a device or make other changes, you will be prompted to do so after step 3. ■

USING SYSTEM RESTORE

If you made a recent change to your system, such as installing a new program or a new device, and problems began after the installation, the System Restore feature can help get your system back into working condition. To see how to access this and other advanced options at startup, refer to step 6 in the previous task, "Opening the Troubleshoot Startup Menu." In this section, you learn how to run System Restore from Control Panel.

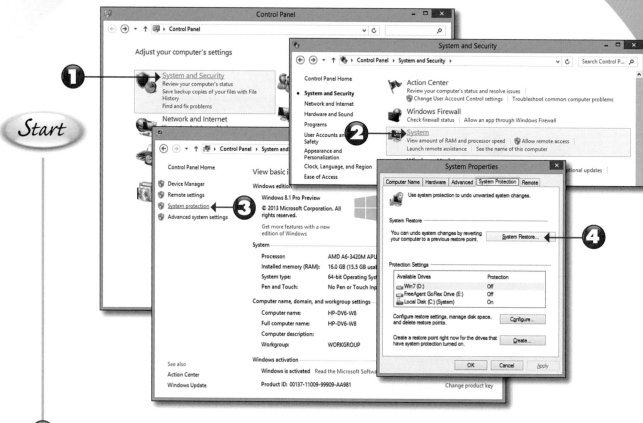

1 From the Control Panel, click **System and Security**.

2 Click **System**.

3 Click **System Protection**.

4 Click **System Restore**.

Continued

NOTE

Create Your Own Restore Point If you are planning to install new hardware or software, don't assume that Windows 8/8.1 will create a restore point for you before the process begins. Use the Create button shown in step 4 to create a restore point manually before you make changes to your system. ■

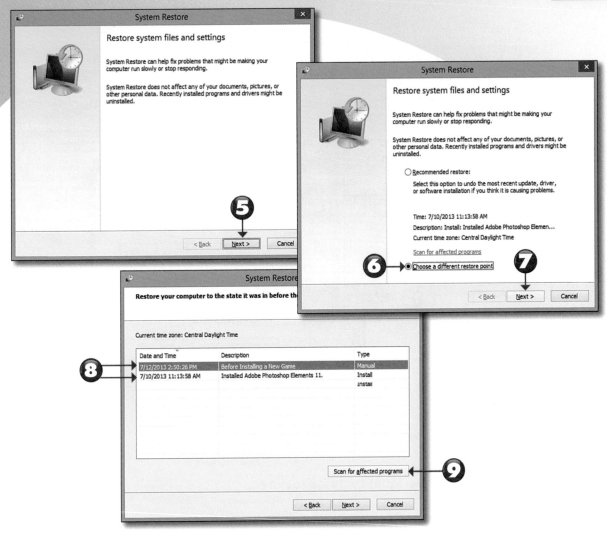

5 Click **Next** if you see this introductory dialog. Skip to step 6 if you don't see this dialog.

6 Click **Choose a different restore point**.

7 Click **Next**.

8 Select a restore point.

9 Click **Scan for affected programs**.

Continued

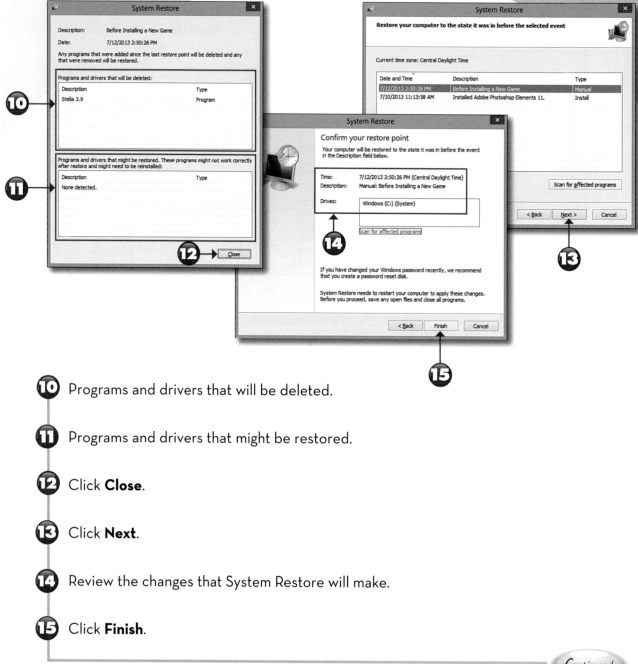

10 Programs and drivers that will be deleted.

11 Programs and drivers that might be restored.

12 Click **Close**.

13 Click **Next**.

14 Review the changes that System Restore will make.

15 Click **Finish**.

NOTE

System Restore and Changes to Your System The programs and drivers listed in step 10 are those installed after the restore point you selected in step 8. The programs and drivers listed in step 11 might need to be reinstalled. ■

Continued

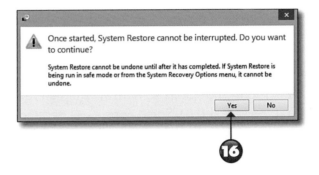

16 Click **Yes**. Your system restarts.

17 After your computer starts, System Restore displays a status report on the Windows desktop indicating success or failure.

18 Click **Close**.

End

NOTE

Undoing System Restore If System Restore indicates that it didn't work correctly in step 18, you can undo it by running System Restore again and selecting the Undo option when it is presented. ■

Glossary

Use this section to bring your-self up to speed on important concepts and terms relating to Windows and to your computer. Definition terms that appear in *italics* are also listed in the glossary.

A

Accelerator A feature of Internet Explorer 10 and 11 that enables you to highlight text in a web document and map, search, or perform other activities using that text without opening up a separate browser window.

access point Device on a Wi-Fi network that provides a connection between computers on the network. Can be combined with a router and a switch.

administrator Windows term for the manager of a given computer or network; only users in the administrator's group can perform some management tasks. Other users must provide an administrator's name and password for tasks marked with the Windows security shield icon.

App Program that runs from the Modern UI (Start screen) in Windows 8 and 8.1. Some apps are preinstalled, while others are available from the Windows Store.

application program Program used to create, modify, and store information you create. Micro-soft Word, Adobe Photoshop, and CorelDRAW are all applica-tion programs.

B

backup Making a copy of a file for safekeeping, especially with a special program that must be used to restore the backup when needed; backups can be compressed to save space. Full backup backs up the entire contents of the specified drive or system; a differential backup backs up only the files that have changed since the last full backup.

Bluetooth A short-range wire-less networking standard that supports non-PC devices such as mobile phones and PDAs, as well as PCs. Bluetooth uses frequencies ranging from 2.402 to 2.480GHz with a range up to

about 30 feet. Data transmis-sion runs at 1Mbps or 2Mbps, depending on the version of the technology supported by the devices. Windows 8 includes Bluetooth support.

boot Starting the computer. A *warm boot* is restarting the com-puter without a reset or shut-down. A *cold boot* is shutdown or reset before startup.

boot disk A disk with operat-ing system files needed to start the computer. Windows 8 and 8.1 DVDs are bootable, as is the Recovery Drive you can create with Windows 8.1.

Broadband Internet Inter-net connections with rated download speeds in excess of 256Kbps. Most common types include cable modem and DSL, but ISDN, fixed wireless, Fiber optic (FIOS and others), and sat-ellite Internet services are also broadband services.

browser A program that inter-prets HTML documents and allows hyperlinking to websites. Windows 8.1 includes Inter-net Explorer 11 as its standard (default) web browser.

BSOD Blue Screen of Death. This is a fatal system error in Windows that stops the system from starting; it is also called a stop error, and is named after the blue background and the white text error message.

C

CD Compact Disc.

CD-R Recordable CD. Contents of CD-R can be added to but not changed.

CD-ROM Compact Disc-Read-Only Memory. Standard optical drive. Most can read CD-R media, but drives require MultiRead capability and a UDF reader program to read CD-RW media.

CD-RW Compact Disc-Rewritable. Rewritable CD. The contents can be changed. A CD-RW drive can also use CD-R media.

Charms bar Windows 8 interface that appears on the right side of the display. Includes charms for search, share, Start screen, devices, and settings.

Compact Flash A popular flash-memory storage standard used by digital cameras. It can be attached to desktop and portable PCs by means of a card reader or PC Card adapter.

Control Panel A Windows feature that sets Windows options.

D

DAE Digital Audio Extraction. The process of converting tracks from a music CD to a digital format, such as MP3 or WMA, at faster than normal 1x analog speeds. Windows 8's Windows Media Player use DAE to rip (convert) audio into digital form.

defragment Reorganizing the files on a drive to occupy contiguous sectors to improve retrieval speed; a defragmenting utility is included in Windows 8.

desktop Windows 8/8.1 use the desktop for program shortcuts, access to components such as the Recycle Bin, and for program windows.

device driver A program used to enable an operating system to support new devices.

Device Manager The Windows portion of the system properties sheet used to view and control device configuration. These include drivers and other configuration options.

Devices and Printers A Windows 8/8.1 feature that displays all devices and printers in a single window for quick access to the management features for each device.

drag and drop Windows term for clicking and holding on an object, such as a file or a tile on the Start screen, dragging it to another location, and releasing it.

DVD Digital Video Disc. Also known as Digital Versatile Disk. High-capacity replacement for CD-ROM.

DVD-R Digital Video Disc-Recordable.

DVD-RAM Digital Versatile Disc-Random Access Memory. A rewritable *DVD* standard developed by Panasonic and supported by the DVD Forum. A few of these drives also support DVD-R write-once media.

DVD-ROM Digital Video Disc-Read Only Memory. Retail and upgrade editions of Windows 8/8.1 are distributed on DVD-ROM media, as are many other application and utility programs from major publishers.

DVD-RW Digital Video Disc-Rewritable. A rewritable *DVD* standard developed by Pioneer Electronics and supported by the DVD Forum. These drives also support *DVD-R* write-once media.

DVD±RW Refers to drives that support both *DVD-R*/RW and *DVD+R*/RW media.

DVD+RW A rewritable *DVD* standard supported by the DVD+RW Alliance and sold by HP, Philips, Sony, and other vendors. Most of these drives also support DVD+R write-once media.

E

email Electronic mail. The contents of email can include text, HTML, and binary files (such as photos or compressed archives). Email can be sent between computers via an internal computer network, a proprietary online service such as AOL, or via the Internet.

F

FAT File Allocation Table. The part of the hard disk or floppy disk that contains pointers to the actual location of files on the disk.

FAT32 32-bit file allocation table. FAT method optionally available with Windows 8/8.1 and earlier versions. It allows 232 files maximum per drive and drive sizes up to 2TB (terabytes). Windows 8 supports FAT32 for data drives only.

file attributes Controls how files are used and viewed and can be reset by the user. Typical file attributes include hidden, system, read-only, and archive; Windows 8 also supports compressed and encrypted file attributes on drives that use the NTFS file system.

file extension Alphanumeric identifier after the dot in a filename; indicates file type, such as .html, .exe, .docx, and so on. Windows 8 does not display file extensions by default, but you can make them visible through the Control Panel's Folder Options utility.

file system How files are organized on a drive; FAT16, FAT32, and NTFS are popular file systems supported by various versions of Windows.

firewall A network device or software that blocks unauthorized access to a network from other users. Software firewalls such as Zone Alarm or Norton Internet Security are sometimes referred to as personal firewalls. Routers can also function as firewalls. Windows 8 includes a software firewall.

font A particular size, shape, and weight of a typeface. 12-point Times Roman Italic is a font; Times Roman is the typeface. Windows 8/8.1 include a number of different typefaces, and you can select the desired font with programs such as WordPad, Paint, and others.

FORMAT A Windows program to prepare a drive for use; hard disks must be partitioned first.

G

GB Gigabyte. 1 billion bytes.

GHz Gigahertz.

GUI Graphical User Interface. The user interface with features such as icons, fonts, and point-and-click commands; Windows and Mac OS are popular GUIs.

H

hard drive A storage device with rigid, nonremovable platters inside a case; also called hard disk or rigid disk.

hardware Physical computing devices.

HDD Hard Disk Drive. Windows 8 is typically installed to an HDD.

Hi-Speed USB Another term for USB 2.0.

home page The web page that is first displayed when you open a web browser; can be customized to view any web page available online or stored on your hard disk.

HomeGroup A Windows network feature that enables two or more Windows 8 or Windows 7 systems to belong to a secure, easy-to-manage network.

I

icon An on-screen symbol used in Windows to link you to a program, file, or routine.

install The process of making a computer program usable on a system, including expanding and copying program files to the correct locations, changing Windows configuration files, and registering file extensions used by the program.

Internet The world-wide "network of networks" that can be accessed through the World Wide Web and by Telnet, FTP, and other utilities.

J

jump list A Windows 8/8.1 feature that enables programs and documents to be started from taskbar shortcuts.

L

LAN Local Area Network. A network in which the components are connected through network cables or wirelessly; a LAN can connect to other LANs via a router.

landscape mode A print mode that prints across the wider side of the paper; from the usual proportions of a landscape painting.

Live Tile Windows 8 feature that uses some tiles on the Start screen to display up-to-date information being fed from local storage (Pictures) or from websites (Weather, People, News, and others).

lock screen This screen appears when Windows 8/8.1 is started or locked. The user must press the spacebar, click a mouse, or press the touch interface to see the login screen. This screen displays the date, time, and a full-screen image.

logging Recording events during a process. Windows 8/8.1 creates logs for many types of events; they can be viewed through the Computer Management Console.

M

mastering Creating a CD or DVD by adding all the files to the media at once. This method is recommended when creating a music CD or a video DVD. Windows 8's built-in CD and DVD creation feature supports mastering.

Microsoft account Account setup option supported by Windows 8/8.1. Log in with a Microsoft account (example: somebody@hotmail.com), and your settings are synchronized between systems. This was previously known as a Windows Live ID.

Microsoft Knowledge Base The online collection of Microsoft technical articles used by Microsoft support personnel to diagnose system problems. Can also be searched by end users by using the http://support.microsoft.com website.

MMC Microsoft Management Console. The Windows utility used to view and control the computer and its components. Disk Management and Device Manager are components of MMC.

monitor A TV-like device that uses either a CRT or an LCD screen to display activity inside the computer. Attaches to the video card or video port on the system. Windows 8/8.1 supports multiple monitors.

mouse A pointing device that is moved across a flat surface; older models use a removable ball to track movement; most recent models use optical or laser sensors.

MP3 Moving Picture Experts Group Layer 3 Audio. A compressed digitized music file format widely used for storage of popular and classical music; quality varies with the sampling rate used to create the file. MP3 files can be stored on recordable or rewritable CD or DVD media for playback and are frequently exchanged online. The process of creating MP3 files is called ripping. Windows Media Player and Windows Media Center can create and play back MP3 files.

MPEG Motion Picture Experts Group; creates standards for compression of video (such as MPEG 2) and audio (such as the popular MP3 file format).

multi-touch A Windows feature that enables icons and windows on touch-sensitive displays to be dragged, resized, and adjusted with two or more fingers.

N

netbook A mobile computing device that is smaller than a laptop and has a folding keyboard and screen (usually no more than about 10 inches diagonal measurement). Netbooks have lower-performance processors, less RAM, and smaller hard disks (or solid state drives) than laptop or notebook computers. Windows 8/8.1 runs on netbooks as well as more powerful types of computers.

network Two or more computers that are connected and share a resource, such as folders or printers.

network drive A drive or folder available through the network; usually refers to a network resource that has been mapped to a local drive letter.

Network and Sharing Center The Windows control center for wired, wireless, and dial-up networking functions.

NTFS New Technology File System. The native file system used by Windows 8 and some earlier versions of Windows. All NTFS versions feature smaller allocation unit sizes and superior security when compared to FAT16 or FAT32.

O

objects Items that can be viewed or configured with File Explorer, including drives, folders, computers, and so on.

OS Operating system. Software that configures and manages hardware and connects hardware and applications. Windows 8, Linux, and Mac OS are examples of operating systems.

P

packet writing A method for writing data to an optical disc in small blocks (packets). This method is used by UDF programs. Packet-written media requires a UDF reader, unlike media created with a mastering program, which can be read without any additional software. Windows 8/8.1's CD and DVD writing feature can use packet writing (UDF formatting).

PAN Personal Area Network. Bluetooth is an example of a network technology that supports PANs.

password A word or combination of letters and numbers that is matched to a username or resource name to enable the user to access a computer or network resources or accounts.

path A series of drives and folders (subdirectories) that are checked for executable programs when a command-prompt command is issued or a drive/network server and folders are used to access a given file.

personal firewall Software that blocks unauthorized access to a computer with an Internet connection. Can also be configured to prevent unauthorized programs from connecting to the Internet. Windows 8 includes a personal (software) firewall.

Photo Viewer A Windows 8 utility for photo viewing and printing.

PIN Personal Identification Number. Windows 8/8.1 supports PIN numbers as an optional login method.

pinning The act of locking a program or document to the Windows taskbar or Start menu. You can use this feature along with jump lists to create shortcuts to your most commonly used programs in either location.

POP3 Post Office Protocol 3, a popular protocol for receiving email.

portrait mode The default print option that prints across the short side of the paper; it gets its name from the usual orientation of portrait paintings and photographs.

power management BIOS or OS techniques for reducing power usage by dropping CPU clock speed, turning off the monitor or hard disk, and so on during periods of inactivity.

PowerShell A Windows utility that runs from the command prompt and enables experienced users and system administrators to write scripts (series of commands) to perform tasks. Included in some editions of Windows 8 as an optionally installed feature.

properties sheet A Windows method for modifying and viewing object properties. Accessible by right-clicking the object and selecting Properties or by using Control Panel. On a tablet or touchscreen-based device, press and hold the object until the properties sheet appears. It is located on the bottom of the screen when run from the Start screen or Apps menu.

Q

QWERTY The standard arrangement of typewriter keys is also used by most English or Latin-alphabet computer keyboards; the name was derived from the first six letter keys under the left hand.

R

Recycle Bin Windows holding area for deleted files, allowing them to be restored to their original locations; can be over-ridden to free up disk space.

Refresh New Windows 8 system recovery feature; enables system and Windows Store software to be reset to their original configuration without losing personal settings or files.

Reset New Windows 8 system recovery feature; resets Windows to its as-installed state. All user changes (new programs, files, and settings) are also wiped out.

resolution The number of dots per inch (dpi) supported by a display, scanner, or printer. Typical displays support resolutions of about 96dpi, whereas printers have resolutions of 600dpi to 2,400dpi (laser printers). Inkjet printers might have even higher resolutions.

Ribbon toolbar The program interface used by many Windows 8 components. Click a tab on the Ribbon to display related commands.

ripping The process of converting CD audio tracks into digital music formats, such as MP3 or WMA.

router The device that routes data from one network to another. Often integrated with wireless access points and switches.

S

safe mode Windows troubleshooting startup mode; runs the system using BIOS routines only. Can be selected at startup by pressing the F8 key repeatedly and then selecting it from the startup menu that appears.

SD card Secure Digital card. Popular flash memory card format for digital cameras and other electronic devices. See also *SDHC card*.

SDHC card Secure Digital High Capacity card. Popular flash memory card format for digital cameras and other electronic devices. Devices that use SDHC cards can also use SD cards; however, devices made only for SD cards cannot use SDHC cards.

shared resource A drive, printer, or other resource available to more than one PC over a network.

shortcut A Windows icon stored on the desktop or in a Windows folder with an .lnk extension; double-click the icon to run the program or open the file.

SkyDrive A Windows online file and photo storage and sharing site. Requires a free Microsoft account (formerly known as a Windows Live ID). Windows 8 provides access to SkyDrive from the Start screen and Windows desktop. This service will change its name in the future because the name SkyDrive infringes on the UK's Sky Broadcasting company.

SMTP Simple Mail Transport Protocol.

software Instructions that create or modify information and control hardware; must be read into RAM before use.

SOHO Small Office/Home Office.

SP Service Pack. A service pack is used to add features or fix problems with an operating system or application program. Windows 8's Windows Update feature installs service packs for Windows and for Microsoft apps such as Microsoft Office automatically when standard settings are used.

spam Unsolicited email. Named after (but not endorsed by) the famous Hormel lunch meat. Many email clients and utilities can be configured to help filter, sort, and block spam.

SSID Service Set Identifier. The name for a wireless network. When you buy a wireless router, the vendor has assigned it a standard SSID, but you should change it to a different name as part of setting up a secure network.

standby The power-saving mode in which the CPU drops to a reduced clock speed and other components wait for activity.

Start screen The new Windows 8 user interface that uses tiles for apps and is designed for touchscreens, but can also be navigated with a keyboard, mouse, or touchpad.

storage Any device that holds programs or data for use, including hard disks, USB drives, DVD drives, and so on.

suspend The power-saving mode that shuts down the monitor and other devices; it saves more power than standby. Windows 8 calls suspend mode sleep mode.

System Restore A feature built in to Windows 8 that enables the user to revert the system back to a previous state in case of a crash or other system problem. System Restore points can be created by the user and are created automatically by Windows when new hardware and software is installed or by a predefined schedule.

T

taskbar A Windows feature that displays icons for running programs, generally at the bottom of the primary display. In Windows 8, the taskbar also contains jump list shortcuts to frequently used programs.

TB Terabyte. 1 trillion bytes.

TCP/IP Transmission Control Protocol/Internet Protocol. The Internet's standard network protocol that is also the standard for most networks.

tile The Windows 8 term for the icons on the Start screen. They can be moved to different places on the Start screen by using drag and drop.

touchpad A pressure-sensitive pad that is used as a mouse replacement in some portable computers and keyboards.

touchscreen A touch-sensitive screen built in to some desktop and most tablet computers. Windows 8's Start screen is designed for touchscreens, but can also be navigated with a mouse or touchpad.

Trojan horse A program that attaches itself secretly to other programs that usually has a harmful action when triggered. It is similar to a computer virus but cannot spread itself to other computers, although some Trojan horses can be used to install a remote control program that allows an unauthorized user to take over your computer. Antivirus programs can block Trojan horses as well as true viruses.

typeface A set of fonts in different sizes (or a single scalable outline) and weights; Times New Roman Bold, Bold Italic, Regular, and Italic are all part of the Times New Roman scalable typeface.

U

UDF Universal Disk Format. A standard for CD and DVD media to drag and drop files to compatible media using a method called packet writing. Windows 8/8.1 supports various UDF versions.

uninstall The process of removing Windows programs from the system.

Universal Disk Format See *UDF*.

URL Uniform Resource Locator. The full path to any given web page or graphic on the Internet. A full URL contains the server type (such as http://, ftp://, or others), the site name (such as www.markesoper.com), and the name of the folder and the page or graphic you want to view (such as /blog/?page_id=38).

Thus, the URL http://www.markesoper.com/blog/?page_id=38 displays the "About Mark" page on the author's website.

USB Universal Serial Bus. High-speed replacement for older I/O ports; USB 1.1 has a peak speed of 12Mbps. USB 2.0 has a peak speed of 480Mbps; USB 3.0 has a top speed of 5Gbps. USB 2.0 ports also support USB 1.1 devices. USB 2.0 devices can be plugged in to USB 1.1 devices but run at only USB 1.1 speeds. USB 3.0 ports support USB 2.0 and 1.1 devices, which run at their original speeds.

username Used with a password to gain access to network resources.

V

virus A computer program that resembles a Trojan horse that can also replicate itself to other computers.

VoIP Voice over Internet Protocol. Enables telephone calls to be transmitted or received over an IP network. Windows 8 includes Skype, which can be used for VoIP calls.

W–Z

WAV A noncompressed standard for digital audio. Some recording programs for Windows can create and play back WAV files. However, WAV files are very large, and are usually converted into other formats for use online or for creating digital music archives.

Web Slice An Internet Explorer 11 feature that displays content from other websites while you view a website in the main window.

WEP Wired Equivalent Privacy. A now-obsolete standard for wireless security. Replaced by *WPA*.

Wi-Fi The name for IEEE-802.11a, IEEE-802.11b, IEEE-802.11g, or IEEE-802.11n wireless Ethernet devices that meet the standards set forth by the Wi-Fi Alliance.

Windows Action Center A Windows 8 feature that combines security and system warnings and notifications into a single interface.

Windows Essentials An optional addition to Windows 8/8.1 that provides support for photo management and editing, blogging, family safety, instant messaging, email, and video editing. These programs run from the Windows desktop, but photo editing, family safety, instant messaging, and email apps that run from the Start screen are included in Windows 8.1.

wireless network The general term for any radio-frequency network, including *Wi-Fi*. Most wireless networks can be interconnected to conventional networks.

WLAN Wireless Local Area Network. Instead of wires, stations on a WLAN connect to each other through radio waves. The IEEE 802.11 family of standards guide the development of WLANs.

WMA Windows Media Audio. This is the native compressed audio format created by Windows Media Player. Unlike *MP3*, WMA files support digital rights management.

WPA Wireless Protected Access. Replaced WEP as the standard for secure wireless networks. Original WPA uses TKIP encryption. An improved version known as WPA2 uses the even more secure AES encryption standard.

WWW World Wide Web. The portion of the Internet that uses the Hypertext Transfer Protocol (http://) and can thus be accessed via a web browser, such as Microsoft Internet Explorer, Google Chrome, and Mozilla Firefox.

Zip The archive type (originally known as PKZIP) created when you use Send To Compressed (Zipped) folder. A zip file can contain one or more files and can be created, viewed, and opened in File Explorer. Formerly also referred to the Iomega Zip removable-media drive.

Index

A

accelerators (IE11), 369
accessibility options, 220-225
accounts
  email accounts, adding to Windows Mail, 149
  Microsoft accounts, 19, 235, 240-241
  user accounts, 396
    administrator accounts, 401
    changing account type, 400-401
    child accounts, 401
    parental controls, 406-415
    picture passwords, 416-419
    PIN number access, 404-405
    selecting to log in, 402-403
    setting up, 398-399
    standard accounts, 401
Achievements (Xbox Games page), 250
addresses (website), entering, 353
administrators, 260, 401
alarm clock feature, 82-85
Alarms app, 82-89
albums, 340-343
app share options, 210
applications. See apps
appointments, 158-159
apps. See also individual apps (for example, Calendar)
  app share options, 210
  app size options, 213
  browsing in Windows Store, 230-233
  compared to desktop programs, 51, 54, 236
  finding, 58-59
  grouping, 60
  installing, 237
  opening, 51
  pinning to Start screen, 186
  rating, 238
  reinstalling, 239
  removing, 239
  searching for in Windows Store, 231, 236
  snapping, 52
  switching between, 52
  uninstalling, 187
  unpinning from Start screen, 187
  viewing
    app information, 234-235
    all apps, 56-57
    open apps, 395
    in Windows Store, 242
Apps screen, 254, 258-259
audio
  audio CDs
    burning, 348-349
    playing, 332-333
    ripping, 336-339
  editing, 96-97
  music. See music
  recording, 94-95
  system volume, 196
AutoComplete feature (IE11), 65
AutoPlay settings, 202

B

background, 388-389
backing up files, 426-427
Bing Food & Drink app, 170-171
Bing Health & Fitness app, 172-173
Blocking popups, 372
brightness, 197
browser. See Internet Explorer 11
browsing
  apps in Windows Store, 230-235
  music, 104
Burn to disc command, 284-285
burning CDs/DVDs, 284-287, 348-349
buying. See purchasing

C

Calculator, 7, 90-93
Calendar, 156-159
calls (Skype), 177-179
Camera app
  cropping photos, 131
  editing photos, 132-133
  self-timer, 128
  shooting photos, 126-127
  shooting video, 129
  Video mode, 129
  viewing photos, 130
Camera Roll, 130, 206
captions, 116-118
category view (Windows Store app), 232-233

CDs

CDs
  burning, 284-287, 348-349
  playing, 332-333
  ripping, 336-339
Character Map, 268-269
Charms bar, 27
child accounts, 401
Cleanup tool, 295
clicking and dragging, 40
closing
  Calculator, 93
  desktop programs, 259
  Internet Explorer, 11, 79
  Internet Explorer tabs, 75
cloud-based storage. See SkyDrive
color
  Start screen settings, 189
  window color, 390-391
compressed files, 292
computers, adding to HomeGroups, 312
configuration. See also customization
  additional displays, 386-387
  desktop background, 388-389
  desktop themes, 393
  devices and printers, 394
  parental controls, 406-411
  PC settings. See PC settings
  picture passwords, 416-419
  PIN number access, 404-405
  screen savers, 392
  touch keyboard, 29
  user accounts, 398-399
  window color, 390-391
  Windows Update, 384-385, 424-425
conflicts in file/folder names, 282-283
contacts, 164-165
Control Panel
  Devices and Printers window, 394
  Network and Internet window, 308-313
controls
  Movie Moments app, 116
  Windows Media Player controls, 334-335
Converter feature (Calculator), 92-93
copying
  audio CDs, 336-339
  files, 280-281
  folders, 280-281
  SkyDrive files, 143

cropping photos, 131
customization. *See also* configuration
    accessibility options, 220-225
    app share options, 210
    AutoPlay settings, 202
    camera roll options, 206
    display resolution, 200
    location settings, 215
    Lock screen, 199
    microphone settings, 217
    mouse and touchpad settings, 201
    notification settings, 211-212
    privacy settings, 214
    screen brightness, 197
    Search options, 209
    SkyDrive storage settings, 204-205
    Start screen
        adjusting tile size, 190-191
        border and color settings, 189
        name groups, 185
        pinning apps to, 186
        pinning folders to, 188
        relocating tiles on, 184
        turning live tiles on/off, 192-193
        unpinning objects from, 187
    sync settings, 207
    time zone, 218-219
    webcam settings, 216
    window color, 391
cutting and pasting SkyDrive files, 142

D

Defragment tool, 295
deleting
    IE11 history list items, 376-377
    SkyDrive files, 140-141
desktop
    background, 388-389
    toolbar, adding apps to, 261
    viewing web pages on, 78
desktop programs. *See also* specific
  programs
    adding to desktop toolbar, 261
    closing, 259
    compared to apps, 51, 54, 236
    finding, 255-257
    maximizing, 259
    pinning to Start screen, 260
    printing from, 270-271
    running as administrator, 260
    sorting, 256-257
    starting from Apps screen, 258-259
    switching between, 262-263
    viewing, 254

desktop themes, 393
device management, 394
Devices and Printers window, 394
directions, getting, 160-163
displays
    adding, 386-387
    resolution, 200
downloading music/video, 111
dragging and dropping, 282
Drive Tools, 294-295, 437
drives
    connecting, 55
    managing, 294-295
    scanning for errors, 438-439
    viewing drive information, 437
DVDs, burning files to, 284-287

E

Ease of Access settings, 220-225
editing
    appointments, 159
    audio, 96-97
    photos, 132-133
    playlists, 345
effects, adding to photos, 132-133
email. *See also* Windows Mail
    marking as junk, 152
    newsletters, viewing, 153
    reading, 150-151
    writing and sending, 154-155
emoticons, 30-31
errors, scanning drives for, 438-439
eSATA drives, 55
Exposure setting (Camera), 127

F

Family Safety
    enabling parental controls, 406-411
    reviewing logs, 412-415
favorites
    IE11
        Favorites bar, 361
        Favorites Center, 360-363
        opening, 368
        organizing, 364-365
        saving tab groups as, 366-367
    Skype, 176
featured music, browsing, 104
File Conflict dialog box, 282-283
File Explorer, 59, 272. *See also* files
    drive management, 294-295
    Drive Tools tab, 294-295
    folders, 280-283

Frequent Places list, 293
    Home tab, 276-277
    nodes and objects, 275
    panes, 275
    Ribbon menus, 276-279
    Share tab, 292
    starting, 274
    View tab, 278-279
File History, 426-429
files
    backing up with File History, 426-427
    burning to CD/DVD, 284-287
    copying, 280-281
    finding, 58-59
    grouping, 288-291
    moving, 280-281
    name conflicts, 282-283
    opening, 314
    recovering, 428-429
    selecting, 288-291
    size, checking, 123
    SkyDrive files
        adding, 138-139
        copying/pasting, 143
        cutting/pasting, 142
        deleting, 140-141
        Open With option, 144-145
        renaming, 140-141
        thumbnails, 137
        viewing, 136-137
    syncing, 346-347
    viewing, 288-291
    Zip files, 292
Finance app, 168-169
finding
    apps, 58-59
        "hidden" apps, 255
        with sort options, 256-257
        in Windows Store, 231, 236
    files, 58-59
    locations, 160-163
FireWire drives, 55
folders
    copying, 280-281
    moving, 280-281
    name conflicts, 282-283
    pinning to Start screen, 188
    sharing in HomeGroups, 315-316
    SkyDrive folders, 138-142
Food & Drink app, 170-171
formatting discs, 285
freeze-frame, disabling, 119
Frequent Places list, 70-71, 293
Friends (Xbox Games page), 250

G-H

games
Games app, 248-249
managing with Games app, 248-249
purchasing from Windows Store, 246-247
Xbox Games page, 250-251
Games app, 248-249
grouping
apps, 60
files, 288-291

handwriting with stylus, 32-33
hardware compatibility, 21
Health & Fitness app, 172-173
help (games), 251
"hidden" desktop programs, finding, 255
hidden networks, connecting to, 302
hiding notifications, 197
High Contrast setting, 222
history list (IE11), 376-377
home page (IE11), 355
Home tab (File Explorer), 276-277
HomeGroups
creating, 304-305, 310-311
folder sharing, 315-316
joining, 307, 312-313
leaving, 317
opening files, 314
passwords, 306

I

images
creating with Snipping Tool, 264-265
desktop background, 388-389
photos
adding to Pictures Library, 320-321
cropping, 131
editing, 132-133
importing, 322-325
photo-organizing programs, 324
printing, 328-329
shooting, 126-127
viewing, 130, 326-327
importing photos, 322-325
InPrivate Browsing (IE11), 68-69, 370
installation
apps, 237
Windows 8, 14-21
Internet Explorer 11
desktop UI, 350
accelerators, 369
favorites, 368
history list, 376-377
home page, 355

InPrivate Browsing, 370
Internet privacy features, 374
links, opening, 356-357
Page Zoom, 358
popups, managing, 372-373
split screen video reviews, 107
starting, 352
tabbed browsing, 354
web pages, 359, 378-381
website addresses, entering, 353
Modern UI, 62
closing, 79
Frequent list, 70-71
InPrivate browsing, 68-69
new features, 9
starting from Start screen, 64
tabs, 66-67, 75
web pages, 70-78
website addresses, entering, 65
Internet privacy features, 374

J-K-L

joining
HomeGroups, 307, 312-313
Skype, 174-175
junk mail, marking messages as, 152

keyboards, 25, 28-29
keyword phrases, searching for apps by, 236

leaving HomeGroups, 317
libraries, Pictures Library, 320-321
links
emailing, 380-381
opening, 356-357
live tiles, 5-6, 192-193
location settings, 215
locations, finding with Maps, 160-163
Lock screen, customizing, 199
locking PC, 46
logging in, 21-25, 402-403

M

Magnifier, 221
Mail
adding email accounts, 149
marking messages as junk, 152
reading messages, 150-151
starting, 148-149
viewing newsletters, 153
writing and sending messages, 154-155
maintenance, 434
drives, 437-439
power schemes, selecting, 436

System Restore, 442-445
Windows troubleshooters, 440
Make offline option (SkyDrive), 141
Maps app, 160-163
marking messages as junk, 152
maximizing desktop programs, 259
messages. See email; text messages
Messages (Xbox Games page), 250
metered connections, 208
microphones, 97, 217
Microsoft accounts, 19, 235, 240-241
Microsoft Digital Camera Codec Pack, 323
Microsoft Windows 8 page, 21
minimizing Ribbon, 279
mouse, 40-43, 201
Movie Moments
adding captions, 118
adding music, 120
adding titles, 118
checking file size, 123
controls, 116
emphasizing text, 119
previewing and saving videos, 121
searching, 110
sharing videos, 122-123
starting, 114-115
trimming and splitting video, 117
moving
files, 280-281
folders, 280-281
tiles on Start screen, 184
music
adding in Movie Moments app, 120
browsing, 104
buying, 108
creating radio stations, 103
downloading, 111
playing, 100-105, 340-343
playlists, 344-345
rating, 341
Music app
browsing music, 104
buying music, 108
creating radio stations, 103
downloading music, 111
playing music, 100-105

N

name conflicts, 282-283
name groups, 185
Narrator, 220
navigating
with mouse, 40-43
Start screen, 26

with touchpad, 40-43
with touchscreen, 34-39
Navigation pane (File Explorer), 275
Network and Internet window, 308-313
networks
disconnecting from, 303
hidden networks, 302
HomeGroups. See HomeGroups
secured private networks, 300-301
unsecured public wireless networks, 298-299
New InPrivate tab button (IE11), 68
New Tab button (IE11), 67
newsletters, viewing, 153
nodes (File Explorer), 275
notes, Sticky Notes, 266-267
notifications, 197, 211-212
nutritional information, finding, 172-173

O

on-screen keyboard, 25
Open With option, 144-145
opening
apps, 51
Apps screen, 254
Calculator, 90-91
Charms bar, 27
desktop programs, 258-259
favorite websites, 368
File Explorer, 274
frequently visited web pages, 70
HomeGroup files, 314
Internet Explorer 11 (desktop UI), 352
Internet Explorer 11 (Modern UI), 64
links, 356-357
Movie Moments app, 114-115
Network and Internet window, 308-309
SkyDrive files, 144-145
Skype, 174-175
Windows Mail, 148-149
Windows Media Player, 330-331
Optimize tool, 295
optimizing performance. See performance optimization
organizing favorites (IE11), 364-365

P

Page Zoom (IE11), 358
parental controls
enabling, 406-411
Family Safety logs, 412-415
passwords
for HomeGroups, 306
password hints, 25

picture passwords, 416-419
viewing, 24
pasting SkyDrive files, 142-143
payment methods, adding to account, 240-241
PC info, viewing, 203
PC settings, 194
accessibility options, 220-225
app share options, 210
app sizes, 213
AutoPlay, 202
camera roll options, 206
display resolution, 200
location settings, 215
Lock screen, 199
metered connections, 208
microphone, 217
mouse and touchpad, 201
notifications, 197, 211-212
PC info, viewing, 203
PC Settings dialog, 198
privacy, 214
Recent Settings pane, 226-227
screen brightness, 197
Search options, 209
SkyDrive storage settings, 204-205
sync settings, 207
system volume, 196
time zone, 218-219
uninstall options, 213
webcam, 216
PC Settings dialog, 198
People app, 164-165
performance optimization
drives, 437-439
power schemes, 436
System Restore, 442-445
personalization. See customization
photo-organizing programs, 324
photos
adding to Pictures Library, 320-321
cropping, 131
editing, 10, 132-133
importing, 322-325
photo-organizing programs, 324
printing with Windows Photo Viewer, 328-329
shooting, 126-127
viewing, 130, 326-327
Photos app, 130
picture passwords, 416-419
pictures. See photos
Pictures Library, 320-321
PIN number access, 404-405
Pin site button (IE11), 72
Pin to Start option, 72, 260

Pin to Taskbar option, 261
pinning
apps to Start screen, 186
desktop programs, 260-261
folders to Start screen, 188
items to Frequent Places list, 293
web pages to Start screen, 72-73
places, finding with Maps, 160-163
placing calls with Skype, 178-179
planning trips with Maps, 162-163
playing
CDs, 332-333
music, 100-105, 111, 340-343
video, 106, 111
playlists, 344-345
popups, managing, 372-373
power options, 47
power schemes, 436
previewing
video, 106, 121
web pages, 359
Print menu, 270
printers, managing, 394
printing, 270-271
HomeGroup passwords, 306
photos, 328-329
web pages, 76-77, 359
privacy, 214, 374
private networks, 300-301
protecting computer. See security
public wireless networks, 298-299
purchasing
games, 246-247
music, 108
video, 108

R

radio stations, creating, 103
rating
apps, 238
music, 341
RAW photos, 323
reading email, 150-151
receiving calls with Skype, 177
Recent Settings pane, 226-227
recording audio, 94-95
recording speeds, 287
recovering files, 428-429
reinstalling apps, 239
relocating tiles on Start screen, 184
removing
apps, 239
picture passwords, 419
web pages from Frequent list, 71
renaming SkyDrive files, 140-141
resizing tiles, 190-191

resolution, 200
restarting, 47
restoring system, 442-445
Ribbon menus, 276-279
right-clicking mouse, 40
ripping CDs, 336-339
Run as Administrator option, 260
Run setup.exe command, 14

S

saving
    tab groups as favorites, 366-367
    videos, 121
    web pages, 378-379
scanning
    drives for errors, 438-439
    for viruses/spyware, 432
scheduling appointments, 158-159
Scientific mode (Calculator), 91
screen brightness, 197
screen savers, 392
Search, 6
Search options, 209
Search tool, 58-59
searching
    for apps
        "hidden" apps, 255
        sort options, 256-257
        in Windows Store, 231, 236
    for locations, 160-163
    Movie Moments, 110
    TV shows and movies, 110
secured private networks, 300-301
security, 420
    File History
        backing up files, 426-427
        recovering files, 428-429
    Internet privacy features, 374
    location settings, 215
    parental controls
        enabling, 406-411
        Family Safety logs, 412-415
    privacy settings, 214
    UAC (User Account Control), 422-423
    Windows Action Center, 430-431
    Windows Defender, 432-433
    Windows Update, 384-385, 424-425
self-timer (Camera app), 128
sending email, 154-155
settings. See PC settings
setting up. See configuration
Share tab, 292
shared music, playing, 102
sharing
    folders, 315-316
    videos, 122-123

shooting
    photos, 126-127
    video, 129
shopping. See purchasing
shopping lists, creating from recipes, 170-171
shortcut keys, 11
shortcuts, 44-45, 59
shutting down, 47
signing up for Microsoft accounts, 19, 235
sizing tiles, 190-191
SkyDrive, 134
    adding files, 138-139
    copying/pasting files, 143
    creating folders, 138-139
    cutting/pasting files, 142
    deleting files, 140-141
    Open With option, 144-145
    opening files, 144-145
    renaming files, 140-141
    renaming folders, 140-141
    storage settings, 204-205
    thumbnails, 137
    viewing files, 136-137
Skype
    joining, 174-175
    placing calls, 178-179
    receiving calls, 177
    selecting favorites, 176
    starting, 174-175
    text messaging, 180-181
Sleep, 47
snapping apps, 52
Snipping Tool, 264-265
software compatibility, 21
sorting apps, 256-257
sound. See audio
sound effects, 393
Sound Recorder
    editing audio, 96-97
    recording audio, 94-95
split screen, 8, 107
splitting video, 117
spyware, 432
standard accounts, 401
Standard mode (Calculator), 90
Start screen
    apps
        grouping, 60
        opening, 51
        snapping, 52
        switching between, 52
        uninstalling, 239
        viewing all, 56-57
    border and color settings, 189
    HomeGroups, 304-307

name groups, 185
navigating, 26
new features, 4
overview, 50
pinning apps to, 186
pinning items to, 72-73, 188, 260
Search tool, 58-59
starting Internet Explorer 11 from, 64
tiles
    adjusting size of, 190-191
    relocating, 184
    turning live tiles on/off, 192-193
unpinning items from, 74, 187
zooming, 60
starting. See opening
Sticky Notes, 266-267
stopwatch, 88-89
stylus, 32-33
surfing the web. See Internet Explorer 11
switching between apps, 52, 262-263
symbols, 30-31
sync settings, 207
syncing files, 346-347
system maintenance, 434
    drives
        scanning for errors, 438-439
        viewing drive information, 437
    power schemes, 436
    System Restore, 442-445
    Windows troubleshooters, 440
System Restore, 442-445
system volume, 196

T

tabbed browsing (IE11), 354
tabs (IE11), 66-67, 75
Task Manager, 395
text, emphasizing in Movie Moments, 119
text messages, 180-181
themes, 393
thumbnails (SkyDrive), 137
tiles
    adjusting size of, 190-191
    live tiles, 192-193
    name groups, 185
    relocating on Start screen, 184
time zone, 218-219
timeline view, 116
timers, 86-87
titles
    adding in Movie Moments, 118
    in timeline view, 116
toolbar, adding desktop programs to, 261
touch keyboard, 28-29
touchpad, 40-43, 201

touchscreen, 34-39
tracks (music), 340-343
trimming video, 117
trips, planning with Maps, 162-163
turning on/off live tiles, 192-193
TV shows, searching, 110

U

UAC (User Account Control), 422-423
undoing System Restore, 445
uninstall options, 187, 213
unlocking PC, 46
Unpin from Start option (IE11), 74
unpinning items
    from Frequent Places list, 293
    from Start screen, 74, 187
unsecured public wireless networks,
    298-299
updating Windows 8
    completing installation, 18-21
    reviewing settings, 16-17
    software/hardware compatibility, 21
    starting installation, 14-15
    Windows Defender, 432
    Windows Update, 384-385, 424-425
URLs, 65, 353
USB drives, 55, 294-295
User Account Control (UAC), 422-423
user accounts, 396
    administrator accounts, 401
    changing account type, 400-401
    child accounts, 401
    parental controls
        enabling, 406-411
        Family Safety logs, 412-415
    picture passwords, 416-419
    PIN number access, 404-405
    selecting to log in, 402-403
    setting up, 398-399
    standard accounts, 401

V

video
    buying, 108
    downloading, 111
    information about, 107
    Movie Moments app. See Movie
        Moments
    searching, 110
    shooting, 129
    viewing, 106
Video app
    buying videos, 108
    downloading and playing videos, 111

information about video, 107
    viewing video, 106
Video mode (Camera app), 129
View tab (File Explorer), 278-279
viewing
    all apps, 56-57, 254
    apps in Windows Store, 234-235, 242
    calendar, 156-157
    drive information, 437
    files, 288-291
    folder sharing settings, 316
    HomeGroup passwords, 306
    newsletters, 153
    open programs and apps, 395
    password, 24
    PC info, 203
    photos, 130, 326-327
    SkyDrive files, 136-137
    video, 106
    web pages on desktop, 78
viruses, 432
volume, 196

W

wallpaper, 388-389
weather, checking, 166-167
Weather app, 166-167
web browser. See Internet Explorer 11
web pages
    adding to Frequent list, 70
    addresses, 65
    emailing, 380-381
    favorites
        Favorites bar, 361
        Favorites Center, 360-363
        opening, 368
        organizing, 364-365
        saving tab groups as, 366-367
    frequently visited web pages, 70
    home pages, 355
    pinning to Start screen, 72-73
    previewing, 359
    printing, 76-77, 359
    removing from Frequent list, 71
    saving, 378-379
    unpinning from Start screen, 74
    viewing on desktop, 78
web surfing. See Internet Explorer 11
webcam settings, 216
website addresses, 65, 353
window colors, 390-391
Windows 7, upgrading to Windows 8
    completing installation, 18-21
    reviewing settings, 16-17
    starting installation, 14-15

Windows Action Center, 430-431
Windows Defender, 432-433
Windows Mail
    adding email accounts, 149
    marking messages as junk, 152
    reading messages, 150-151
    starting, 148-149
    viewing newsletters, 153
    writing and sending messages, 154-155
Windows Media Player
    albums, 340-343
    CDs
        burning, 348-349
        playing, 332-333
        ripping, 336-339
    file syncing, 346-347
    playback controls, 334-335
    playlists, 344-345
    starting, 330-331
Windows Photo Viewer, 326-327
Windows Store, 228
    adding payment method to account,
        240-241
    browsing apps, 230-233
    installing apps, 237
    learning more about apps, 234-235
    purchasing games, 246-247
    rating apps, 238
    reinstalling apps, 239
    removing apps, 239
    searching for apps, 231, 236
    viewing apps, 242
Windows troubleshooters, 440
Windows Update, 384-385, 424-425
wireless networks
    disconnecting from, 303
    hidden networks, 302
    HomeGroups. See HomeGroups
    secured private networks, 300-301
    unsecured public wireless networks,
        298-299
WordPad, 268-269
writing email, 154-155

X-Y-Z

Xbox Games page, 250-251
Xbox Video. See Video app

Zip files, 292
zooming Start screen, 60

easy
Windows® 8.1
See it done. Do it yourself.

Mark Edward Soper

FREE
Online Edition

Your purchase of *Easy Windows 8.1* includes access to a free online edition for 45 days through the **Safari Books Online** subscription service. Nearly every Que book is available online through **Safari Books Online**, along with thousands of books and videos from publishers such as Addison-Wesley Professional, Cisco Press, Exam Cram, IBM Press, O'Reilly Media, Prentice Hall, Sams, and VMware Press.

Safari Books Online is a digital library providing searchable, on-demand access to thousands of technology, digital media, and professional development books and videos from leading publishers. With one monthly or yearly subscription price, you get unlimited access to learning tools and information on topics including mobile app and software development, tips and tricks on using your favorite gadgets, networking, project management, graphic design, and much more.

Activate your FREE Online Edition at
informit.com/safarifree

STEP 1:   Enter the coupon code: JBGJDDB.

STEP 2:   New Safari users, complete the brief registration form.
          Safari subscribers, just log in.

If you have difficulty registering on Safari or accessing the online edition,
please e-mail customer-service@safaribooksonline.com